# HETERODOX VIEWS OF FINANCE AND CYCLES IN THE SPANISH ECONOMY

# Heterodox Views of Finance and Cycles in the Spanish Economy

MANUEL ROMAN

Routledge
Taylor & Francis Group
LONDON AND NEW YORK

First published 2002 by Ashgate Publishing

Reissued 2018 by Routledge
2 Park Square, Milton Park, Abingdon, Oxon OX14 4RN
711 Third Avenue, New York, NY 10017, USA

*Routledge is an imprint of the Taylor & Francis Group, an informa business*



A Library of Congress record exists under LC control number: 2001098027

ISBN 13: 978-1-138-72530-0 (hbk)
ISBN 13: 978-1-138-72524-9 (pbk)
ISBN 13: 978-1-315-19196-6 (ebk)

# Contents

# List of Figures and Tables

# Preface

Classical economists excluded credit from the conceptual structure of their development theories because they wished to investigate the limits to capital accumulation imposed by the evolution of profitability. When Thomas Malthus in the early 19th century introduced the possibility of effective (consumption) demand lagging behind the growth of capacity and hence undermining its growth, he laid the grounds for the seminal idea that growth trends could not be separated from cyclical fluctuations.

In contrast with Classical Political Economy, Keynesian economics put forth the claim that the absence of savings, should be no obstacle to expansion. Keynes's message proclaimed the independence of investment from savings and hence from budget constraints. Cyclical downturns could be avoided, and aggregate income expanded, as long as timely injections of credit lifted investment spending to the appropriate level. In the mid-1960s Richard Goodwin developed the formal apparatus behind the notion of growth cycles. In contrast with Malthus and Keynes, however, Goodwin's model linked the dynamics of accumulation to the inverse relationship between profits and wages.

I examine in this book five models of endogenous growth cycles in order to evaluate in theory and practice the role of credit finance in the persistence of cycles. My theoretical investigation distinguishes between those closer to the classical tradition, like Goodwin's or Shaikh's, from others with a Keynesian foundation like Minsky's. Is accumulation hampered by inadequate money supply growth as in Foley's model? How these models view the growth of the money supply, as endogenous credit-money or externally set by the monetary authority helps to settle this question. Then I use the experience of the Spanish economy as my reference to assess the theoretical claims of the models presented. I derive from the Spanish data definite conclusions that highlight the growing significance of business savings as the chief source of funding for capital accumulation. When looking at the role of credit finance, I take stock of its hidden side. By this I mean the depressing effect on accumulation exerted by a growing burden of debt. I find overwhelming evidence to support the claim that firms tailor their investment plans to their internal budgets. In Spain, only in the second half of the 1970s did credit take precedence over internal funds as the main source of accumulation finance.

# Acknowledgements

I wish to credit my wife, Ascension, for her technical support in the complex task of creating and formatting the manuscript for publication. But her companionship was my most valuable asset in this project. I owe my teachers at the New School for Social Research, Prof. Thomas Vietorisz and Prof. Anwar Shaikh, life-long gratitude for sharing with me their impressive intellectual achievements and their friendship. I would be happy if the book's content managed to convey that message. I need to acknowledge my appreciation for Prof. Jamee Moudud's magnificent research in the field of endogenous growth cycles as well as his sound advice on matters of method. I am indebted to Prof. Steve Pressman and Prof. Susan Feiner for the meticulous and constructive suggestions that they made to improve the manuscript's contents. I cannot forget that without the many *Series* data diskettes Prof. Carlos Sebastian sent me from Spain, I could not have fleshed out my theoretical claims. Prof. Sebastian, of course, is not responsible for my interpretations of the data. I feel grateful to Mr. Adam Hickford, Commissioning Editor, for his prompt and kind messages regarding procedures. Last, but not least, I am indebted to Ms. Pauline Beavers, my Desk Editor at Ashgate, for her sensitive reading of the manuscript and her incisive advice designed to improve its presentation. I thank her as a friend.

# 1 Introduction

The central object of my investigation concerns the role of finance in economic growth and its link with the persistence of business cycles in Spain. It is my contention that the roots of what are now considered heterodox views of these matters can be traced to the dynamical approach pioneered by Classical Political Economy. A case study of this kind provides invaluable testing grounds to assess the relevance of some accepted conventions found in contemporary theories of growth and cycles. In particular I will stress the fact that that some of the stylized facts found in this literature are not present in the Spanish case, for example the capital-output ratio was not constant at all but rather rose sharply from the early 1960s through the early 1980s and less rapidly thereafter. After a sharp fall in the mid-1970s, the share of profits trended upwards from the early 1980s through the present. Despite the crucial role of bank credit to prop up standing firms in the depression phase (from the mid-1970s through the early 1980s) evidence that the share of internal funds to finance business investment increased is strong. This is why I believe that the Spanish experience provides support for my understanding of the Classical approach.

After presenting two succinct views of what constitutes the Classical approach from a heterodox perspective, I will outline my own version derived from Lowe's synthesis (Lowe, 1954) and will then proceed to link up the main thrust of these interpretations with the central tendencies of the Spanish economy. Then I will lay out the contrasting views of the monetarist and Post-Keynesian traditions regarding the role of money and credit in business activity. I will conclude outlining a theory of inflation elaborated by A. Shaikh as an extension of his model of finance, accumulation and cycles. I will show its connection with the Classical approach and finally its empirical strength applied to the Spanish case.

## The classical approach

The Classical Economists took growth for granted as long as structural barriers did not hamper the extraction of the economic surplus from productive employment. The consumption of workers in this pursuit was a cost of production to capitalist firms advancing circulating capital. Capitalist consumption of goods or the services of unproductive labor was viewed as a subtraction from business savings. Internal finance was sufficient to sustain capital accumulation and no stimulus from government deficits or bank lending was essential for its growth.

Abstracting from the differences in the works of Smith, Ricardo, Malthus and Marx, Classical growth models according to Donald J. Harris share as a basic assumption:

> recognition that accumulation and productive investment of a part of the social product is the main driving force behind economic growth and that under Capitalism, this takes the form mainly of the reinvestment of profits (Harris, 1987, p. 445).

Kaldor's understanding of the characteristic features of the Classical approach also brings out the primacy of profits:

> profits were assumed to be largely saved and invested, whilst wages are consumed, the share of profits in income also determines the share of investment in total production, and the rate of accumulation (Kaldor, 1965, p. 180).

Adam Smith saw technical change fostering the division of labor, raising labor productivity and expanding both employment and the surplus since population expansion would in due course put a lid on the growth of wage rates. Higher productivity leading to expanding profits would promote higher accumulation and a growing demand for labor, but wage rates would only rise temporarily because if wages went up, net birth rates would increase and population growth would surpass the labor demand.

Ricardo brought out the link between accumulation and the class distribution of income. He examined how structural changes in the class distribution of the surplus between productive capitalists and landowners could slow down or even bring to a halt accumulation altogether. Initially accepting Smith's view of growing employment with rising accumulation, Ricardo saw the secular rise in wage rates coming about as a result of expanding accumulation. As cultivations bumped against the boundaries of the best soil for growing food, capitalist farmers would be forced to cultivate progressively lower grade areas. The rising cost of food at the margins would push wage rates higher, thus allowing the landowners of the better lands to capture an increasing share of the surplus in the guise of differential rents. Ricardo then argued that if the surplus retained by capitalists declined, so would accumulation. Finally in contrast to Smith, Ricardo also allowed that labor saving technical change and declining accumulation would reduce the demand for labor, harming employment.

Malthus on the other hand questioned the viability of exuberant accumulation in the absence of external sources of effective demand. If workers consumption demand was limited by subsistence wages and capitalist consumption was constraint by competition and the drive to accumulate, where would the final demand for the growing output to be found? This question led Malthus to theorize the necessity of cycles as an organic feature of secular growth. For Malthus the accumulation drive would widen the gap between the growing capacity to produce commodities and the insufficient growth of final consumption demand. Hence periodic slumps would punctuate this growing imbalance and their destructive force would temporarily reduce the existing gap.

Malthus then was instrumental in laying the grounds for the modern Keynesian theories of effective demand, growth and cycles. Classical economists including Malthus and Marx were aware of the fact that unexpected shocks occurred periodically, giving rise to market turbulence that accentuated the systemic imbalances out of which central tendencies emerged. Neo-Classical economics on the other hand treats shocks as perturbations of an otherwise balanced growth path.

## The Spanish economy and the classical approach

I think that this is not only a fair view of the Classical approach to the determinants of accumulation, but also captures the actual central tendencies behind the structural changes in Spanish growth. The fundamental dynamics of growth underlying the Classical school were discernible in Spain, particularly if the boundaries of that school are extended to include Marx's analysis of the effect of technical progress on profitability via the rising capital-output ratio. Then the relevance of the Classical approach linking the evolution of profits and accumulation is decisive.

The Spanish economy traversed through a decade of development in the 1960s, followed by a period of depression lasting from 1975 through the early 1980s, a faltering recovery ending in the 1993 slump and a new cyclical upturn ending the century. Despite these sharply contrasting phases of its development, some structural features common to all stand out distinctively. My reading of the turbulent experience in Spain suggests a definite answer to some basic theoretical questions.

In this light, a basic question underlies all others, was economic growth endogenous, once capitalism was in full sway? Despite the financial support rendered by a variety of external sources at different stages of development, I will argue that the evolution of profits set the central tendency for the changes in the rate of accumulation.

Related to this question, was economic growth linear along a balanced path, or rather, were cycles endogenous to growth? An examination of the systemic changes brought about by technological progress, such as the rise in capital-output ratios for over twenty years of development, point to a non-linear growth path running trough sharp fluctuations in accumulation growth rates.

Was there a "knife-edge" corridor evident in the growth experience of the Spanish economy? If growth took place through cycles, were there attractors that kept the fluctuations within bounds, in other words, was the growth path stable? The answer to this question is complicated by the onset of depression from the mid-1970s through the early 1980s. I would argue that intractable systemic forces caused the slump, namely the impact of rising mechanization on capital-output ratios and its effect on profitability. Attractors were present, nevertheless. As accumulation plunged and unemployment soared structural changes were underway depressing the share of wages and raising that of profits. Phases of rapid growth after the early 1980s on the other hand expanded employment and reversed the growth of the profit share somewhat, although the overall trend was never altered.

During the years of depression large infusions of credit salvaged the integrity of the businesses that remained standing. Once the banking system came to the rescue, did credit contribute to lift the path of accumulation or did it merely have a temporary boost that dissipated as the accumulated debt was repaid with funds that were no longer available to finance investment? Accumulation was negatively impacted by the stagnation of profits in the 1970s and positively affected by its recovery in the late 1980s, but the accumulation path remained distinctly lower than it was in the 1970s.

In my view then the rise, stagnation and recovery of the profits mass, the residual after subtracting wages and depreciation from the business sector GDP, was the key force shaping the trajectory of the accumulation path in Spain for the past half-century. After the 1980s, business savings increased as the trend in the share of profits and that of retained earnings relative to profits went up. Indeed running through the contrasting phases of growth, depression and recovery in Spain, the relentless pursuit of structural changes favorable to the expansion of profits gained momentum.

I will endeavor to show, moreover, that questions previously excluded from the Classical approach to development, such as the role of credit in capital accumulation and its effect on short-term fluctuations, can be answered without abandoning the basic principles of that paradigm.

**The long-run growth trend**

Business practice alone should suffice to shed light on the significance of profits for capital accumulation and output growth. We would expect that because the pursuit of profits by business enterprise is paramount, the growth of output must be closely related to the dynamics of the profit rate. From the Keynesian perspective the derivation of this conclusion follows from the equilibrium condition for income determination. Assume that government expenditures, G equal taxes, T. The equilibrium level of income requires that $I = S = s\Pi$. Further assume that all savings, S is a portion, s of actual profits, $\Pi$. Now define normal profits, $\Pi_n = \frac{\Pi}{u}$, that is actual profits divided by capacity utilization, u. Then actual profits are equal to normal profits only when capacity utilization, u equals 1. The equilibrium condition accordingly becomes: $I = s\Pi = s\,u\,\Pi_n$. Expressing this equality relative to the capital stock, K we have:

$$\frac{I}{K} = su\frac{\Pi_n}{K} = g_K = su\,r_n$$

This key expression says that the growth rate of fixed capital is a function of the propensity to save (out of profits) and the profit rate and only when $u = 1$, will the growth rate, $g_k = sr_n$. In Spain as profits grew larger, capital investment growth rates rose from the mid-1950s through the early 1970s. Falling profitability after the mid-1960s, however, had a dampening effect on the growth of accumulation. After the early 1970s the growth rate of fixed capital investment could no longer compensate for the decline in profitability and the mass of profits stagnated. The collapse of profits after the mid-1970s dragged output growth rates down as the rewards of accumulation practically vanished. The neat historical record of their growth and collapse leaves no doubt concerning the non-linear nature of the system's growth path.

My chief concern here centers on the dynamics of short-term GDP fluctuations and its relation to credit cycles in bank lending to finance excess demand by business and government. My view is that these cycles occurred around a trend set by the long-wave dynamics of the profits mass. Examination of the growth path of the Spanish economy after the mid-1960s reveals the presence of persistent short-term fluctuations. I believe the marshaled evidence will confirm the presumption that these cyclical movements were connected with matching cycles in short-term credit growth. As long ago as the 1930s, however, John Strachey found it necessary to remind his Keynesian readers that the existence of credit did not imply the absence of a budget constraint. While seeking to explain the genesis of the deep depression then engulfing the world economies, he indulged his fancy in a playful exercise comparing a "creditless" economy with one in which external finance was available:

> If we can imagine a creditless capitalism in which every transaction was mediated by hard cash, then it is true that the oscillatory form of the crisis, but not the crisis itself might be abolished. We should get a slow, steady decline of the rate of profit which would act upon the system like a creeping paralysis (Strachey, 1935, p. 313).

Figure 1.1 shows the simple correlation between the nominal business-sector GDP yearly change and the private sector yearly credit supply change in log scale. The yearly credit supply is the average of the monthly credit supply. Both start in 1964 because reliable data for credit growth before that date is not available. I do not believe that these GDP fluctuations were caused by the vagaries of an exogenous supply of credit-money. On the contrary, the state of current business profitability combined with expectations of future sales motivated the demand for and provision of credit. In my view, the supply of credit-money is fundamentally endogenous to the needs of business for short-term working capital.

**Figure 1.1 Yearly GDP and credit supply change**

*Sources:* Series 832000 and 970000T.

My concern with the role of credit in the formation of growth cycles cannot overlook the underlying forces shaping the long-term behavior of accumulation. In this regard the marginal profit rate, defined as the change in profits between two consecutive years relative to investment spending with one-year lag, proved to be a good harbinger of investment growth. The dynamics of profitability set the non-linear growth path for the economy. Its driving force from the early 1960s to the early 1980s was the remarkable technical revolution that radically transformed the composition of the capital stock. The mechanization of production led to a rising capital-output ratio that dragged profitability way down from its initially lofty levels. In addition to technical change shaping the trend, after 1970 empirical evidence supports the existence of two medium-term growth cycles akin to Richard Goodwin's theoretical constructs. Goodwin's growth cycles reflect the effect on accumulation of changes in the wage-share, abstracting from credit and finance except in so far as they affect profitability. My findings show that after the late 1960s medium-term changes of the wage share punctuated the long-run trend in profitability and modulated its downward bent.

## External finance and accumulation

Because I relied so heavily on the perspective found in Classical Political Economy regarding profits and growth, it was necessary to locate the role played by external finance in accumulation. Classical economists from Adam Smith on to Marx were well aware of the role of credit and banks in support of economic activity. Their chief objective, however, was to lay bare the laws of Political Economy applying to a growing economy absent external finance. Hollander for instance cites Adam Smith's criticism of Hume for taking a position that allowed him "to have gone a little into the notion that public opulence consists in money" (Hollander, 1987, p. 177). By following this line of thinking, Classical economists could focus their attention on the intrinsic mechanisms that brought about the growth of capital and led to the expansion in the wealth of nations. They were able to gauge the full potential for growth contained in systems whose core dynamics hinged on capital accumulation. The springboards necessary for the growth of capital as well as its structural limits were found within the system itself. External credit played no structural role in its development path.

This means that a rise in the rate of accumulation assumed a corresponding fall in consumption spending. It is clear that in Adam Smith "extra capital investment from a given total of profits and rents will only be attainable if there is an equivalent reduction in consumption from these"

(Eltis, 1984, p. 79). Marx was even more explicit on this issue than Adam Smith ever managed to be, despite the fact that both dealt extensively with banking practices. In the transition from "simple" to "expanded" reproduction, the source of the additional funds required by capitalists to raise the rate of accumulation above its current level was their own current consumption budget. To drive this point home Marx remarked that:

> it was presupposed in our presentation of simple reproduction that the entire surplus-value in departments I and II was spent as revenue. In point of fact, however, one portion of surplus-value is spent as revenue, and another portion transformed into capital. Only with this precondition does real accumulation take place (Marx, 1981, p. 579).

Marx's conceptual schemes of expanded reproduction worked out in Volume II of Capital showed how capital accumulation and balanced growth can happen when profits are reinvested and certain proportions are strictly observed. External credit or deficit financing were not present or required for accumulation. In fact capitalist savings must rise in Smith and Marx in order to finance higher investment (larger employment of productive workers in Smith). There is no "income multiplier" effect in the Classical approach to accumulation precisely because any increases in the ratio investment/profits necessarily will be matched by a decline in the consumption/profits ratio. This is a consequence of considering as possible sources of accumulation only internally available finance. The classical economists sought to formulate the laws of development applying to capital free from any elements capable of obscuring the nature of its intrinsic dynamics.

## The post-Keynesian reversal

Post-Keynesians engaged in the interpretation of a "monetary theory of production" have gone to the opposite extreme. They generally praise Keynes for restoring the primacy of credit over investment and investment over saving. In Keynes a rise in investment spending above its current equilibrium level (investment = saving) led to an income multiplier effect because no previous reduction in consumption spending (no previous rise in aggregate savings) was required to finance it. Instead, the higher investment spending would be financed by bank loans. Without external credit no such expansion is possible. In the Keynesian perspective firms engage in deficit spending as a matter of course. Writing as a radical Keynesian, Bleany has argued that Marx's schemes of reproduction "tend naturally towards the Keynesian formulation" because:

> The existence of a banking system, paper money and credit facilities means that a capitalist can extend his production without proportionately cutting back on his own consumption, or that of his fellows. If this happens, a situation of excess demand is created (Bleany, 1976, p. 107).

The hidden link between H. Minsky's financial fragility hypothesis and Keynes's own work can be traced to Minsky's identification of the banking system as the chief source of external funding for business expenditures:

> Banks are the central financial organization of a capitalist economy. Once the assets and liabilities of banks are set, the economy's financing framework is largely determined (Minsky, 1986, pp. 318-319).

While agreeing with Minsky's general approach to finance, J. Toporowski has questioned his "banking perspective" (J. Toporowski, 1999) arguing that in the "English-speaking countries" it must be acknowledged that "the banking system does not cover the whole financial system". This is not the case in Spain, where a few major banks make-up the hub of the financial system and capital markets remain in its periphery.

Following this line of reasoning to its logical conclusion, Colin Rogers took the decisive step of elevating to the rank of a production factor the finance mode that Classical theory had previously done without. It is obvious to him that "Credit is now—and always has been—an interdependent part of capitalist production, i.e. it is in effect a factor of production" (Rogers, 1989, p. 290). The justification for this conclusion is, of course, that Post-Keynesians see credit financing of all current costs of production as a necessary "input" of the final product. Reimbursement of these loans out of sales at regular intervals, however, begs a paradoxical question. How can firms that borrowed to finance their costs of production obtain sufficient revenues to pay back principal plus interest at the end of each period? The authoritative post-Keynesian answer is that "firms borrow the amount of interest they have to pay upon their credit, as they borrow to cover the other costs" (Deleplace and Nell, 1996, p. 15).

On the face of it, the Post-Keynesian approach seems to disregard the ruling discipline of markets. On the heels of the Keynesian revolution in theory and policy, John Strachey cautioned that credit would not suspend the rules set by profitability:

> Credit makes the cash nexus which unites the dealers of an exchange economy into an elastic nexus. It allows production to swing out beyond the limits imposed upon it by the social system. But then, and to the same extent, it pulls production in within those limits (Strachey, 1935, p. 313).

I will seek to demonstrate on the basis of Chapter 2 that this perspective on credit, properly formalized and meticulously developed by A. Shaikh (Shaikh, 1989 and 1992) proved to be exceedingly helpful in the arduous effort required to interpret Spanish data. Indeed external finance allowed firms to engage in deficit spending, that is, expand beyond their own means. This did not mean, however, that the discipline of the prevailing "social system" was ignored. The budget constraint facing firms not only remained unscathed, but gained weight as a result of the acquired debt. Short-term credit for working capital bridged the time gap between production expenditures and revenue flows from sales. Sales realize profits and the results will confirm whether previous investments were justified. Profitability trends, on the other hand, will be set by the evolution of the capital-output ratio and real unit labor costs reflecting the evolution of real wages and labor productivity. Changes in these variables stem from complex dynamics related to mechanization and employment/wage cycles unrelated to finance regimes. Finally, firms' credit-worthiness will largely depend on their past and prospective profitability.

## Monetarism versus Post-Keynesian endogenous credit

The monetarist approach focuses on the demand for money as a buffer stock, a reserve of cash that avoids its holders unnecessary transaction costs associated with recurrent purchases. Post-Keynesian studies emphasize finance, the need for credit-money to fund all planned business spending throughout the production stages preceding sales. Monetarists see the supply of money as being determined by central bank policy independently of the finance needs expressed by entrepreneurs. From their perspective money plays no role in the adjustments that drive goods and factor markets to full-employment balance. They argue that the supply of money and its changes affect the price level only through adjustments in spending flows and the stock of money reserves held. Post-Keynesians locate the chief source of new money in the creation of credit lines by banks responding to the demand by firms for working capital. From their standpoint, the supply of credit money does not exist apart from the demand for it, but rather it is endogenous to the finance needs of the real economy and its growth. The transmission mechanism between credit supply flows and changes in the purchase of inputs needed to produce the final output is transparent, while fluctuations of the credit flows are driven by demand and the burden of past borrowing.

Banks are profit-seeking entities that aggressively will acquire whatever liquid reserves are needed to accommodate their clients' needs for finance. Monetarists are keen on warning against excessive growth of the money supply because having first assumed full employment the only possible outcome is inflation. Since the money supply is taken as being exogenously driven by government fiat, budget deficits are usually blamed for the excesses fueling inflation. The chief concern of monetarists regarding borrowing is the public debt, linked to the profligate habits of governments and the growth of their budget deficit.

Post-Keynesian economists such as R. Wray on the other hand typically support public deficits as providing the stimulus necessary to sustain the growth of aggregate demand and prevent recessions (Wray, 1993). Generally Post-Keynesian economists trace the rise of inflation to the excessive growth of wages, that is, wages rising faster than productivity. In the event firms prevent the resulting profit squeeze by raising prices. While they see the expansion of private business debt as the other side of the creation of credit-money by the banks, they ignore explicitly the effect of this debt on new business spending.

For Paul Davidson and other Post-Keynesian theorists credit will be required to finance the planned working capital spending by firms even when the scale of production is held steady. New loans are required to cover the costs of current production. The reason is that costs precede revenues and proceeds from past sales were used to repay previous borrowing. Even in the case of a constant activity level, current sales must provide the wherewithal to repay past loans. Moreover, with a constant level of output, higher wages or materials costs require additional borrowing. In short, current borrowing will cover the finance needed to bridge the interval between production plans and realized sales. Placing credit finance as the starting point of modern industrial enterprise, that is, as a "pre-condition to production", leads Post-Keynesian theorists to conclusions diametrically opposed to monetarism. From this perspective, bank lending takes precedence over the creation of bank deposits. There is a general agreement among Post-Keynesian economists that "the creation of credit ex nihilo, more than financial intermediation, is then the specific attribute of banks" (C. Delaplace and E. J. Nell, 1996, pp. 11-12).

Post-Keynesians argue that if banks failed to provide firms with the initial finance for wages, materials and fixed capital investments money sales could not be large enough to cover costs. Prominent Post-Keynesians have explicitly raised the intriguing question, "how firms who borrow a given sum can reimburse it and pay interest, if all money comes from credit?" and given a no less paradoxical answer, namely that firms need to borrow enough credit to match the interest payments due (Delaplace and Nell, 1996, pp. 14-15).

The fact that government deficit spending under certain conditions will expand the supply of money apart from the deficit spending by private firms adds a new twist to the Post-Keynesian story, while the primacy of credit finance remains unchallenged. Now considered from the standpoint of its sources not its forms (currency plus bank deposits), the supply of money, $M_S$, includes both high-powered money, $H_S$, issued by the government (currency in circulation plus bank reserves), and bank loans, $L_S$, made by commercial banks. The change in the stock of money, $\Delta M_S$, is given by the change in loans advanced to the private and public sectors, $\Delta L^a$, plus the net change in high-powered money, $\Delta H^n$. This refers to the change in high-powered money, $\Delta H$, net of discount-window borrowing by the banks, $\Delta BR$, that is the change in bank reserves.

Alternative ways of financing the public deficit have a different impact on the money supply. When the Treasury purchases bonds from commercial banks, the reserves of the banking system will expand, but whether or not the money supply increases depends on the demand for loans. If commercial banks dispose of their excess reserves by purchasing bonds, the money supply will expand once the government spends the newly acquired money. On the other hand, if the government runs a deficit that needs financing, the alternatives are as follows. In the United States the U.S. Treasury can engage in open-market operations, and as a result bank reserves will increase but not necessarily the money supply. Secondly, if the Treasury sold bonds to the non-bank public or banks holding no excess reserves money will simply exchange hands and both the stock of high-powered money and the supply of money will remain unchanged. Finally if the central bank purchased the Treasury bonds, the stock of high-powered money in the system will increase, and according to Barro this procedure would lead to the same results as if the changes occurred due to "helicopter drops" (Barro, 1993, p. 377).

Once public spending is introduced, the finance needs of the public sector must be accounted for alongside those of the private sector. The problem that such an inclusion puts forth is that since the money supply includes high-powered money as well credit-money, fulfilling the finance requirements of the public sector may add up to a total money supply at variance with the aggregate money demand. In light of this complication, the leading monetarist D. Laidler has observed that:

> A fiscal deficit can therefore become an independent source of monetary expansion when the monetary authorities are treating the interest rate as their policy instrument, namely that it is not only the extension of credit to the private sector, but also to the fiscal authorities, which leads to the creation of money (Laidler, 1982, p. 60).

The question of the relationship between the money supply and the price level enters the monetarist model after the adjustments necessary to achieve market equilibrium in the commodity and factor markets have been thoroughly carried out. This is so whether or not the analysis involves general or partial equilibrium methodology.

## The supply of money and the price level

A general equilibrium outcome stipulates that all markets will be balanced and all resources will be fully employed. To this end, price adjustments must work timelessly in response to the existence of positive or negative excess demand. The mechanism leading to this optimal result requires two institutional arrangements. One is the presence of an elusive auctioneer reconciling the notional bids advanced by buyers and sellers in commodity and factor markets. Secondly, a "centralized system of accounts", where goods will be placed by suppliers and collected by demanders. Money as means of exchange or historical time for that matter, are not involved in the matching of bids or collection of goods.

Only after the full employment aggregate output level compatible with general equilibrium is obtained will the supply of money be exogenously introduced. Post-Keynesian theorists like Paul Davidson have rejected the whole methodology of general equilibrium analysis:

> The necessary assumptions underlying the Walrasian equations set up producers and consumers free of uncertainty, sure of their tastes, resource productivity, and market conduct, and certain that the price system will pre-reconcile all choices before any production or exchange is undertaken. In essence these models are *timeless* systems, in which market events and market information are universally possessed (Davidson, 1977, p. 283).

Both general and partial equilibrium theorists posit the real aggregate output and employment as determined apart from the money supply. Monetary authorities fix the quantity of money. Once the money supply is so determined, it will merely affect the price level for the aggregate product, not the matrix of relative prices that regulated its production and will govern its exchange. The road to monetarist results is covered with artificial props, for as D. Laidler has acknowledged, we can always:

> produce monetarist results if we assume full employment, and then postulate that the major source of disturbance is variations in the level of--or rate of change of--the nominal money supply... To put matters this way is, in effect, to say that monetarists' belief in the quantity theory as a theory of money income boils down to the view that sustained inflation is caused by an expanding money supply (Laidler, 1982, p. 10).

## The Post-Keynesian alternative

A large portion of the spirit animating the Post-Keynesian revolt against Monetarism may have been captured in the phrase of an economist not fully identified with the Post-Keynesian paradigm: "it is not money that makes the world go round, but credit" (Stiglitz, 1988, p. 64). In the Post-Keynesian approach money is "willingly held" as a reserve, to use Barro's terminology (Barro, 1993, p. 134) because as P. Davidson observes "bankers are willing to make additional bank-debt contracts available under the rules of the game" (Davidson, 1982, p. 227). Such was the lesson brought home by the *Treatise on Money* where Keynes (Keynes, 1930, p. 3) recognized that money "comes into existence along with debts, which are contracts for deferred payment and ... offers of contracts for sale or purchase".

As W. Godley sees it, there is no question that firms require initial finance. In the nature of things the firms' universe is Post-Keynesian since they share:

> their perception that investment, production and distribution processes which take up historical time—a period which must elapse before sales can take place, hence generating a systemic need for finance (Godley, 1996, p. 2).

In contrast to the monetarist haven of timeless tranquility and perfect knowledge of predefined outcomes, the world of Post-Keynesian economics is crowded with the phantoms of risk and ignorance looming behind every long-term business decision. Past borrowing by firms often results in a burgeoning debt that must be serviced at given intervals out of current revenues. While firms may anticipate that future sales will be large enough to meet their financial obligations to their creditors, events may prove them otherwise.

Paul Davidson has expressed disdain for "The fictional world of Walrasian general equilibrium, where money is superimposed on the system only after all the real elements of exchange are resolved" (Davidson, 1977, p. 283). In such a world, without uncertainty about present or future conditions, as Frank H. Hahn pointed out, it would be irrational for anyone to hold money as a reserve (Hahn, 1971). Rational agents would instead pile-up interest-yielding assets, expected to mature at a specific date. Davidson judges such a world-view as "an impediment to a serious theory of money".

In light of the Post-Keynesian withering critique of Monetarism, alternative explanations for holding money reserves need be considered. In Goodhart's account, the demand for money as a "buffer stock" exists as a result of the uncertainty inherent in market outcomes (Goodhart, 1984). W. Godley explicitly assumes in his analysis of money, finance and national income determination that "all decisions have to be taken in a state of uncertainty, without agents knowing what their sales or income are going to be" (Godley, 1996, p. 2). Keynes was aware of the fact that unexpected shortfalls or delayed revenues are common events justifying the holding of reserves, "assets in the same standard as that in which future liabilities may fall due" (Keynes, 1977, p. 237).

Barro's approach on the other hand stresses the convenience of holding cash rather than facing the uncertainty involved in business decisions. For Barro it "is typically more convenient to allow receipts to accumulate for a while as cash before spending these funds or converting them into bonds" (Barro, 1993, p. 98). This is so due to the *transaction costs* involved in trading assets for money. It is wise and therefore advisable to keep money on hand because rational agents wish to minimize the costs of finding buyers for their assets when cash is needed. In Barro's interpretation, however, uncertainty enters the picture in the guise of external shocks. The rational response of agents to the relentless shocks that impact their pursuits leads to the maintenance of reserves, both goods and liquid assets.

Regarding cash reserves, the size of these "buffer stocks" will vary according to changes in agents' liquidity preference. Once the effect of the public deficit is taken into account, and if the chosen fiscal policy leads to the expansion of the money supply, there is no assurance that the money stocks agents wish to hold will match the augmented money supply. Prominent monetarists have tackled this problem with various degrees of success. D. Laidler tracked the way in which the discrepancy could arise even if monetary policy explicitly aimed at balancing the credit markets:

> Even if, at a particular rate of interest, the values of income, prices, the rate of return on capital and so on are such as to render the supply of money and bank

> credit compatible with portfolio equilibrium on the part of the banking system and the non-bank public, that in no way guarantees either that the fiscal authorities' budget is in balance or that, if it is not, the private sector will be willing to absorb just the right number of new government bonds to finance whatever deficit is being incurred (Laidler, 1982, p. 60).

In general, the imbalance arising when the actual stock of money reserves differs from the desired stock will lead to spending changes. Then when fluctuations of the actual stocks of reserves are due to windfall gains or losses the changes in spending that follow will not necessarily match the changes in aggregate output. The challenge to Monetarism proffered by W. Godley questions the very foundations of its conceptual structure:

> The "supply" of money is a redundant concept—there is no such thing. Even the term "demand" for money strains language; for it badly describes a situation where people aim to keep their holdings of money within some normal range but where the sums they end up with are determined in large part by impulse purchases, windfalls and other unexpected events. It is unfortunate that the stock of money measured ex-post should have become generally known as the "money supply"—a term which invites the supposition that a supply exists independently from what people wish to hold (Godley, 1998, pp. 9-10).

Changing grounds from the methodology of general to that of partial equilibrium, we encounter a major "black box" hiding the secret of the quantity theory of money (Laidler, 1982, p. 64), much like we found the auctioneer of general equilibrium in the midst of it all. The "black box" contains a "complex transmission mechanism" (Laidler, 1982, p. 62) that translates changes in the quantity of money into changes of nominal income via price movements. The problem is that how exactly this is brought about remains unsolved. Laidler challenged his fellow travelers to spell out the way in which:

> the typical agent receives a windfall gain in money holdings and sets in motion expenditure which enables him to adjust his money holdings towards their long-run level (Laidler, 1982, p. 50).

Barro's and Laidler's accounts of what happens in the "black box" start out with the initial assumption that the demand for money is positively related to income and inversely related to the implicit interest rate. Laidler's explanation (Laidler, 1982, pp. 126-127) also assumes that money, just as any other asset that households or firms may possess, provides a diminishing marginal utility to its holder. Now if asset equilibrium prevails to begin with, an unexpected increase in money stocks held by agents will bring about a decline of its implicit interest yield. In response to this, agents will change their array of desired assets in favor of securities, thereby driving down their rates of return. The decline in asset yields will then enhance the appeal of consumption, causing thereby a rise in spending for non-durable goods, which translates into a rise in sales. At this point Laidler's story includes an "accelerator" effect, as the expansion of sales will prompt firms caught with inadequate inventories to increase their investment spending. Laidler's story needs the accelerator effect because by linking the growth of investment to a rise in consumption spending, the focus is directed to the supposedly ubiquitous inventory shortfalls, hence to the immediate price increases that will follow.

Barro's version carries Laidler's story one step further. After the initial windfall gains, agents rearranged their asset portfolios in favor of securities, hence bond prices rose and their yields declined. But once goods prices go up, as Laidler expects they will, higher expenditures will prompt agents to reduce their bond holdings and increase their money stocks. In the end, interest rates will bounce back to their initially higher levels and only higher goods prices will make the difference. The moral of the story being that, contrary to Keynesian economics, the expansion of the money supply will cause inflation and no decline in interest rates (Barro, 1993, p. 136).

I believe that W. Godley's expressed frustration with the method and scope of Neo-Classical economics issues to a large extent from his reading of the colorful but wholly unreal character with which neo-classical writers conceptualize the money supply. In this regard, Godley noted that even "Modigliani…gives banks (with regard to their assets) no role other than to hold government bonds; and Milton Friedman famously used a helicopter when he wanted to get more money into the system". Not mincing his words, Godley decries the fact that:

> Modern textbooks on macroeconomics treat money in a remarkably uniform—and remarkably silly –way. In the primary exposition the stock of "money" is treated as exogenous in the two senses, a) that it is determined outside the model, and b) that it has no accounting relationship with any other variable (Godley, 1996, p. 1).

In order to confirm Godley's findings, one needs to go no further than Barro's textbook, *Macroeconomics*. When he deals with the question of expanding the money supply *ad hoc* windfall gains take the main stage. In Chapter 5 of his celebrated textbook the layout of the problem is as follows:

> We consider, in other words, a permanent increase in the quantity of money. The change would arise if the government, on a one-time-only basis, printed up some extra money and gave it to people. In Chapters 7 and 17 we shall examine more realistic ways in which new money gets into the economy (Barro, 1993, p. 135).

In Chapter 7, however, Barro avoids the issue again, advising that, "we sidestep the theory of the money supply in this and the next chapter". Chapter 8, however, contains the section *Monetary Growth and Transfer Payments* and in it, we find again Milton Friedman's "popular story" featuring "transfer payments as arising via a 'helicopter drop' of cash". The celebrated vignette is once again promoted as the "simplest possible way to introduce monetary growth into the model" (Barro, 1993, p. 188).

Victoria Chick has pointed out the central role that windfall gains play in the monetarist story. When the stock of money increases via helicopters or similar guises, "the new money is clearly a windfall. No effort has been expended to earn it, so it is perceived as an increase in wealth, not income. It comes all at once, not gradually as payment for goods or services" (Chick, 1985, p. 96). Hence the desired monetarist conclusion is locked-in with the initial premise that the money will be spent not saved. Indeed the monetarist result is part of the parable precisely "because of the way the money enters the system", that is, as a windfall gain.

What is missing here is the recognition that money chiefly enters the system as credit finance to cover the working capital of firms and their long-term investments, when internal funds are insufficient. Godley has also noted that Neo-Classical texts avoid this alternative: "Usually the role and even existence of bank credit is simply ignored". V. Chick on the other hand finds that the single-minded focus on money stocks, not financing of working capital, leads to preposterous suggestions:

> I have seen, not infrequently, references in the literature to the borrowing in order to increase one's money holding. Outside the (rather trivial) finance motive, this strikes me as patently absurd. Indeed, in an overdraft system, overdrafts and the money supply do not expand until those granted an overdraft actually make use of it (Chick, 1985, p. 98).

Two conclusions follow from this. First, the availability of overdraft accounts should provide a measure of flexibility to reduce the chances of stock imbalances. Secondly, contrary to the monetarist assumption of automatic transmission, as J. Moudud has stressed, the growth of bank reserves will only result in the expansion of the money supply *desired* by banks, not necessarily the growth of the actual money supply, which depends on the credit demand (Moudud, 1998a, 1998b, 1999).

## Critique of the Post-Keynesian alternative

Banks issue loans to credit-worthy clients. Borrowers need to show that their future revenue flows are likely to be large enough to pay back principal plus interest. The future is uncertain and banks as well as firms face the risk of default. These are truisms. The growth of external finance presupposes the ability of firms to expand their sales at a rate sufficiently high to allow for repayment of rising debts and no negative effect on their investment growth. Post-Keynesian economics fails to go beyond this valuable insight, although it is a great leap forward compared to the timeless world of general equilibrium.

An alternative view would make the following connections. When planned spending by firms exceeds their available internal funds, drawn from past sales, external credit provides an alternative option whose weight depends on their assessed liquidity. New borrowing will reduce that liquidity measure to the extent of the growth in liabilities, and will impose definite horizons for the retirement of the contracted debt. Future revenues earmarked for debt repayment will reduce the sum of internal funds available to finance circulating plus fixed investment spending. On balance, positive excess demand will emerge when total spending exceeds internally accessible funds and in the aggregate, realized sales will be larger than before. But the discipline inherent in debt accumulation by firms will reverse the sign of excess demand once loan repayment lowers the firms' available internal funds and thus the potential spending flow in future.

## The multiplier and debt

Money, indeed, enters the non-bank sector in the form of credit, and drawing the implications of debt expansion is generally not an integral part of the Monetarist research program, except when it concerns the effects of the public debt. Post-Keynesians characteristically fail to include in the expenditure function of their investment models the negative effects of a growing debt. The Keynesian story of the income multiplier is typically presented as if the acquired debt had no impact on the outcome of the expansion.

Starting in the mid-1980s, A. Shaikh was first to subject this approach to a scathing critique in his New School University (New York) Graduate Seminar on *Marx, Keynes and Kalecki*. My version of it derives from his pioneering teachings. The story develops out of an initial equilibrium position, where current investment spending is fully financed by firms' savings (retained earnings) plus household savings, in short, total savings. Then a jump in investment breaks the balance between savings and investment flows and requires a first round of external (bank) credit. New rounds of credit finance will be needed as long as the advancing level of savings fails to match the higher level of investment. The gap between investment and the rising (but not equal) savings level needs filling with new external credit. It is precisely the fact that the sustained level of investment exceeds the (advancing) level of savings what expands aggregate income. Once the expansion of income allows for a level of savings (internal finance) as high as investment, income growth comes to a halt.

We can show that the total injections of credit adds-up to the total expansion of aggregate income. How then will this newly acquired debt be retired? At the new equilibrium achieved by the income multiplier, internally available funds are sufficient to finance current investment, but not to retire the debt. If the debt is not paid, it will grow without limit due to compound interest. The claims advanced on behalf of the Keynesian income multiplier will remain shaky as long as the story fails to include a satisfactory account of the consequences derived from the acquired debt.

Figure 1.2 shows the dynamic simulation of a Keynesian model moving from one equilibrium position to another. A. Shaikh created the model and Tutsim simulation in the mid-1980s and it took me several years later to replicate it. In this simulation, zero excess demand defines the initial equilibrium level of income, the condition where savings equals investment. The equilibrium condition persists for a time until investment spending jumps up and sets into motion the sequence of flows that raises aggregate income to a higher level.

The dynamic simulation reflects the rising wave of positive excess demand, as the jump in investment spending relative to current savings injects new funds into the system. Current savings refers to internal funds, while the rise in investment requires new credit borrowing. The wave in excess demand reflects the cyclical adjustment of savings to investment spending all the way through, until the gap vanishes and a new equilibrium emerges. Figure 1.2 displaying the model's simulation, shows that even after the new income equilibrium is attained and the higher investment spending fully financed out of internal funds (savings), the acquired debt will continue to grow without limit due to the inherent effects of compound interest. Clearly this cannot be so, and therefore the Keynesian model needs to recognize explicitly how the debt will be retired and what the effects will be on excess demand when it so happens.

Barro's monetarist approach might superficially seem compatible with Post-Keynesian economics, since he allows for the fact that "Financial institutions use the funds generated from deposits to make loans to households, businesses, and the government" (Barro, 1993, p. 483). Post-Keynesians, however, do not see banks as mere intermediaries between savers and borrowers but rather as active creators of credit-money. Credit-finance, in their view, precedes the implementation of firms' production plans. Only because of their willingness "to enter into additional debt contracts with the banking systems" are firms and government able to offer work contracts to labor and purchase other inputs from their producers.

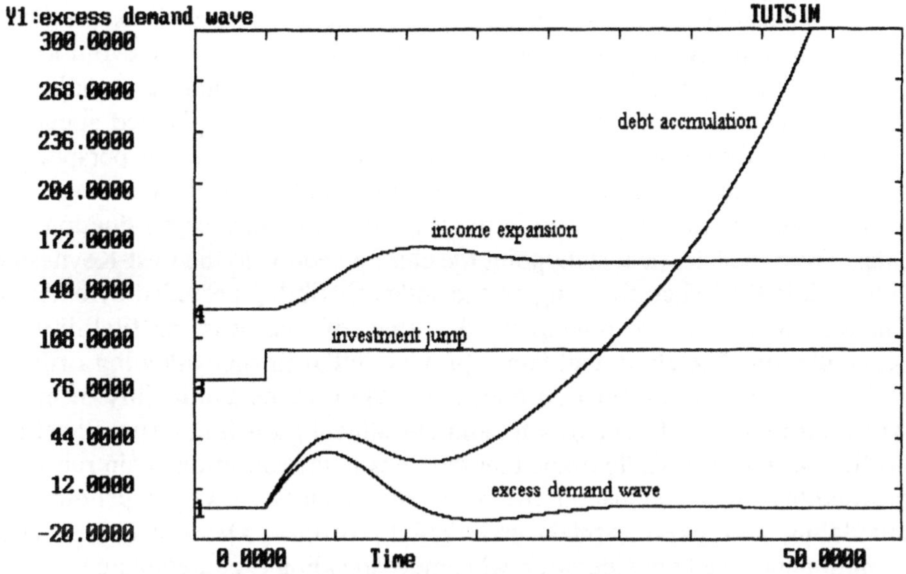


**Figure 1.2 Simulation of Shaikh's dynamic model of the Keynesian income multiplier with explicit debt**

In the Spanish case, it would seem as though the Post-Keynesian connection between credit finance of working capital and business activity is empirically validated. Indeed adding up the full measure of finance needed annually to cover wages, investment, depreciation and taxes in the business sector provides a reliable gauge of the credit supply issued by banks to the private sector.

This empirical support of the link between the estimated finance needs of the business sector and the credit supply to the private sector held good for the last thirty years. When the funding of the public sector is taken into account, and particularly its deficit spending, the level and growth of the total credit supply falls roughly into place.

Yet the equally close fit between fixed capital investment and the reported data for business retained-earnings strongly suggests that the evolution of internal funds was a major factor accounting for the pace of accumulation. The Classical growth dynamics of Smith, Ricardo and Marx relied on profits to provide the wherewithal for capital accumulation. Marx's Volume II worked out schemes of expanded reproduction showing how growth was possible fueled exclusively by internal funds, not credit. The injection of external credit into the schemes of reproduction, alas, would not free accumulation from the inherent discipline of the profit constraint.

My alternative approach differs from Monetarism as well as the Post-Keynesian approach because I see a straight link connecting the evolution of profits, and especially retained earnings, with capital accumulation. Admittedly, short-term credit fills the time gap between planned spending finance and future sales revenues. Indeed, the Post-Keynesian perspective appears to render spending and accumulation independent of savings and profits. But this can only be so in the short-interval between production and sales. From the Classical standpoint the chief objection to the Post-Keynesian approach is that when focusing on the added flexibility provided by external finance, it seems to downplay the role of business profitability in accumulation. The claim that banks provide initial finance allowing firms to purchase factors of production does not mean that the availability of credit will determine investment growth, and investment growth in turn will set the profitability path. I would argue that the links in the causation chain run from profitability to decisions on the scale of business activity (spending on circulating and fixed capital) and then to finance. Of course past debt commitments need consideration when new spending is contemplated.

## Investment, profits and inflation

I can readily accept the findings of Post-Keynesian economists concerning the link between the working capital spending carried out by firms and short-term bank credit. The question is whether access to credit as such provides capital growth. It is true that access to short-term credit finance will allow firms to purchase the resources necessary to complete production plans in advance of sales. The spending, however, will be justified only if sales revenues are high enough to provide the expected profit margin after repayment of the loans. Taking into account the iron discipline of debt, requiring repayment of principal plus interest, the sum returned to the creditors must be larger than the amount received. Profits are not only the object of business enterprise but also the means to achieve that goal, providing the wherewithal to acquire and harness new productive inputs. Profit growth remains the prime object of enterprise and firms' spending growth cannot be justified in its absence. It follows from this that credit finance cannot be thought of as the fuel for the growth engine of capital unless enterprise profits are present.

As I have argued, firms' investments growth plans and attendant credit finance will fluctuate around their intrinsic profitability path. The highest investment rate will be achieved when all available enterprise profits are plowed back in the guise of productive inputs. Therefore the maximum rate of capital accumulation, $g_K$, cannot exceed the profit rate, r, without affecting the rate of inflation. In symbols, the maximum rate of investment follows:

$$I_{max} = \Pi, \text{ so that } \frac{I}{K}\max \equiv g_K \max = \frac{\Pi}{K} = r$$

J. Moudud's (Moudud, 1998a) integration of the classical theory of credit money and the dynamics of growth cycles provides an elegant definition of excess demand. The supply of money, $M_S$, consists of high-powered money issued by the government, $H_S$, plus credit-money, $L_S$, (loans) granted by commercial banks. Aggregate excess demand, E, is the difference between nominal aggregate demand, $Y_D$, and aggregate supply, $Y_S$. From the standpoint of the money stock, aggregate excess demand is the difference between the money supply, $M_S$, and the quantity of money demanded, $M_D$. The expression for excess demand in symbols becomes:

$$P(Y_D - Y_S) = E = (M_S - M_D)$$

## Inflation and excess demand

Monetarists have traditionally focused their attention on the growth of public deficits as the main cause of inflation flares. In the Spanish experience, for example, public deficits were typically financed through borrowing from the banking system.

This practice has been frequently criticized as conducive to the rise in inflation. But public deficit spending occurred largely after the early 1980s, a period in which overall excess demand was negative (total investment in fixed and circulating capital plus capitalist consumption plus public deficits was lower than total profits) and the rate of inflation was falling.

Expanding the credit supply to private firms whose spending plans outpace their profits growth, as happened in Spain from the mid-1970s through the early 1980s, will cause a rise in positive excess demand and therefore inflation, the virulence of which will depend on the size of the spending deficit involved. Whether the recipient of external finance to cover deficit spending is the public or the private sectors, pushing total investment spending above the growth of profits amounts to a violation of the intrinsic loop between profits and their transformation into productive inputs useful for capital accumulation.

According to Anwar Shaikh, when investment grows relative to profits, the *throughput* coefficient (Shaikh, 1999) will rise, signaling growing inflationary pressures. For Shaikh price inflation is a sign that the profit mass has failed to grow sufficiently to accommodate the growth of investment spending. The theoretical roots of Shaikh's classical theory of inflation reach deep into Von Neumann's model of maximal balanced economic growth. In that model Von Neumann reduced the consumption of workers, as a necessary subtraction from the system's output, to a hypothetical minimum and assumed that its entire surplus would be available for accumulation (Kregel, 1971, Makarov and Rubinov, 1987, pp. 824-825, Chakravarty, 1989).

In addition, Marx outlined the foundation for one of the analytical streaks in Shaikh's view on inflation, namely the link between the surplus and the *throughput* of productive inputs. Marx focused on possible bottlenecks impeding the transformation of the surplus into productive inputs for accumulation. In his *Theories* comment, a general rise in prices will occur if profits are growing so fast that their transformation into productive inputs encounters bottlenecks. While Marx discussed elsewhere the effect of stagnant or falling profits on the rate of accumulation, in his *Theories of Surplus Value* he did not take up the issue of steady accumulation in thc face of stagnant or falling profits:

> if the production of surplus capital takes place at a very rapid rate, and its re-transformation into productive capital so increases the demand for all the elements of the latter that real production cannot keep pace, and consequently there is a rise in prices of all commodities which enter into the formation of capital (Marx, 1952, p. 371).

For as long as profits were growing and the economy enjoyed high employment inflation in Spain was relatively mild. Significantly, the rise in inflation coincided with the stagnation of profits, large infusions of bank credit and the rapid growth in unemployment. From Shaikh's classical perspective, *stagflation,* the joint appearance of growing unemployment and price inflation ceases to be a Keynesian anomaly. From a classical perspective, *stagflation* now emerged as the natural manifestation of a warped slump, reacting to credit-fueled investment expenditures pressing against stagnant profits.

## General conclusions

I will endeavor to show in the nine chapters that follow how the movements of profitability and excess demand set the path for the growth trend and cycles of accumulation in the Spanish economy. In so doing I will be guided by the dynamical approach pioneered by the Classical economists and modeled by A. Shaikh. I am mindful of the fact, nonetheless, that Post-Keynesian economics goes a long way to provide a more realistic and useful approach to the link between modern finance and capital accumulation than monetarism ever did. Post-Keynesian analysis breaks the artificial dichotomy between the real economy and money. It generally entertains no presumption that full employment is normally present. The world of uncertainty and risk that surrounds business decisions is fully recognized and the need for money reserves duly appreciated. My reservations stem from the fact that placing external finance ahead of production decisions based on profitability and budget constraints disregards the fundamental discipline of capital accumulation because it underplays the role of profits behind it. After the early 1980s in Spain internal funds loomed larger as the chief source of finance for business investment and correspondingly credit growth diminished in that period. Overall, the dynamics of profitability and its impact on accumulation trends set the trend for the observed cycles in the business sector demand for credit finance.

# Part I: Heterodox Growth and Cycles Models

# 2 Shaikh's Model of Finance and Accumulation

One path-breaking line of research pursued by Anwar Shaikh since the mid-1980s has focused on formalizing the effects of external finance on accumulation as an extension of the Classical tradition. A. Shaikh's contribution to the analysis of growth and cycles includes two dynamical models (Shaikh, 1989 and 1992). His approach to modeling is dynamical because the structure of his system is built with ratios whose variables are normally growing. Structural adjustments involve changes in the growth rates of these variables around their trends. It is assumed that growth can be normally achieved through capital accumulation, involving the reinvestment of disposable profits. Other factors, such as technical change or population growth do not rank as elements intrinsically necessary to achieve economic growth. There is no presumption in any of Shaikh's models that actual growth will produce full employment of labor, even though average capacity utilization will fluctuate around its normal or average level and profitability will cycle around its normal trend as well.

In his first model, presented in this chapter, Shaikh made borrowing and the attendant debt an explicit argument of his accumulation function. Holding the profit margin and the interest rate constant, the requirement that business debt be paid periodically in the midst of shocks gave rise to persistent cycles. Shaikh's second model (1992) seeks to generalize the theory of effective demand, provides a fuller explanation for the persistence of cycles of different duration and suggests a solution to Harrod's puzzle of the warranted path's instability.

Shaikh's conceptual structure allows him to formalize the determinants of short-term as well as medium-term cycles. First, he works out the dynamics of a fast cycle responding to the perennial adjustments between aggregate demand and aggregate supply. The fast cycle, lasting 3-5 years, is produced by the adjustments carried out to correct the emerging disparities between actual and desired business inventories. The slower fluctuations emerge as a result of averaging the adjustments between growing aggregate supply and growing capacity. Changing fixed investment growth rates occur in response to rising capacity utilization and produce the slower cycle, stretching 7-11 years. Capacity growth in turn is the natural consequence of net fixed investment growth.

While questioning the propriety of any equilibrium solution, Shaikh's analysis concluded that indeed the actual growth of the system followed a cyclical path around its warranted growth trajectory. In short, in the long-run average aggregate supply will be roughly equal to average capacity output. The important finding was that internal mechanisms exist that ensure the system's growth and dampen any explosive deviation from its warranted growth path.

I believe that his work provided the dynamic conceptual structure most effective to study the persistence of business cycles in Spain. To that end I wish to confront Shaikh's model of accumulation and effective demand with the experience of Spain's growth fluctuations from 1964 to the present. In his first model Shaikh worked out the implications of business borrowing for the growth path of firms engaged in deficit spending. If accumulation can be (at least) partially financed with bank credit, will this free investment decisions from the constraints set by their internal funds?

For purposes of empirical testing, however, I was obliged to reduce the complex dynamics of the model to its bare bones. To begin with, I believe there is one major structural difference between Shaikh's object of investigation and mine. In his model, Shaikh sought to analyze the dynamics of credit finance under normal conditions of accumulation. Spain's growth experience after the mid-1970s can be described as anything but normal. Early in that decade, business profits and confidence collapsed. A deep and prolonged depression unraveled the channels required for expanded reproduction and its reverberations never really ended despite a brief mini-boom in the second half of the 1980s.

In the wake of the depression jolt a rising tide of inflation sharpened the divide with the previous phase and banks pumped credit into insolvent firms. With the gathering momentum of the slump, banks infused large amounts of credits into firms experiencing an unprecedented contraction of profits. Lacking the necessary internal finance firms raised their necessitous levels of bank borrowing in order to sustain spending plans carried over from the pre-depression period. The build-up of debt that followed towards the end of the 1970s however forced them to increase their retained earnings, reduce expenditures and struggle to restore solvency. Maintaining good standing with the banks allowed the borrowing firms no other alternative. In order to prevent the free fall in economic activity that could be expected from the reduction in private sector effective demand, deficit spending in the public sphere soaked up additional credit.

**Excess demand equations**

Shaikh's model realistically assumes that aggregate demand need not be equal to aggregate supply. Firms have access to external credit when their growth plans exceed the limits of their internal funds and their standing with creditors remains good. Debt repayment is built into the financial dynamics. An initial episode of credit borrowing will give rise to diminishing cycles of (positive) excess demand as the new funds are spent but are followed by a period of debt repayment and reduced spending as business liquidity is built up. Consequently, business will have a reduced need for borrowing and so on. This means that in the absence of new financial shocks, excess demand would cyclically decline and the long-run accumulation path would be shaped by the dynamics of profits, (profits being the chief source for internal funds). If periodic financial shocks occur, the availability of external credit will ensure the persistence of excess demand and debt cycles around the path of potential profits.

In Shaikh's models, the source of business internal funds is sales minus desired inventories. The timing of purchases and sales, borrowing and repayment of loans is of crucial importance. All expenditures required to produce the goods offered for sale are identified in the model. In the absence of shocks, the revenues derived from the sales in each period must cover the purchases of inputs in the previous one. With these protocols in mind, we can see that the aggregate supply price will be equal to:

$$Q_t = M_{t-1} + W_{t-1} + Dep_{t-1} + \Pi_t \tag{2.1}$$

M and W represent the cost of materials and wages purchased in period (t-1). $Dep_{t-1}$ stands for depreciation of the capital stock with one period lag, and $\Pi$ is potential profits. The model then identifies the uses of funds normally required. These include not only the purchase of materials and capital goods, M+IG, but also the payments of wages, W, dividends, $R_t$ and $F_t$ the finance charges due to past borrowing plus the desired change in liquid reserves $CMR_t$:

$$M_t + IG_t + W_t + R_t + F_t + CMR_t$$

Aggregate demand emerges as the sum of spending on materials, fixed investment goods, $IG_t$ plus the consumption of workers and capitalists out of dividend income ($ConW_t$ and $ConR_t$) plus desired inventories:

$$D_t = M_t + IG_t + ConW_t + ConR_t + CINV_t \quad (2.2)$$

Excess demand = $E_t = D_t - Q_t$ and if we assume that workers' consumption equals their wage, ($ConW_t = W_t$) the equation for excess demand will be:

$$E_t = M_t + IG_t + ConW_t + ConR_t + CINV_t - [M_{t-1}+W_{t-1}+Dep_{t-1}+\Pi_t]$$

$$= \underbrace{(M_t-M_{t-1}) + (W_t-W_{t-1})}_{A_t} + \underbrace{(IG_t-Dep_{t-1})}_{I_t} + CINV_t + ConR_t - \Pi_t$$

$$E_t = A_t + I_t + CINV_t - (\Pi_t - ConR_t) \quad (2.3)$$

Shaikh's symbol for the accumulation of circulating capital is $A_t$ and $I_t$ for the accumulation of net fixed capital. As I indicated earlier, my empirical tests will necessarily be stripped-down versions of the model. To begin with, I will have to disregard the desired level of inventories $CINV_t$ in my empirical tests due to the lack of such data.

**Borrowing equations**

Equation (2.3) indicates that total spending for circulating, fixed capital plus capitalist consumption each period, ($A_t+I_t+ConR_t$) will realize aggregate business profits in that period, in other words, aggregate purchases equal potential profits plus excess demand $A_t+I_t+ConR_t = \Pi_t+E_t$. The difference between profits realized and dividends disbursed equals the internal funds available to business firms. Expenditures above these limits must be financed through borrowing. There are two borrowing channels. One is internal to the circuit of business finance, namely the stock and bond markets that mediate the reflux of capitalist personal savings, SAVR. This is the residual available after capitalist consumption, ConR is subtracted from dividend income, R. Banks are typically the external source for borrowing. Positive excess demand results when total spending in any one period is larger than the revenues received from the aggregate sales in the previous period. Borrowing the difference from the banking system injects into the system new purchasing power that must be repaid out of the available internal funds available in the future.

At the start of each period firms formulate their spending plans taking into account the extent of their disposable internal funds, $X_t$. These include the realized profits available from the previous period $(\Pi+E)_{t-1}$ minus the finance charges due as a result of past borrowing $F_t$. Borrowing is necessary when firms engage in deficit spending, that is, when financing production plans plus the financial payments coming due exceed their internal funds. Total borrowing, including a portion of the funds previously paid out as dividends and now mediated by the financial markets will amount to: $B_t + SAVR_t = M_t+W_t+IG_t+F_t+R_t+CMR_t - [((M_{t-1}+W_{t-1}) + Dep_{t-1}+\Pi_t) - CINV_t]$

$$= (M_t-M_{t-1}) + (W_t-W_{t-1}) + (IG_t-Dep_{t-1}) + CINV_t+F_t+CMR_t - (\Pi_t-R_t)$$

$$B_t + SAVR_t = A_t + I_t + CINV_t + [(F_t+CMR_t) - (\Pi_t-R_t)]$$

$$B_t = A_t + I_t + CINV_t + (R_t-SAVR_t) - \Pi_t+F_t+CMR_t$$

Potential profits minus the disbursement of dividends ($\Pi_t$ - $R_t$) makes-up firms' retained earnings. Dividend income minus capitalist personal savings $R_t$-$SAVR_t$ is the personal consumption of capitalist families ($ConR_t$). Then the equation for borrowing can be written as:

$$B_t = A_t + I_t + CINV_t + (ConR_t-\Pi_t) + F_t+ CMR_t = E_t + F_t + CMR_t$$

It follows from this expression that excess demand in any one period is equal to bank borrowing minus finance charges due in the same period:

$$E_t = (B_t - F_t) - CMR_t \tag{2.4}$$

Because Shaikh's model requires that the debt must be retired within one period, financial charges will be = $F_t = (1+i)\ B_{t-1}$ and finally, if we abstract from the desired changes in liquid reserves by firms $CMR_t$ (for which I have no data), the equation specifying the borrowing requirements becomes:

$$B_t = E_t + (1+i)B_{t-1} \tag{2.5}$$

**Closure of Shaikh's model**

Shaikh assumes a constant propensity to consume out of profits c, and a constant rate of fixed capital accumulation k. In addition, the model is built around a constant profit margin, m, defined as the ratio of the change in profits over circulating capital in the previous period. This is equivalent to the incremental rate of return on circulating capital.

By definition, $ConR_t = c\Pi_t$ and $I_t = k\Pi_t$ while the profit margin:

$$m = \frac{\Pi_t - \Pi_{t-1}}{(M_{t-1} + W_{t-1})} \tag{2.6}$$

The equations for excess demand (2.4) and for borrowing (2.5) plus the expression for the profit margin, m (2.6), a proxy for the incremental rate of return on circulating capital, serve as the structural foundation for Shaikh's first dynamical model of effective demand and accumulation. Rearranging equation (2.3), we find that the profits realized each period ($\Pi_t$+$E_t$), the sum of potential profits plus excess demand, are equal to aggregate spending, = $A_t$+$I_t$ + $ConR_t$. When firms form their spending and borrowing plans for the period ahead, the internal funds at their disposal $X_t$ will consist of the profits realized in the previous period minus the financial charges due as a result of past borrowing:

$$X_t = (\Pi+E)_{t-1} - (1+i)B_{t-1} \tag{2.7}$$

Dividing $A_t$ and $X_t$ by $\Pi$ we have the change in the rate of accumulation in circulating capital $\frac{A_t}{\Pi_t} = a_t$ and the model's accumulation reaction function simply requires that the desired change in $a_t$ each period should be proportional to the percentage excess of internally available funds over potential profits previously achieved:

$$a_t - a_{t-1} = h\left[\frac{E-(1+i)B}{\Pi}\right]t-1 \tag{2.8}$$

Dividing the terms in equation (4.3) by potential profits, $\Pi$, and writing e $= \frac{E}{\Pi}$; $a = \frac{A}{\Pi}$; $k = \frac{I}{\Pi}$; $c = \frac{ConR}{\Pi}$, the equation for excess demand becomes:

$$e = a + k + c + 1 \tag{2.9}$$

Finally, expressing the continuous change in the rate of accumulation in circulating capital as $\dot{a}$ the accumulation reaction function can be written as:

$$\dot{a} = h[e - (1 + i)b] \tag{2.10}$$

Then applying the same procedure to equation (4.5) for borrowing, that is changing $\frac{B}{\Pi} = b$. Substituting, $\dot{b} = \frac{\dot{B}}{P} - \left(\frac{\dot{P}}{P}\right)b$; as well as, $\dot{e} = \frac{\dot{E}}{\Pi} - \left(\frac{\dot{\Pi}}{\Pi}\right)e$; while bearing in mind that financial charges, $F_t$=(1+i)$B_{t-1}$ we have:

$$\dot{B} + B = (1 + i)B + \dot{E} + E$$

$$\frac{\dot{B}}{\Pi} + b = (1 + i)b + \frac{\dot{E}}{\Pi} + e$$

$$\dot{b} + \left(\frac{\dot{\Pi}}{\Pi}\right)b + b = b + ib + \dot{e} + \left(\frac{\dot{\Pi}}{\Pi}\right)e + e$$

$$\dot{b} = \dot{e} + ib + e + \left(\frac{\dot{\Pi}}{\Pi}\right)(e - b) \tag{2.11}$$

In equation (2.9), the c and k ratios are assumed constant in the short-run, $\dot{e} = \dot{a}$. From (2.6) we know that $\frac{\dot{\Pi}}{\Pi} = ma$, and from (2.9) a = e+1-(c+k). We may label d=1-(c+k) so that a =e+d. Carrying out the substitutions, the final form of the two non-linear differential equations of the model will be:

$$\dot{e} = h[e - (1 + i)b$$

$$\dot{b} = \dot{e} + (1 + i)e + (md - i)(e - b) + me(e - b)$$

The path followed by these two differential equations changes depending on the presence or absence of random shocks. Because their solution is enormously complicated, simulation appears as an attractive compromise to visualize their trajectory. There is no question that the actual path of market economies is strewn with random shocks. This does not mean that structural forces do not drive the overall performance of macroeconomic variables. It simply means that the emerging patterns of growth are frequently obscured by short-term deviations from the critical path.

The simulation of these two differential equations in Figure 2.1 shows how in the absence of random shocks, excess demand (line 1) and borrowing (line 2) cyclically converge to zero around a growth path whose trajectory is determined by the evolution of potential profits.

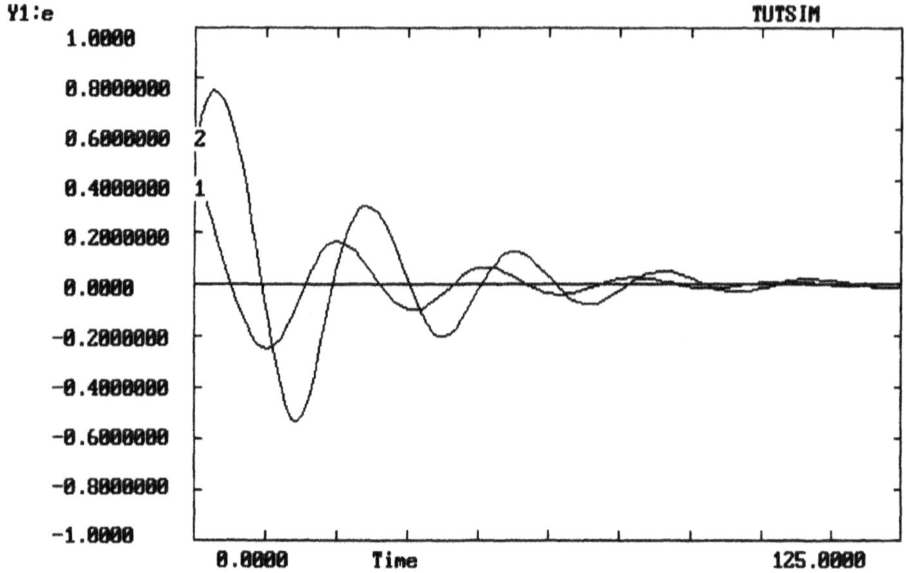


**Figure 2.1 Excess demand and debt without persistent shocks**

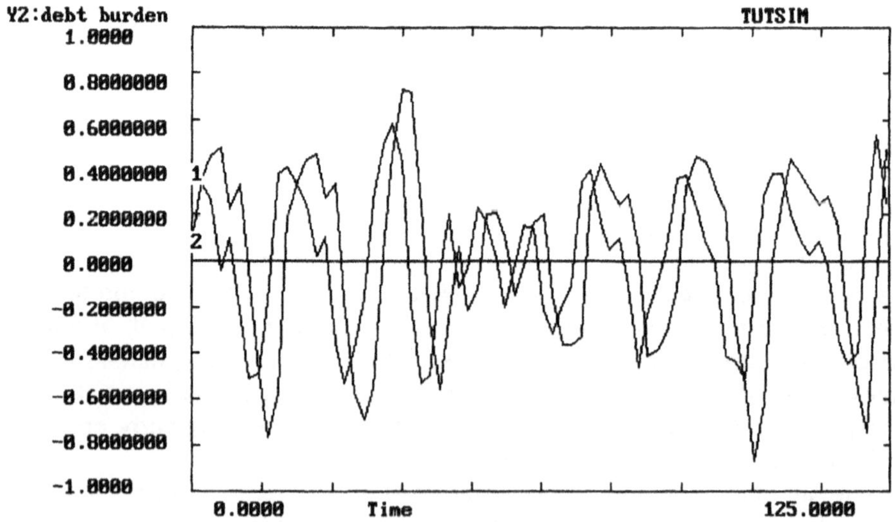


**Figure 2.2 Excess demand and debt fluctuations with persistent shocks**

When random shocks perturb the adjustment mechanism previously outlined, the fluctuations of excess demand and borrowing persist through time as the Figure 2.2 simulation clearly depicts.

## The multiplier and its critics

As I will show in Chapter 3, the intrinsic dynamics linking investment to profitability (in this case the profit share), will give rise to medium-term endogenous cycles even without the benefit of shocks. It is likely, however, that changes in expectations impacting on spending plus the inevitable shocks that shattered them, unleashed the persistent excess demand fluctuations that circled around the longer accumulation wave.

My critique of Neo-Classical and New Keynesian interpretations of the various downturns in Spain after 1970 (taken up in Chapter 8) fundamentally questions the assumption that absent random shocks balanced and steady growth would be actually realized. On the contrary, in Shaikh's model external financing of investment plans that rise above the internally generated funds leads to the accumulation of business debts and in due course the loans must be repaid. As an unintended consequence, future investment plans must be curtailed to release the necessary repayment funds and periods of positive excess demand will be then followed by downturns in accumulation and output.

First, however, it is necessary to unravel the hidden side of the Keynesian multiplier in order to reveal its unsustainable foundations. In 1938, Keynes offered a detailed account of the ends to which business firms could apply their funds, both internal and borrowed (Keynes, 1987, p. 230). The list included one 'inactive' component, meaning a cash reserve needed as a precaution against uncertainty, the size of which depended on the state of business confidence and expectations. The 'active' category consisted of the cash required to finance working capital expenses, varying according to the level of planned activity and was subdivided into two parts. One was the finance needed to implement the decisions made regarding investment. The other included the finance required by firms to bridge the time lags between their wage payments and the reflux of revenues caused by wage earners purchases. After he recognized how firms depended on bank credit to finance working capital expenditures, Keynes ignored the possibility that they could fall into a liquidity crisis. Robertson raised this issue originally in response to Keynes's interpretation of the 'finance motive'. Quite simply, the problem arose as an insolvency threat, a situation in which firms were unable to implement their investment plans and simultaneously service their debt obligations. Instead, Keynes focused only on the unlimited solvency of the banks:

> the demand for cash, due to the requirements of 'finance', is automatically at an end as soon as the finance is expended. But I agree that the demand for cash due to the time lag between the receipt and disposal of income, etc., has still to be provided for (Keynes, 1987, p. 230).

The fact that the ratio of outstanding bank credit to GDP has been rising for the past thirty years in the Spanish economy appears to confirm, at first sight, the Keynesian theory of a revolving fund that is also expanding. A closer examination of the trend, however, will open the question of limits to the debt pile-up. Note that the increase in the stock of credit/GDP ratio has by no means been confined to the Spanish economy. A similar development is present in Canada, France, the U.S. and other advanced market economies (Seccareccia, 1996, p.400, Pollin, 1986, pp. 205-235).

## Credit cycles and profitability

The volatility of judgments regarding future business conditions plays a major role in Keynesian economics, particularly in the theory of investment based on long-term profit expectations. According to Shackle, "The Fundamental Equations of Keynes's Treatise on Money were a highly efficient shorthand for stating a comparison between expected and realized results" (Shackle, 1988, p.119). The investment plans of business firms are shaped by profit expectations, and due to the uncertainty surrounding future business conditions, they are subject to quick reversals. As Hansen observed, "Expectations consist in part in volatile waves of pessimism and optimism, but they are nonetheless rooted in real factors" (Hansen, 1953, pp. 209-210).

A possible outcome of this wavering is that maintaining aggregate demand at the level corresponding to full employment cannot be assured. For a long time the question of how these investment plans were financed was not deemed to require special attention. As noted earlier Keynes himself recognized a finance motive for holding money prior to the implementation of investment decisions. Both Keynes and Kalecki explicitly acknowledged the necessity of external credit to fund new investments when spending plans exceeded the current level of internal funds.

The income expansion attributed to the (diminishing) spending rounds in the transition to a new equilibrium occurred precisely because new credit was pumped into the spending stream. Bringing forth all the implications of the

Keynesian multiplier in the presence of borrowing revealed the hidden side of income expansion, that is, the accumulation of business debt. Paradoxically a good number of studies found evidence that investment is overwhelmingly financed out of internal funds and thus support the classical view on accumulation (Kopcke, 1993, Kopcke and Howrey, 1994, Gilchrist and Himmelberg, 1999).

Table 2.1 provides a bird's eye view of the weight gained by bank credit in the finance share of GDP in Spain and the U.S. The U.S. ratios reflect nonfederal credit stock minus home and residential mortgages relative to GDP. I can advance the conclusion that drawing out the implications of this trend will place my analysis at loggerheads with monetarism.

**Table 2.1 Credit stock/GDP in Spain and the U.S.**

| | 1965 | 1975 | 1985 | 1995 | 1998 |
|---|---|---|---|---|---|
| Spain | 0.50 | 0.80 | 0.90 | 1.00 | 1.09 |
| U.S. | 0.74 | 0.80 | 0.96 | 0.88 | 0.94 |

*Sources:* Spain: Series, Ministry of the Economy; U.S.: Flow of Funds, F1 and F2.

To begin with, there is no evidence that this credit expansion was matched by a proportional growth of money reserves by the private sector. I cannot accept the doctrine relating changes in price levels exclusively to exogenous changes in the money stock caused by the central bank. When commercial banks take the center stage as credit providers, a new perspective on the importance of money (credit money flows as means of payment versus money as a stock of liquid reserves) and its sources must be considered.

Post-Keynesian economics recognizes the significance of bank credit and the attendant expansion of debt by businesses in a growing economy. Indeed Post-Keynesians and Circuit theorists have advanced elaborate research programs that focus on bank credit as the chief source of external finance, allowing businesses to effect payments in anticipation of revenue flows. As forcefully stated by C. H. Whalen, a prominent Post-Keynesian economist writing in appreciation of H. Minsky's reconstruction of Keynes's and J. Schumpeter's approach to cycles and growth:

> While standard economic theory emphasizes exchange, Minsky's recognition of historical time caused him to emphasize that production precedes exchange—and that finance precedes production. Thus, credit and finance are at the center of capitalist development (Whalen, 1999, p. 4).

While Post-Keynesian economics identifies the repayment of business debts to the banks as the means by which credit-money is destroyed, it is equally clear that its practitioners are prone to neglect the negative consequences of borrowing for capital accumulation (Shaikh 1989). Tracing the gist of the controversy between Keynes, Robertson and Ohlin will allow me to establish a bridge between their findings and Shaikh's Classical models on accumulation and finance. Then I will evaluate from Shaikh's perspective the available data on credit finance in order to account for the output fluctuations in the Spanish economy.

## Endogenous money and the banking school

Adam Smith argued that the supply of money and credit was endogenous to the needs of trade. Smith held that "the quantity of coin in every country is regulated by the value of the commodities which are to be circulated by it". (Smith, 1965, p. 408) Moreover, "The value of goods annually bought and sold in any country requires a certain quantity of money to circulate" (Smith, 1965, p. 409). Adam Smith thought that shortages of gold and silver coins relative to the value of goods in circulation would be self-correcting: "Buying and selling upon credit…will supply it with less inconvenience" (Smith, 1965, p. 405). The reason being that "The business of the country is almost entirely carried on by means of the paper of these different banking companies, with which purchases and payments of all kinds are commonly made" (Smith, 1965, p. 281).

Smith favored the replacement of bank credit for commodity money because the capital necessary to produce the precious metals would then be available for accumulation in productive industries. As a result, the aggregate output of commodities capable of further productive use would expand faster. The growth of the money stock would have no effect on interest rates because in the classical tradition the movement of interest rates was driven by the profitability of non-financial capital. After an extended period of rapid accumulation, low interest rates would reflect the existence of a large stock of productive capital and a low profit rate. The low profit rate would reflect the relative exhaustion of profitable investment opportunities and the attendant intensification of competitive skirmishes.

The circulation of bank credit should be restricted to people who were creditors in real market transactions. Once the debtor paid up in commodity money, the credit borrower could clear his position with the bank (Foley, 1987b). Under the "real bills" doctrine, a merchant could borrow from his bank against bills of exchange. Having access to "cash accounts" allowed him to finance his expanding trade. Smith warned however that banks should avoid excessive lending because:

> A bank cannot consistently with its own interest advance to a trader the whole or even the greater part of the circulating capital with which he trades; because, though that capital is continually returning to him in the shape of money, and going from him in the same shape, yet the whole of the returns is too distant from the whole of the out-goings, and the sum of his repayments could not equal the sum of his advances within such moderate periods of time as suit the convenience of a bank. Still less could a bank afford to advance him any considerable part of his fixed capital (Smith, 1965, p. 291).

With these observations in mind, Kregel found it proper to posthumously induct Adam Smith into the Banking School (Kregel, 1996, p. 655). By the mid-1840s the Banking School and its chief advocate, Thomas Tooke developed Adam Smith's views in opposition to the dominant Currency School. Rousseas has reminded enthusiasts of the post-Keynesian position that the root of their endogenous money interpretation reaches back to the Banking School:

> The idea of an endogenous money supply, however, is not quite the postwar "discovery" it is sometimes made out to be. In less rigorous form, and lurking somewhere in the background to which it had been assigned, the "banking principle" supported the notion of the money supply spontaneously accommodating "the needs of trade" via a passive financial structure (Rousseas, 1992, p. 68).

The Banking School argued that the price level determined the amount of money and credit needed in circulation, and that prices ultimately reflected the incomes of the final consumers. This formulation effectively reversed the Ricardian chain of causation between the money stock and the price level.

The growing awareness that bank credit financed business activities led Tooke to widen his inquiries into the possible links between credit growth and wealth creation. For Tooke: "Nine tenths, or more probably ninety-nine hundredths, of the purchases of the wholesale markets, are transacted through the medium of book debts, or simple credit, and cheques on bankers". Could over-expansion in the supply of credit money inflate prices? In his 1844 pamphlet *An Inquiry into the Currency Principle*, Tooke developed a credit growth theory of price fluctuations, not of the price level:

> We have thus seen, that neither the amount of the circulation (bank notes) or the rate of interest or discount, to the extent to which it has hitherto varied can be

> considered as exercising a direct influence on the prices of commodities, but that the greater part, if not the whole of the fluctuations of prices which are over and above those that are necessarily incidental to the nature of the commodities, are attributable to the expansion and contraction of credit, under the influence of the opinion of dealers or speculators, more or less exaggerated, of the prospects of markets (Arnon, 1991, p. 114).

As part of his theory of short waves (Arnon, 1991, p. 172), Tooke argued that fluctuations in trade itself were not caused by factors directly tied to the banking system. He cautioned, however, that unless lending was restrained in prosperous times and expanded in lean years, bank credit would accentuate price cycles without creating new wealth (Arnon, 1991, p. 172). In the final analysis, Tooke did not propose any measures to control the quantity of credit advanced by the banks and failed to explain how market forces could exert any pressures to that end (Arnon, 1991, p. 115).

## Credit finance and the multiplier

Shortly after the publication of the *General Theory,* Keynes spelled out the nature of the finance motive for borrowing credit. He was prompted by Ohlin and Robertson to admit that in order to implement the decision to raise investment above its current level, (when investment spending was financed out of current savings) firms would require new bank credit to carry it through. After Keynes complied, Robertson appreciated Keynes's acknowledgement and pointedly went on to:

> welcome the explicit recognition of the fact that banks sometimes lend money to entrepreneurs for use in their businesses, instead of being merely corporations for the purpose of buying/selling gilt-edged securities from/to persons governed by the 'speculative motive', as a reader of the General Theory might suppose (Keynes, 1987, p. 227).

Robertson did not accept the benign effects of the Keynesian multiplier. He showed how the hidden key to the workings of the income multiplier should be found precisely in the injection of new bank credit. This new lending was necessary in the interval between the initial rise in investment and the progressively smaller gaps left between the higher investment level and the rising but not equal (until the end) savings (Robertson, 1940, Chick, 1983, pp. 257-263). Since the new equilibrium could only obtain after the income multiplier had completed its rounds, business spending would exceed the reflux of internal funds until the final step of the income multiplier sequence was completed. The fact that a rise in savings would occur only after increased spending focused his attention on the sources of investment finance.

It was clear to Ohlin "that not much can be gained through a refined analysis, unless it is made to run in terms of a time-using process" (Keynes, 1987, p. 197). Applying such a method, it was clear to him that new bank credit should precede the rise in income and savings. Robertson was able to show that in fact the rise in income would be matched by the rise in total bank credit, that is to say, additional business debt. From Robertson's perspective, the workings of the income multiplier implied an equal expansion of debt and he complained that its consequences were completely ignored by Keynes (or his followers, whether Neo or Post-Keynesians).

Robertson's criticism of the income multiplier was aimed at unraveling the consequences of debt accumulation for the growth plans of firms. It can be argued that the appeal of Keynesian economics during and after the Great Depression of the 1930s was highly enhanced by leaving debt out of the dynamics of the multiplier. Income would rise by a multiple of investment without any sacrifice of consumption (indeed consumption would rise). Unwarranted side effects to this recovery were not contemplated. Robertson himself did not contend that investment finance necessarily required prior savings. As Chick has noted, "Once the banks were able to 'create credit in excess of savings' to a significant extent" (Chick, 1983, p. 190) the precedence of investment over savings was granted. Keynes and his revolving fund, however, failed to persuade Robertson that the liquidity of the banks, and much less that of the indebted firms, would be restored as soon as the entrepreneurs spent their loans. Robertson remained unconvinced and insisted that:

> I cannot see that any revolving fund is released, any willingness to undergo illiquidity set free for further employment, by the act of the borrowing entrepreneur in spending his loan. The bank has become a debtor to other entrepreneurs, workpeople etc. instead of to the borrowing entrepreneur, but that is all. The borrowing entrepreneur remains a debtor to the bank: and the bank assets have not been altered either in amount or in liquidity (Keynes, 1987, pp. 228-229).

Keynes sanguine treatment of business borrowing and his theory of the "revolving fund" for working capital as a whole could be linked to Adam Smith's theory of credit "reflux". While not overlooking the matter of debt repayment on the part of the borrowers, Smith spelled out the chain of payments leading to the credit reflux:

> The banks, when their customers apply to them for money, generally advance it to them in their own promissory notes. These the merchants pay away to the manufacturers of goods, the manufacturers to the farmers for materials and provisions, the farmers to their landlords for rent, the landlords repay them to the merchants for the conveniences and luxuries with which they supply them, and the merchants again return them to the banks in order to balance their cash accounts, or to replace what they may have borrowed of them; and thus almost the whole money business of the country is transacted by means of them (Smith, 1965 p. 283).

## Credit and costs of production

Keynesian traditionally conceded that new investment, but not consumption output required previous bank finance, on the assumption that the sale of consumer goods "automatically" covered the costs of production involved. Graziani has pointed out that there are no "reasonable" grounds for such a consensus (Graziani, 1996, p. 146). Financial advances on the part of banks allow industry to fund not only the production of investment but also consumption goods. Public deficits aside, industry dependence on commercial bank credit to finance working capital and fixed investment is the basis for the persistence of a revolving debt. Commercial banks themselves must look to the central bank as a lender of last resort. The difference between Keynes's approach and the Post-Keynesians' was duly acknowledged by Rousseas's observation that:

> The failure to question Keynes's liquidity preference theory and its reformulation ultimately into an asset-portfolio model missed the opportunity to emphasize that the demand for money is for financial credit primarily, under normal conditions, by the business sector and not, as overwhelmingly represented, for assets by utility-maximizing people. Linking the demand for money to the financing of investment and the problem of capital accumulation would have yielded a far more promising prospect for the development of monetary theory (Rousseas, 1996, p. 673).

Assume that since wages are largely spent on consumption, financing consumption is the equivalent of financing wages. Now if industry borrowed all the money needed to finance wages and means of production, how could they repay their loans plus the interest due and still make profits? The answer given by Post-Keynesians is that the funds needed by industrial firms to make their interest payments to the banks are also borrowed from them. This is part of the total finance required, along with the credit needed to cover all other costs of production (Deleplace and Nell, 1996, p. 15).

The controversy as to what needs funding in the conventional Keynesian model could be readily settled using Robertson's discovery that new injections of credit money are needed to finance the income multiplier. It can be shown that the total debt will include the initial loan to cover the rise in investment plus additional credit to finance the rise in wages that provides the means for a rise in total consumption.

The sequence involved in the expansion of income is as follows. Once the credit obtained in order to finance a rise in investment is spent, income will rise as much. This rise in income will now lead to a rise in consumption, the size of which will depend on the MPC. A rise in savings will now occur. The difference between the rise in investment and the insufficient rise in savings, however, will have to be filled with new credit until the income expansion reaches its last step (when $\Delta S = \Delta I$). What is it that this new credit finances? Clearly this new credit will fund the rise in wages associated with the rising employment caused by the initial jump in investment. The means for a rise in total consumption is provided by this rise in wages. The total rise in income will be a multiple of the rise in investment, because of the induced rise in wages and therefore total consumption. The addition to the total debt in fact will exactly match the rise in investment and wages, as long as interest payments are not added to the liabilities incurred by industry. If they are so added, the change in total liabilities will exceed the rise in income. The following table sums up the structure of the period multiplier including the emerging pile up of debt. Table 2.2 shows the expansion of income in discrete steps in response to the initial rise in investment spending of 10 in period $Y_0$ -- thus $\Delta I_0 = 10$, and therefore $\Delta Y_0 = 10$.

**Table 2.2 Period multiplier including debt**

| | Investment change $I_t$ | Savings each period $S_t$ | New credit each period $I_t$-$S_t$ | Total income each period $Y_t$ |
|---|---|---|---|---|
| 0 | 10 | 0 | 10 | 10 |
| 1 | 10 | 10-b10 | b10 | 10+b10 |
| 2 | 10 | $10\text{-}b^2 10$ | $b^2 10$ | $10+b10+b^2 10$ |
| 3 | 10 | $10\text{-}b^3 10$ | $b^3 10$ | $10+b10+b^2 10+b^3 10$ |
| - | - | - | - | - |
| n | 10 | $10\text{-}b^n 10$ | $b^n 10$ | $10+b10+b^2 10+b^3 10 \ldots b^n 10$ |

Changes in consumption spending are a function of income in the previous period, so $\Delta C_1 = \Delta Y_0 * MPC = 7.5 \rightarrow \Delta Y_1$. This additional income will then give rise to new increases in consumption, so that $\Delta C_2 = b^2 \Delta Y_0 \rightarrow \Delta Y_2$ and consequently the change in consumption at the end of the rounds, $\Delta C_n = b^n \Delta Y_0 \rightarrow \Delta Y_n \rightarrow 0$.

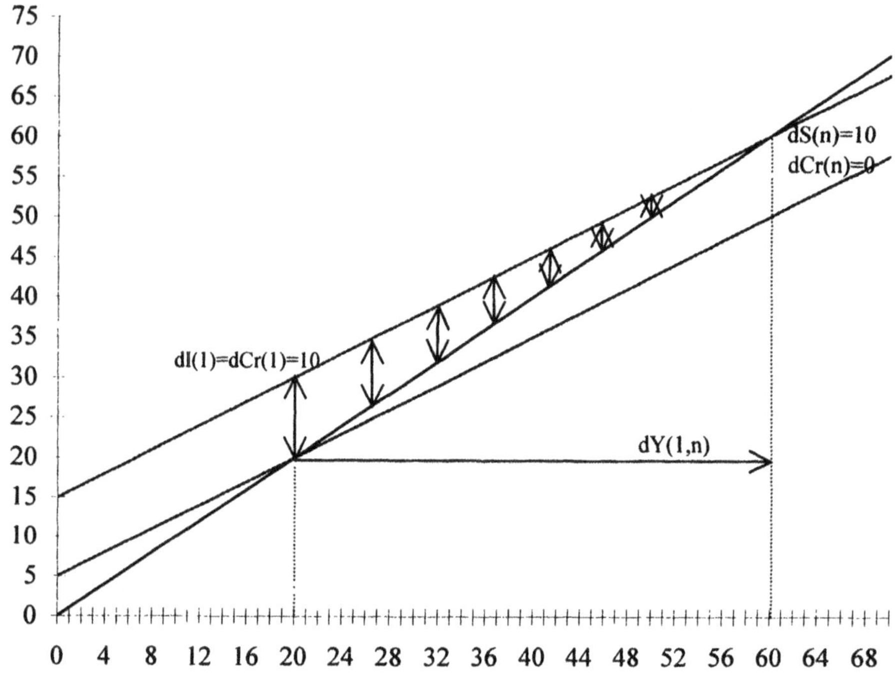


**Figure 2.3 The Keynesian multiplier and credit expansion**

There is a major difference, however, between the standard presentation of the income multiplier adjustment sequence and that developed by A. Shaikh in his Seminar on Marx, Keynes and Kalecki at New School University. Shaikh's chief contribution in this regard consists in uncovering the financial gap that, while getting smaller, remains open until the expansion is complete, and the borrowing required to fill it all the way through. It is worth noting that between $Y_0$ and $Y_n$ the change in investment, $\Delta I > \Delta S$. The difference between the sustained change in investment and the sequential change in savings shows the finance gap facing firms (the deficit in the savings reflux coming back to them through the financial markets). This borrowing will take place on top of the initial loan required to finance the rise in investment in period $Y_0$. By definition, $\Delta S_t = \Delta Y_{t-1} - \Delta C_t = \Delta Y_0 - b^t * \Delta Y_0$, and the financial gap that firms must cover by way of extra bank credit will be $\Delta I_t - \Delta S_t = \Delta I_t - b^t * \Delta Y_0$.

Of course, firms must have access to bank credit when total savings, including their own and those of households are insufficient to cover their needs for working capital. It turns out that the rise in additional debt *after* the initial borrowing to finance the higher investment equals at each step the additional rise in consumption and income. In short, the rise in total consumption is equal to the rise in additional debt and equals the rise in income after the initial jump in investment.

On the (Kaleckian and Post-Keynesian) assumption that consumption spending roughly equals wages, we can conclude that the rise in consumption following the initial growth in fixed investment spending, will be financed by the additional credit provided by the banks. These expenditures will cover the growth in wages related to the higher employment associated with the rise in investment. To sum up, the initial borrowing covers the initial rise in investment and the new borrowing covers the related growth in wages. The sum of the two add-up to the expansion of total income and are equal to the new total debt incurred by business firms from beginning to end. Will the revenues obtained from the sale of investment and consumption goods suffice to retire the accumulated debt, principal and interest? Considering the expectations built into conventional Keynesian theory, some unexpected results will appear once autonomous consumption, A, and debt, B, are made explicit, both as an accumulated stock as well as a flow.

The standard theory says that the change in income, $\Delta Y$, will equal the change in investment, $\Delta I$, times the multiplier, m. We have seen that the rise in income will be matched by a rise in external borrowing, $\Delta B$. This flow of borrowing must be added to the accumulated stock of business debt already outstanding, A+B, as follows:

$$\Delta Y = \Delta I * m = \Delta B$$
$$Y = (A + I) * m = A + B$$

Then the growth rate of income would be:

$$\frac{\Delta Y}{Y} = \frac{\Delta I}{I}\left(\frac{I}{A+I}\right) = \frac{\Delta B}{B}\left(\frac{B}{A+B}\right)$$

And since both $\left(\frac{I}{A+I}\right)$ and $\left(\frac{B}{A+B}\right)$ <1 it is clear that the growth rate of income will be lower than the growth rate of investment as well as the growth rate of the stock of debt. The growth rate of the stock of debt would equal the growth of income only if autonomous consumption, A=0.

$$\frac{\Delta B}{B} = \frac{\Delta Y}{Y} * \left(\frac{A+B}{B}\right) \geq 1 \quad \text{Since} \left(\frac{A+B}{B}\right) > 1$$

**Empirical caveats**

While following Shaikh's approach to the link between finance and accumulation, I will make the following general assumptions in order to make sense of the data on credit provided by *Series* of the Ministry of the Economy in Spain.

I will assume with the Post Keynesians that at the beginning of each production period businesses will borrow short-term finance to cover their working capital needs, plus the difference between their fixed capital investment plans and their retained earnings. Businesses must pay out taxes and dividends and so they keep only a portion of their gross profits as retained earnings ("business savings"). The difference between firms retained earnings and their investment plans sets their extended borrowing needs beyond the short-term financing of working capital.

I will further assume that at the end of each production period and under normal circumstances businesses pay back to the banks the loans taken for working capital along with the total interest due. In order to do this, their aggregate sales must provide sufficient revenue to service their outstanding short-term debt. In the light of these assumptions, we will expect total credit demand for working capital to rise more or less in step with the total product. Short-term business borrowing will rise as working capital expands. The short-term debt will be repaid as revenues come in. Borrowing to finance capital goods investment will then depend on the scale of the investment plans, the evolution of retained profits and the availability of bank credit. The supply of bank credit, of course, will be contingent upon the bank's perception of its clients' credit worthiness.

A crucial measure of business solvency suggested by Wolfson consists of gross profits plus depreciation plus interest payments relative to interest payments, known as the "interest coverage ratio" (Wolfson, 1994, pp. 155-156). Fluctuations in this ratio reflect the changing liquidity position of non-financial firms. For example, a fall in the "interest coverage ratio" implies a rise in interest payments relative to internal funds profits. While data on interest payments is not available, the financial gap between business investment and retained earnings is. Conversely, the ratio retained earnings to investment shows that after the early 1980s Spanish firms moved from a deficit position to a surplus one. They did so by simultaneously increasing the share of undistributed profits in gross profits and lowering their rate of accumulation.

## Conclusions

In Shaikh's first model, external finance allows firms to expand spending beyond their internal means and because of that positive excess demand emerges. The build-up of business debt however serves as an inhibitor of uncontrolled expansion, as debt retirement is explicitly required within a definite time horizon. In a variation of this approach, Shaikh's second version developed in Chapter 10 allows for profit margin changes driving the transition between phases and having an impact on the dynamics of excess demand growth. Initially a boom phase occurs when input prices have been depressed by the slack of recession. The profit margin will rise because aggregate spending raises output prices proportionately more than input prices. As the boom matures the relationship between the growth of input and output prices is reversed, reflecting the increasingly tight input markets and the growth of aggregate supply. Thus in Shaikh's models either the build-up of business debt, or falling profit margins are the attractors of his dynamical system preventing booms from becoming explosive. The existence of these two separate attractors suggests the possibility of their acting together. What clear signal will trigger banks change of perception regarding increasing risk and the need to cut back lending better than falling profit margins? Thus, all downturns and reversals in excess demand are not economic crises. As shown in Chapter 10, using Shaikh's model guidelines, the empirical reconstruction of excess demand provides the foundation to unravel the actual dynamics of accumulation and output growth in the Spanish economy.

# 3 Goodwin's Growth Cycles

My choice of the classic Goodwin growth cycles model took into account the extent to which its chief claims were verifiable. After working out the conceptual structure of the Goodwin model, I will present a brief contribution by Di Matteo (1984) introducing financial variables. Because Semmler's model of credit overshooting (1988, 1993), aptly formalizes Minsky's approach to cycles I included it in Chapter 4. This model belongs in a class separate from Shaikh's second model (1992) developed in Chapter 10. Finally, Foley's model (1987a) included in Chapter 5 elegantly shows the relationship between profitability and accumulation cycles.

Are short and medium-term cycles produced by inadequate credit supply growth as in Foley, overshooting in debt accumulation as in Minsky and Semmler or the discipline of credit debt repayment as in Shaikh? These are questions whose answers require a comprehensive review of the alternative models. It is important to my investigation that empirical evidence be available to make the final determination of the relevant analytical framework. Only then can we move on to evaluate the soundness of the models' structure as a guide to the Spanish economy. To anticipate the results, however, the Goodwin and Shaikh's models outrank all others as far as empirical verification is concerned, even though some of their explicit assumptions need modification to fit the Spanish case.

## Central tendencies in accumulation

It is my view that the downward pressure on profitability exerted by the rising capital-output ratio set the long-term trend for capital accumulation in Spain. This movement was not steady or smooth. Feedback effects from changes in the demand for labor and the wage rate linked to spurts in accumulation caused the medium-term growth fluctuations. Wage rate changes had an inverse effect on the accumulation rate, and wages were affected by its fluctuations, giving rise to endogenous growth cycles. My frame of reference is R. M. Goodwin's dynamical system developed in his classical form, "A Growth Model". In this model, Goodwin presents a clear and concise analysis of the interplay between the dynamics of growth and endogenous cycles. Goodwin's stated objective in "A Growth Model" was:

> My thesis is that the very structure of capitalism constitutes a homoestatic mechanism which functions by means of variations in distribution shares but does so in such a way as to keep them constant in the long run. If real wages go up, profits go down: if profits go down, saving and investment lag, thus slowing down the creation of new jobs. But the labor force is continually growing both through natural increase and through men "released" by technological progress. The reserve army of labor grows, wages lag behind the growth of productivity, profits rise and accumulation is accelerated back up to a high level. This in turn gradually reduces unemployment, wages rise, and so it goes on, indefinitely (Goodwin, 1972, p. 442).

In the last forty years, the Spanish economy has experienced periods of rapid growth and stagnation. Major transformations in its core structure actually happened in cycles of various spans and amplitudes. The over-all growth trend was markedly non-linear, fitting the contours of a long-term wave. The ascending phase of the late 1950s and early 1960s led to the prolonged downturn of the second half of the 1970s and early 1980s. I believe that these national phenomena were the manifestation of general tendencies inherent in the evolution of the global economy. I focused on the dynamics of profitability in the previous chapter because in my view it was decidedly the driving force behind capital accumulation and the chief gauze of its progress through time.

Each business enterprise necessarily operates in a competitive, free-for-all environment. Its quest for profits encounters the challenge of multiple competitors pursuing identical goals. As the market grows, so does the power of these competitors. While their number may dwindle, their power grows. As A. Shaikh has so aptly put it, technological change provides the arsenal needed to engage opponents in competitive battles with a good chance of success (Shaikh, 1990, p. 310). Better techniques translate into higher labor productivity and lower unit costs, hence lower prices and higher market shares for the winners. Success carries a price, however, it is not free of charge, and in the real world that price is high and many cannot bear it. It is clear that the development of new techniques is costly and typically requires huge investments both in the phase of research and development as well as in their deployment. Large masses of capital are necessary and only successful and already profitable firms have access to them.

Economies that fall behind the growth stages of more dynamic systems, as the Spanish economy certainly did relative to other countries in Western Europe, enjoy the opportunity of adopting superior technologies created by others. It would seem paradoxical that falling behind conveys advantages in the form of free technical blueprints unattainable to industry leaders. This advantage will be enjoyed only if the new techniques are thoroughly mastered by capable management, in conjunction with cheap (but well-trained and disciplined) labor.

When the technological gap is so large that the transformation must be completed quickly, industrial renewal will raise the degree of mechanization throughout the system. Finance is less of a problem if profitability has risen prior to the breakthrough. Even if foreign exchange is available in sufficient quantities (either through remittances as in the case of Spain, or borrowing as in Asia), the initial blessings are no guarantee of uninterrupted success. Considering that the rate of profit is defined as:

$$r = \frac{1-u}{\left(\frac{K}{Y}\right)}$$

$$\text{Where } u = \frac{\left(\frac{W}{L}\right)}{\left(\frac{Y}{L}\right)} = \frac{w}{m} = \frac{\text{real wage rate}}{\text{productivity}} = \text{real unit labor cost (RULC)}$$

I have argued that the dynamics of average profitability crucially hinge on the evolution of the capital-output ratio and the aggregate real unit labor costs, RULC (Roman, 1997). From the early-1960s through the mid-1980s the tempo of accumulation and technical progress in Spain led to an increasing capital-output ratio, K/Y, and after 1973 this rise had a more lasting impact on profitability than the cyclical movement of the aggregate RULC. Intensive capital deepening led both to the displacement of large masses of labor as well as to the growth of fixed capital outpacing that of real output. Measured by any conventional standards (i. e. the capital stock estimates of the OECD for the business sector, relative to value-added) the capital-output ratio in Spain rose markedly from the mid-1960s to the early 1980s. The increase in the capital-output ratio lowered the profitability trend, eventually leading to depression. This decline in profitability in turn had an impact on the rate of accumulation and its effects were translated into fluctuations in the demand for labor and the growth rate of real unit labor costs. For a given capital-output ratio, however, falling real unit labor costs raised the share of profits and the profit rate. The cyclical behavior of the profit share produced medium-term accumulation and employment cycles around the profitability path set by the rising capital-output ratio. There is a major difference, however, between Goodwin's model and Spanish reality.

In Goodwin's model, the capital-output ratio remains constant and indeed distribution shares stay "constant in the long run". Goodwin's model examines the joint dynamics of capital accumulation and endogenous cycles. To that end, Goodwin makes some basic assumptions that he considers convenient for the understanding of growth under capitalism.

**Seven fundamental assumptions**

There are seven fundamental assumptions in Goodwin's Growth and Cycles model:

a) The model assumes the presence of persistent, steady (and disembodied) technical progress. Technical change of this kind underlies the growth in labor productivity, $a = \frac{Y}{L} = a_0 e^{\alpha t}$;
b) The labor force is growing at a steady rate, $N = N_0 e^{\beta t}$;
c) There are only two factors of production, labor and "capital" (capital represents plant and equipment);
d) All quantities are real and net;
e) All wages are consumed by workers, all profits saved and invested by capitalists;
f) The capital-output ratio, $\frac{K}{Y} = k$ remains constant, despite steady technical change;
g) The real wage rate rises as the system moves towards higher employment ratios.

The rate of profit plays a central role in the model's dynamics. Indeed Goodwin accepts the basic principle of the Classical approach linking accumulation to profitability. In the version that he uses, all profits are invested, thus $s_c = 1$ and therefore the growth rate equals the profit rate:

$$g_k = \frac{\left(\frac{S}{Y}\right)\left(\frac{Y}{\Pi}\right)}{\left(\frac{K}{Y}\right)\left(\frac{Y}{\Pi}\right)} = \frac{\left(\frac{S}{\Pi}\right)}{\left(\frac{1}{r}\right)} = s_c r_n$$

This equation will establish the basic relationship between profitability and capital accumulation.

Goodwin needs these assumptions to ensure the stability of what Harrod called the "warranted growth path". Harrod defined the warranted growth rate $g_w$ as the product of the propensity to save out of profits, $s_c$ and the profit rate obtaining when capacity utilization is at the normal level. Assuming that $s_c = 1$, the warranted growth rate $g_w$ obtains when profitability is normal and all profits are re-invested. The Goodwin model's dynamics produce a homeostatic mechanism, allowing the warranted rate to match the natural growth rate, $g_w \cong g_n$.

In his model, Goodwin abstracts from issues of effective demand and he allows for (disembodied) steady technical change to raise the productivity of labor without increasing the capital output ratio. He assumes that aggregate demand matches aggregate supply (Z=Y) throughout and makes actual output equal to capacity output (Y=Y*). With these assumptions in mind, the profit rate $r = g_k$:

$$= \frac{\left(\frac{\Pi^*}{Y_n}\right)}{\left(\frac{K}{Y^*}\right)} = s_c \frac{\left(1 - \frac{W}{Y}\right)}{\frac{K}{Y^*}} \text{ and the profit share} = \frac{\Pi}{Y} = g_K \frac{K}{Y}$$

Since K/Y is assumed to remain constant (although Goodwin points out that this should be an empirical question rather than a foregone conclusion), the profit rate and hence the growth of capital depend entirely on the profit share. Goodwin lays out his conceptual structure proving that in fact the actual trend for capital accumulation, $g_k$ will be set by the normal growth rate $g_n$, defined as the sum of population and productivity growth rates = m+n. The trend for the profit share, $\frac{\Pi}{Y}$ is the product of the natural growth rate $g_n$ and the (normal) capital-output ratio = $g_n$ (K/Y*). Since the profit rate is the ratio of the profit share over the capital-output, that is, $r = \frac{\frac{\Pi}{Y}}{\frac{K}{Y}} = \frac{g_n \frac{K}{Y}}{\frac{K}{Y}} = g_n$, it follows that the rate of profit entirely depends on the natural growth rate.

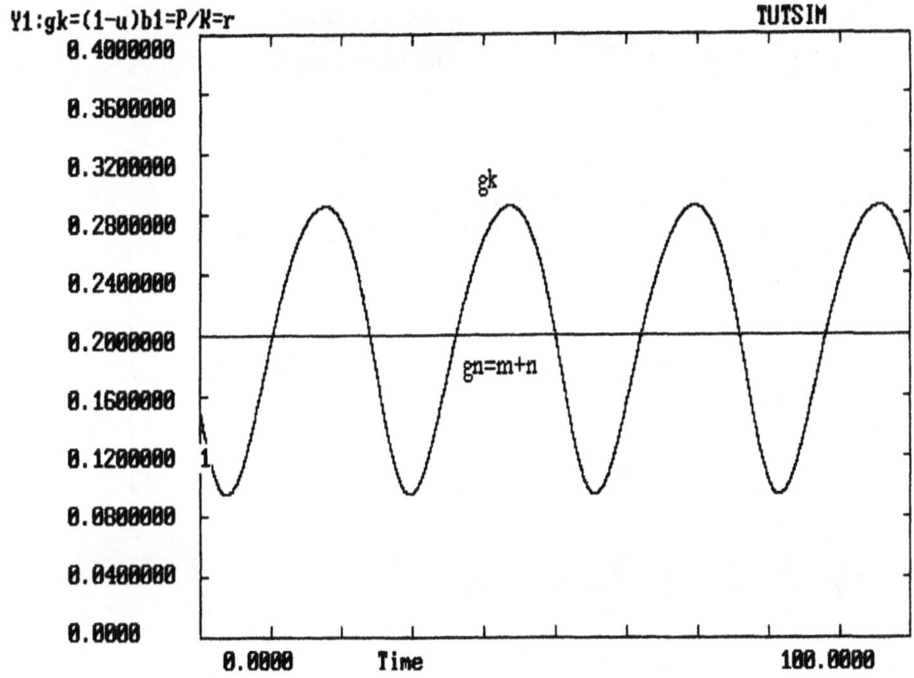


**Figure 3.1 Potential and actual accumulation growth path: Goodwin's model simulation**

It follows from this analysis that not only is growth exogenously given (by the growth of population and technical progress) but also the profit rate since the capital-output ratio is taken as a constant. Because Goodwin assumes that the capital-output ratio and the growth rate of the labor force are constant, in his model changes in profitability depend on the profit share.

The actual adjustment between these two variables proceeds through the inverse movement of the profit and employment shares: as the employment share falls the profit share rises. In Goodwin's model, a higher growth rate of the effective labor supply, $g_n$, will lower the wage share and raise the normal profit rate. On average over the cycle, the employment share, v, defined as the ratio of employed labor to the (growing) labor force, $L/N \cong$ constant and $< 1$. Unemployment is always present. Goodwin's Growth Cycle model consists of two non-linear differential equations with linear coefficients. The system of differential equations follows. By assumption all profits are invested, that is, $\Pi=S=I$. The variables involved are defined as follows:

$$v = \frac{L^E}{L^T} = \text{employment share} = \frac{\text{labor employed}}{\text{total labor supply}}$$

$$u = \frac{W}{Y} = \text{wage share} = \frac{\text{total wages}}{\text{income}} = \frac{\left(\frac{W}{L^E}\right)}{\left(\frac{Y}{L^E}\right)} = \frac{w}{\left(\frac{Y}{L^E}\right)}$$

$$\left(\frac{\hat{Y}}{L^E}\right) = \hat{Y} - \hat{L}^E = m = \text{growth rate of labor productivity} \qquad \begin{cases} \hat{Y} = \frac{\dot{Y}}{Y} \\ \hat{L}^E = \frac{\dot{L}^E}{L^E} \end{cases}$$

The growth rate of accumulation will be:

$$\hat{Y} = \frac{\dot{Y}}{Y} = \frac{\Pi}{K} = \frac{I}{K} = \frac{\dot{K}}{K} = b_1(1 - Y)$$

That is to say:

$$g_k = \frac{\dot{Y}}{Y} = \frac{\Pi}{K} = \frac{Y}{K}\left(1 - \frac{W}{Y}\right) = b_1(1 - u) \qquad \begin{cases} \frac{W}{Y} = u \text{ and} \\ \frac{Y}{K} = b_1 \end{cases}$$

The growth of the employment share will be:

$$\hat{v} = \frac{\dot{v}}{v} = g_k - g_n = b_1(1 - u) - (m + n)$$

Now this expression can be simplified, making $b_1$ - (m+n) $\equiv a_1$. Thus, we can write the first differential equation of the model as:

$$\dot{v} = (a_1 - b_1 u)v$$

To develop the second equation now we need to remember the definition for the wage share = u = W/Y. Dividing numerator and denominator by the employed labor force $L^E$ we have the (real) wage per worker over labor productivity, that is the real unit labor cost. Its growth rate is given by the growth rate of the wage rate minus the growth rate of labor productivity. The wage rate was $\frac{W}{L^E} = w$ and its growth rate, $\hat{w} = \frac{\dot{w}}{w}$, therefore the growth rate of the (real) wage share $\hat{u} = \hat{w} - m$

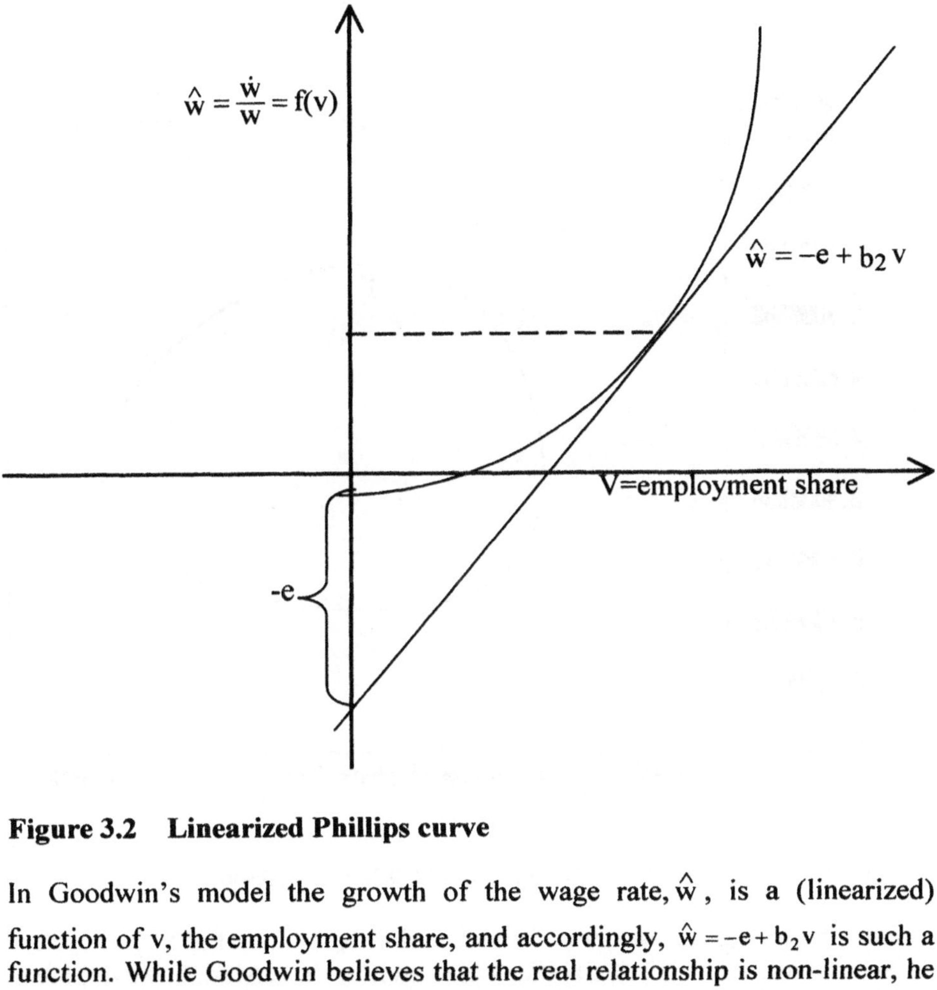


**Figure 3.2 Linearized Phillips curve**

In Goodwin's model the growth of the wage rate, $\hat{w}$, is a (linearized) function of v, the employment share, and accordingly, $\hat{w} = -e + b_2 v$ is such a function. While Goodwin believes that the real relationship is non-linear, he uses a linear function as an approximation derived from Phillips empirical work (Figure 3.2). Thus the growth of the wage share:

$$\hat{u} = -e + b_2 v - m$$

And writing $a_2$ in place of e + m, we have the expression:

$$\hat{u} = b_2 v - a_2$$

Finally, we have the second differential equation:

$$\dot{u} = (b_2 v - a_2)u = -(a_2 - b_2 v)u$$

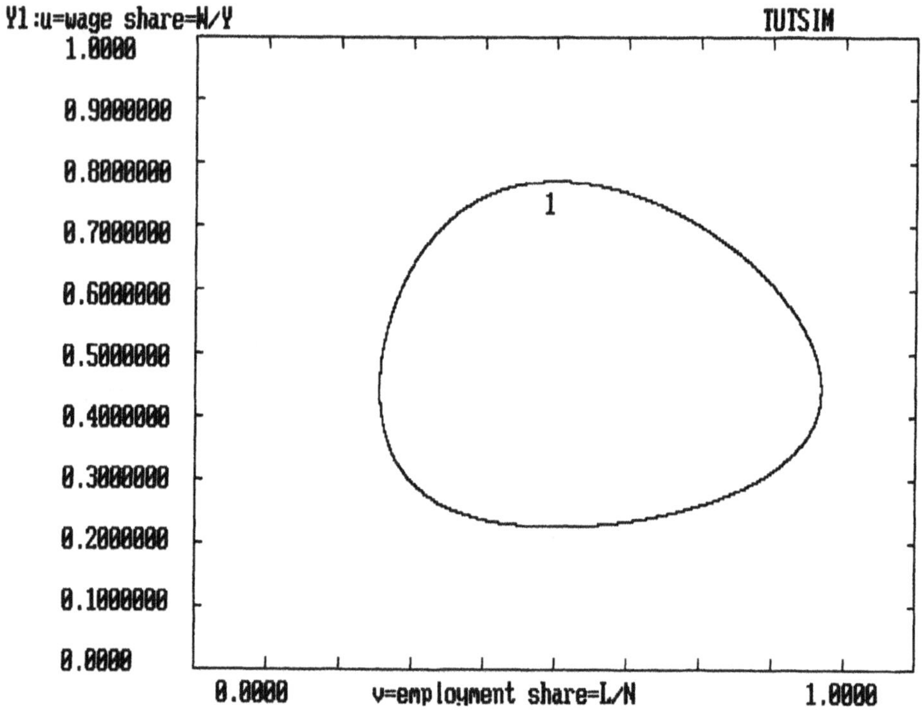


**Figure 3.3 Goodwin's model simulation: phase diagram**

Goodwin's model was meant to formalize Marx's outline of short-run cycles, presented in Chapter 25 of Capital, Vol. I. In Marx's version, however, labor productivity growth is zero because the organic composition remains constant. The growth of the labor force plays no role whatever.

All variables in the model are real, money and price movements play no explicit role. When the rate of accumulation rises above the natural growth rate, the demand for labor grows faster than the effective labor supply and the reserve army of labor declines. Hence, the real wage rate grows faster than labor productivity. The real unit labor costs will rise and the profit share will fall. Given the constant capital-output ratio, the rate of profit will fall. Thus, the rate of accumulation will start decreasing, the demand for labor will shrink below the growth of the effective labor supply and the reserve army of labor will grow back. The real wage will now grow less fast than labor productivity and the profit share will expand once again. The cyclical movement will go on around the normal average growth of the system. The structure of this kind of non-linear model leads to results that are independent of initial conditions. The fluctuations are self-generating and immanent to growth. They do not require shocks for their persistence. The phase diagram of Goodwin's model shows a self-reproducing orbit.

Di Matteo (1984) sought to introduce money and prices into Goodwin's model, making the inflation rate behave pro-cyclically in response to the movement of the real unit labor costs. The supply of money could be either exogenous or endogenously given. His model includes an investment function, augmented with the growth of the money supply:

$$I = Y - \left(\frac{W}{p}\right) l + \sigma K \left(\frac{\dot{M}}{M} - \mu \frac{\dot{Y}}{Y}\right) \tag{3.1}$$

Noting that $\dot{K} = I = b\dot{Y} = g_k$ and substituting,

$$Y - \left(\frac{w}{p}\right) l + \sigma K \left(\frac{\dot{M}}{M} - \frac{\dot{Y}}{Y}\right) = b\dot{Y} \tag{3.2}$$

$$Y - \left(\frac{w}{p}\right) l + \sigma b Y \left(\frac{\dot{M}}{M}\right) - \sigma b Y \left(\frac{\dot{Y}}{Y}\right) = b\dot{Y} \qquad \left\{ \left(\frac{w}{p}\right) l = u \right. \tag{3.3}$$

$$\left(1 - u + \sigma\, b \frac{\dot{M}}{M}\right) Y = (1 - \sigma) b\dot{Y} \tag{3.4}$$

$$\left(\frac{\dot{Y}}{Y}\right) = r = \frac{1 - u + \sigma b \dfrac{\dot{M}}{M}}{b(1 + \sigma)} \tag{3.5}$$

The inflation rate is a function of the growth of the money wage rate and real labor productivity, which ultimately depends on the growth of the real unit labor cost:

$$\frac{\dot{p}}{p} = \frac{\varepsilon}{(1+\varepsilon)}\left[\frac{\dot{w}}{w} - m\right] \tag{3.6}$$

Finally, the demand for money is a function of the price level, output and the rate of interest:

$$M^d = F(p, Y, i) \tag{3.7}$$

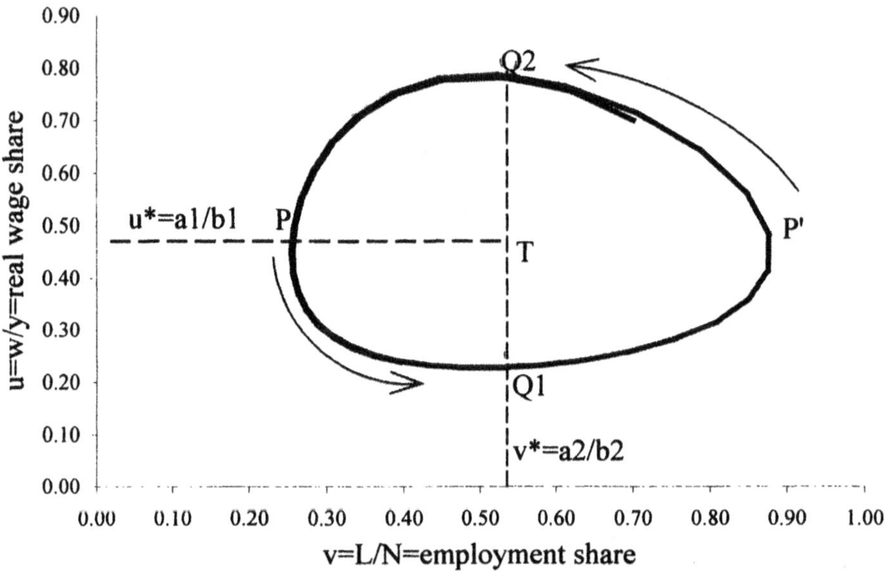


**Figure 3.4 Goodwin's phase diagram: model simulation with money**

As Figure 3.4 shows, we may trace the cycle's motion starting with the recession phase. Then as the growth of money wages falls below that of productivity and the real unit labor costs are falling, the rate of inflation is negative. On the other hand, when the employment share is above the average ($v^*=a_2/b_2$) the inflation rate turns positive but prices will rise at a lower rate than labor productivity. Consequently the growth of profitability will slow down until it reaches its average level at the peak of the expansion P'. Profitability then will fall further from P' to $Q_2$ as the downturn gains momentum. In that phase of the cycle, the growth rate of wages will surpass that of productivity and inflation will flare-up again. At point P the employment share is well below the average (the unemployment rate is well above the system's average), and in fact, this point represents the trough of the employment cycle. In these circumstances, the real wage rate is rising well below the growth of labor productivity (in the extreme case it might even be falling). Since the wage share growth is negative from $Q_2$ to P profitability growth will be on the rise, hence the employment share will improve from P to P'.

## The Goodwin cycles in U.S. perspective

In the United States the Goodwin cycles are somewhat less symmetrical than is the case for the Spanish economy, but the employment and wage-share dynamics is discernible in the historical data. Periods of rising wage-shares witnessed the decline in the employment-shares, albeit for a short-term. Indeed the trends were reversed at some point. Such a pattern occurred in the 1980s preceded by a tortuous climb in wage-shares and declining employment carried over from the 1970s. The employment slide of the 1980s reversed the trend in wage-shares set in the 1960s and managed to reduce its levels, although the definitive push was carried out in the 1990s. From this perspective, for example, after 1992 the growth in the employment share would be induced by the fall of wage shares and the corresponding rise in the share of profits.

Dore (1993) reproduced a less-than-adequate phase diagram of the Goodwin cycle for the U.S. economy constructed by Solow for the period 1947-1986 and on the basis of the patterns displayed in it disparaged its historical significance. He recognized, nevertheless that Goodwin's model is supported by U.S. data in some important ways. As Dore puts it:

> There are periods or episodes in which employment is rising because real wages are relatively low and the resulting high profits have led to increased investment and production. These alternate with periods or episodes in which real wages are relatively high compared to productivity, and the profit-driven impetus to faster-than-average growth is blunted. The alternation of these episodes is *endogenous,* induced by the real-wage Phillips curve (Dore, 1993, pp. 209-10).

Solow himself felt that Goodwin's model ignored the exogenous as well as endogenous fluctuations in effective demand that lie behind the short-run (three to four years) business cycle. While this is undoubtedly true, it would be mistaken to assume that Goodwin cycles belong to the short-run domain of contemporary business cycles. Solow's conclusion was that, "My feeling is that the model does capture something real. At least I can think of episodes that conform to that pattern" (Dore, 1993, p. 210).

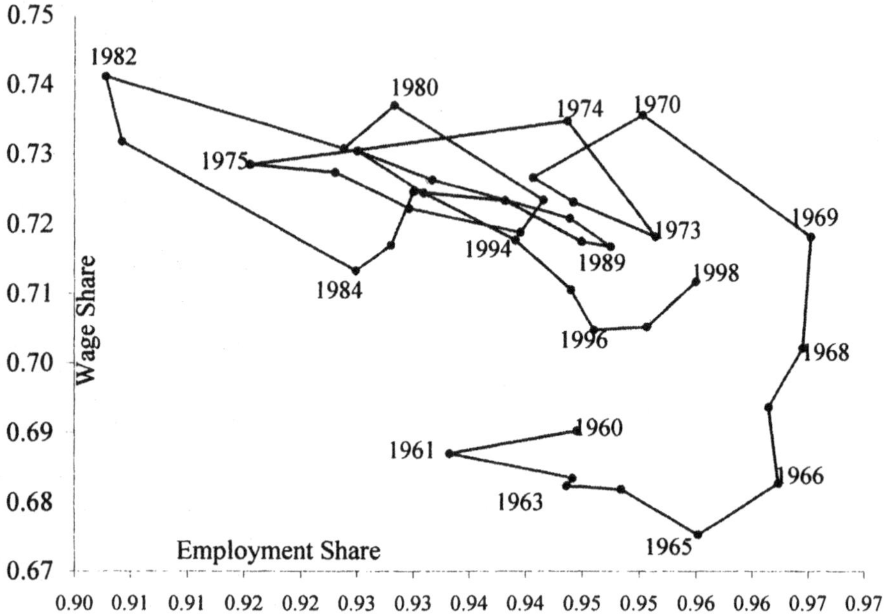


**Figure 3.5 Goodwin cycles in the U.S. economy: 1960-1998**

*Source:* Economic Report of the President 1999.

## Advance findings

Goodwin's medium-run dynamics of accumulation, employment and wage shares are capable of extension with financial variables, with empirically verifiable results. Strong empirical evidence supports the view that Goodwin medium-term cycles (about ten years) set the central tendencies for shorter fluctuations associated with the dynamics of credit driven excess demand. I believe that these claims are verified by the actual dynamics of the Spanish Economy after 1970.

# 4 Minsky's Financial Fragility

Minsky's contribution to Post-Keynesian views of the relationship existing between an endogenous credit supply and the gestation of financial crises deserves special attention. His dynamical approach "represents one of the most important links between post-Keynesians and Institutionalists" (Papadimitriou and Wray, 1997). Indeed, Minsky's theory concerning the deterioration of financial structures resulting from the changing balance between profits, investment and credit will serve as reference for an alternative approach.

Minsky viewed the market system as being in continuous motion, moving through distinct phases of recovery, expansion and booming euphoria leading to a crash. Endogenous forces cause the transformation of each phase, pushing it to its terminal state, thus creating the conditions necessary to usher in a qualitatively new stage. In the course of this cyclical transformation in behavioral patterns, market participants experience drastic changes in expectations. Expansion euphoria leads to excesses in investment and borrowing, resulting in unsustainable debt build-ups and at some point inevitable panics. Firms' borrowing relative to their profits, closely related to their borrowing relative to investment, $\lambda$, typically undergoes drastic changes as the phases of the business cycle unfold. Firms constantly take stock of their prospects, anticipating the likelihood of future profits in the light of recent experience. They shape their investment plans and assess their finance needs accordingly.

When the economy emerges from a slump, a number of things have already happened. First many firms have already disappeared. The surviving firms are the strongest financially. While profits are low, so are their debts as well as the interest rates they are facing. At some point, profits will recover and investment will rise. At the initial steps of the recovery is the time when the borrowing-investment ratio is relatively low, financial good health is the norm, and optimism flourishes. Minsky's approach places the profit flows of industry and banks at the heart of the inevitable fluctuations modulating business activity. Minsky understood that the uniqueness of profits derived from two coincident properties. Profits provide both "a flow which enables businesses to validate debt and because anticipated profits are the lure that induces current and future investment" (Minsky, 1984, pp. 34-35).

As Paul Davidson and other Post-Keynesians have insisted, Minsky saw the business environment where investment decisions are hatched swept by winds of uncertainty. Business practices seek protection against excessive volatility through forward contracts and trust in forecasts of the future based upon conventional market models. If profit growth exceeds the expectations projected in these forecasts, business confidence burgeons and investment spending will rise. Firms normal risk aversion will be assuaged in the pursuit of profit opportunities, real or imagined. Banks will participate in the confidence upswing, aggressively extending new loans to the energized businesses. Borrowing by firms, relative to their expected profits as well as investment spending will rise.

It is noteworthy that despite the prominent role played by profits in Minsky's recovery from the trough, both as growing flows providing internal finance and gauges of business confidence in the future, the expansion phase ultimately does not come to an end due to their decline. Minsky's choice to account for the turning point at the peak of the upswing is not declining profitability but rising debt. Profit flows will rise as the expansion matures and something like full employment comes within sight. At this stage in the cycle profit expectations have reached lofty heights propelled by the experience of the profit growth gathered in the upswing. Investment spending rose because confidence increased and in Minsky as well as in Kalecki it is investment that drives profit growth, not the other way around. As the economy moves towards full employment, investment spending reaches its maximum level and profit flows crest. Debt growth encounters no such cyclical limits, growing as long as lenders are willing to ignore the increasing risk of default and borrowers remain oblivious to its consequences.

The transition to a state of financial fragility stems from the dichotomy between the limit to profits and investment imposed by the full employment barrier, and the boundless growth of potential debt. Even if profit flows remained unchanged, firms leverage would expand unless debts were promptly repaid. In the unlikely case that business confidence was never shaken by unexpected events, lenders' risk would be rising as leverage expands. Any hint that business revenues could be in jeopardy or that the current pace of activity could not be maintained will impact not only on interest rates but also on the willingness of banks to continue extending credit. On the road to full employment, the gap between expected profitability and interest rates will narrow and the demand price for capital assets will fall relative to the supply price of investment goods. When this happens, the decline in capital asset prices will likely trigger a stock market correction that may further aggravate bearish sentiments regarding future profits and drag investment down further.

W. Mitchell focused his attention on the deterioration of profit margins as the upswing matured to explain the turning point of the business cycle. In Minsky's view, the downturn will be caused by the accumulation of debt rising excessively relative to profit flows. At what point this debt burden looms "excessive" relative to profits will depend on the perception of growing risk on the part of creditors. In Minsky-type models, dependence on external finance inevitably leads to a state of "financial fragility". When such a thing happens rising interest rates will trigger a business contraction and if a severe credit cut-off follows will push the economy into a slump. In his own words:

> The instability of a financial regime heavily weighted by speculative and Ponzi finance is due to the impact of changing interest rates that develop as an investment boom matures. As financial and product markets react to profit opportunities in an investment boom, the demand for financing increases interest rates. As a result, the margin between the present value of assets and the investment output decreases. If carried far enough a present value reversal occurs: that is, the value of capital assets falls below the supply price of investment. Rising interest rates diminish or eliminate the margins of safety that make the financing of investment possible (Minsky, 1986, pp. 214-215).

## Empirical findings and Minsky's financial crisis

The empirical tests conducted by Robert Pollin on the genesis of financial crisis as proposed by Minsky revealed that "the profit rate, for Minsky, is a much more ambiguous and less significant analytic category" than it is from the perspective of Classical economics (Pollin, 1986, pp. 205-235). Following Kalecki, Post-Keynesian economists, including Minsky, generally reverse the Classical chain of causation going from profitability to investment. Profitability, according to the Post-Keynesian view, follows and reflects the strength of investment spending.

After empirically evaluating the alternative approaches to the study of financial crises, M. Wolfson ranked his results according to their analytical significance. Topping his list, he found that indeed as Minsky's models predict, in the upswing of the business cycle financial structures deteriorate, as optimism fosters growing indebtedness and firms become more aggressive in their willingness to undertake risky projects. Borrowing ratios relative to profits or investment typically rise. Secondly, Wolfson found that the chief endogenous change leading to a financial crisis was the decline of profit margins (Wolfson, 1994, p. 15). He did not find factual support, however, for

Minsky's assumption that profit flows are a relatively stable share of output. Wolfson's findings regarding the genesis of financial crises, provide empirical support for the view that:

> The important consideration is the relationship between debt payments and the means to repay the debt—profits. It is when profits can no longer keep up with spiraling debt charges that the real trouble begins. It is for this reason that point 2 associates the debt repayment problems of the corporations with the decline in profits (Wolfson, 1994, p. 159).

In my judgment, Wolfson's attention to the dynamics of profitability and debt places his approach within the confines of Classical economics and lends theoretical consistency to his findings. I will close this section with a critique of H. Minsky's approach to cycles derived from Eatwell and Milgate.

## Uncertainty and irrational expectations

Minsky's financial fragility hypothesis is largely based on the psychological misperception of the fundamental forces at play behind any expansion of accumulation. The void created by the general uncertainty surrounding future events is filled with subjective views that take a life of their own. The tempo behind the formation of these anticipations leads to irrational exuberance in the upswing and wretched pessimism in the contraction phase. It is the opposite of rational expectations. This is why any dark cloud in the euphoric horizons of an asset bubble can wreak havoc to its foundation. Duncan Foley has offered a vigorous defense of Minsky's approach, arguing that:

> His theses on financial fragility and instability stem from his vision of the financial process as an essentially human confrontation of the present with the future, mediated by all the psychological baggage humans carry to major life decisions: their self-deception, opportunism, and insecurity as well as their faith, imagination, and steadfastness (Foley, 1998).

Post-Keynesian economics in general makes much of uncertainty and its consequences for the stability of the growth path. Reacting against the timeless logic of General Equilibrium analysis, Post-Keynesians support the necessity of rejecting neoclassical economics in order to develop a model or paradigm firmly rooted in the real world and historical time. From the Post-Keynesian perspective, future outcomes are uncertain in a world of limited information and unmanageable complexity. The MIT Dictionary of Economics offers a very cogent summary of the main structural components sustaining Post-Keynesian thought. The entry says that the major figures among Post-Keynesian economists:

> Stress the dynamic nature of an economy which uses money and which is subject to uncertainty. The nature of time is such that markets do not always clear. Individuals in those markets do not always receive the correct signals to encourage optimal behavior. Post-Keynesian economists emphasize the institutional setting of the economy and the social relationships therein. Following the classical tradition they provide a theory of distribution and employment based on the investment behavior of the class of individuals who control capital (Pearce, 1992, p. 337).

While welcoming the call to realism and the move away from the timeless adjustments of General equilibrium, other Post-Keynesians, such as Eatwell and Milgate (1992) find the heavy reliance on uncertainty troublesome. The presence of uncertainty surrounding all decisions involving historical time leads some prominent Post-Keynesians (notably J. Robinson and Shackle) to deny completely the possibility of long-run tendencies. Leading Post-Keynesians like Paul Davidson find uncertainty to be the main reason for the necessity of money. From that basic insight, they move on to derive theories for the persistence of labor unemployment. For Davidson, a monetary economy operating in an uncertain environment induces a certain kind of behavior in decision makers who:

> feel queasy about undertaking any actions which will commit their current claims on resources on to a path which can be altered, if future events require, only at a very high cost (Davidson, 1982, p. 222).

Looking at the murkiness surrounding decision-making in the real world Post-Keynesians like Paul Davidson saw investment plans bedeviled by the pervasive uncertainty of future outcomes. Searching for a stabilizing rudder in business expectations, Davidson located rigid money wages as the decisive element. Rather than being an obstacle to the clearing of the labor market, rigid or sticky money wages turned out to provide much needed support for the system's stability.

> Money wage rates are normally set by contract over a period of calendar time. If this labor contract fixes money wages relative to productivity for a period which exceeds in calendar time the gestation period for production to occur, then entrepreneurs can undertake production commitments with predictable

> production costs. If profit margins remain fixed for the same period, then prices of newly produced goods are unchanged. Inflation (a general rise in the price level of newly produced goods) will occur only if wage increases outstrip productivity increments and/or profit margins or mark-ups rise (Davidson, 1977, p. 287).

This is a remarkable and succinct statement reflecting one of the most influential trends in Post-Keynesian analysis. Here we find the link between exogenously determined money wage rates, the stability conditions for decision-making, mark-up prices and the foundation for a theory of inflation. Neoclassical theory blames excessive growth of the money supply for inflation, while Davidson and others finds excessive wage increases to be the culprit.

> The post-Keynesian, wage-cost markup model of Weintraub (1978) emphasizes the growth of wages relative to the growth in labor productivity as the main determinant of inflation (Atesoglu, 2001, p. 512).

From this trove of conceptual claims we can infer a certain theory of imperfect competition in which the degree of monopoly sets the mark-up over wage costs and a theory of inflation in which wage-push behavior leading to mark-up boosts are the responsible forces.

The selection of wage-push or cost mark-ups reveals a certain view of oligopoly markets as natural settings for power struggles between capital and labor. Further, in contrast to the conventional Keynesian view of inflation, this problem is not perceived as being caused by effective demand pressures exerted on the economy's limited resources, but rather, as a result of class struggles impacting on the distribution of income.

Minsky dynamical approach shares two basic assumptions with Shaikh's. For Minsky and Shaikh equilibrium is not a state but rather "a moving target" and cycles are fundamentally transient episodes of an economic system never achieving equilibrium but subject instead to the influence of equilibrating forces (Minsky, 1975, p. 61). On the other hand, Minsky's dynamics differ from Shaikk's in the identification of the driving force behind the transition of the cycle's phases.

## Psychology versus structural determination

Aberrant psychology in Minsky's view gives rise to irrational exuberance and is the culprit behind the emergence of financial fragility. Surprisingly the banks are caught in it as if they were unconcerned observers. Minsky elaborates a compelling view of how perceptions of an uncertain future feed on themselves and fly in the face of reality until the bubble bursts.

The credit boom that fueled excess demand in the second half of the 1980s in Spain is a good example of the irrational exuberance that characterizes Minsky's cycles. In this episode, business balance sheets deteriorated sharply as debts grew and the credit controls instituted by the Central Bank in the early 1990s brought the economy to its worst recession in ten years. The question is whether the accumulation of debt by itself would have reversed the mini-boom of the 1980s, even if the Central Bank had not imposed credit rationing. In Shaikh's models expansion is driven by rising profitability justifying higher borrowing and spending. While expectations may get out of line with reality, the weight of the rising debt exerts a sobering influence on future spending.

The problem with Minsky's approach is that irrational exuberance replaces the rational expectations of neoclassical economics and the economy moves continuously from boom to bust. The possibility that economic crises could break out absent irrational exuberance is excluded from Minsky's approach, despite the fact that booms and busts are the center of his analysis. Semmler and Sieveking's model following the presentation of Minsky's approach is closer to Minsky in its content than it is to Goodwin or Shaikh. Semmler and Sieveking examine formally the effects of increasing risk on credit availability and the possibility of bankruptcy. In this model, risk aversion on the part of banks accentuates the liquidity crunch in a downturn.

## Imperfections and market breakdowns

There is a sense, however, in which all of these tactical concessions to the real world, including the focus on misperceptions as the cause of booms and busts, create a barrier to the pursuit of a better theoretical strategy than neoclassical economics provides. Murray Milgate, J. Eatwell and Marco Magnani contend that in order to differentiate their own approach from other Post-Keynesians the term "imperfectionist theory" should be used to attribute recessions and the growth of unemployment to the presence of interferences with the neoclassical theory of rational expectations and market clearing.

Imperfectionist theory would apply to those research projects seeking to undermine the import of neoclassical theory by pointing out irrational behavior or the existence of rigidities in the name of realism and offering them as causation for market breakdowns. Milgate and Eatwell argue that the emphasis on imperfections and irrational behavior that some Post-

Keynesians rely upon tends to legitimate and even strengthen the neoclassical claims made on behalf of orthodox theory concerning how markets clear given rational expectations and absent rigidities. Milgate and Eatwell would rather favor an approach unencumbered by neoclassical residues:

> although the theory of effective demand indicates that this self-adjusting process (i.e. the operation of the market mechanism as it affects employment) does not tend to produce those desirable outcomes that it was asserted to produce according to the orthodox demand-and-supply characterization of the market mechanism, it is not to frictions and rigidities (or 'obstacles' to the normal operation of the market mechanism) that Keynes appeals for his results (Eatwell and Milgate, 1992, p. 265).

Milgate and Eatwell deny that in the purest of all neoclassical worlds full employment will be achieved, as long as rational expectations and flexible price adjustments between different assets exist. Regardless of the ease with which any discrepancies between independently set asset-prices and their cost of production are reconciled, slumps would occur. They argue instead that achieving full employment requires a certain level of effective demand, one that is not at all influenced by any changes in relative prices, money wages or profitability. Eatwell qualifies his denial that changes in profitability will have an effect on the level of effective demand by allowing that indeed the relationship between the rate of profit and the investment level "must be located in the more general context of the process of accumulation" (Eatwell, 1992, p. 125). Unfortunately, however, Eatwell locates the link within a nebulous area, for he views the process of accumulation as something contingent on the "specific circumstances of any given time and place" (Eatwell, 1992, p. 126), a framework loose enough to encompass all sorts of conditions.

In general, Eatwell and Milgate see the promise of Post-Keynesian theory in proving that, despite rational expectations and the smoothest operation of the market economy, free from distortions, the long-term outcome of market forces, exerting their natural weight on transient phenomena, will produce persistent unemployment. Not willing to renounce the long-term tendencies of the market economy does not blind Eatwell and Milgate to the presence of transient rigidities, but they point out that, in long-term perspective it becomes increasingly difficult to attribute all the shortcomings of capitalism to irrational psychology and market imperfections.

Admittedly, the perfect knowledge assumption required by neoclassical models of pure competition is not merely a distortion of the real competition (the "free" competition of Adam Smith and Classical Political Economy), but an ideal construct removed from the world we know. Real competition is neither pure nor perfect, but a turbulent affair with unintended outcomes. Yet, the free interaction of market forces that produces outcomes contrary to the participants' expectations also reveals the nature and direction of the economy's structural laws. These laws are not arbitrary or ideal constructs of the actual evolutionary path. Denying the existence of long-term adjustments capable of overcoming transient disruptions (the approach chosen by Joan Robinson, Shackle, Davidson and Minsky) carries with it a heavy price. It is not merely leaving the theoretical corpus of neoclassical theory unharmed, but also breaking away from the central tendencies of Classical Political Economy, including those formulated by Smith, Ricardo, Malthus and Marx.

## Credit crunches and slumps

Now I turn to W. Semmler and M. Sieveking (1988, 1993) for a classic example of models that focus on the impact of pro-cyclical financial flows on the tempo of business activity in order to derive cycles and a possible collapse. As an introduction, I wish to highlight some works by Eckstein and Sinai, (1977) as well as A. Wojnilower, (1980, 1985) for their suggestive insights into this link. These contributions have enriched the tradition connecting the dynamics of the business cycle to endogenous changes in the financial liquidity of firms and banks.

Wojnilower saw cyclical downturns as the outcome of credit rationing by risk-averse banks once the danger of loan defaults crossed a certain conventional threshold. His conclusion was that credit crunches develop naturally as business expansions near their peak and banks suddenly move to cut their potential losses by restricting any further lending (Wojnilower, 1980). According to Eckstein and Sinai (1986), after the mid-1950s credit crunches preceded and provoked all recessions in the U.S. These credit policy reversals standout as visible limits on the system's growth given by the size of the stock of liquid reserves kept by financial institutions. As business activity gains momentum, particularly in the mature phase of the upturn, the demand for credit accelerates. Eckstein and Sinai also assume that in this phase inflation will be rising and contributing to the growth in credit demand. Responding to the overheated rhythm of activity, at some point the central bank will decide to cool-off the system and impose credit controls. Then banks' liquidity will decline not only due to the restrictive policy of the central bank but also because deposit inflows have slowed-down as the expansion progressed. The likely outcome will be the rise in interest rates, signaling to the banks the need for credit rationing in order to avoid excessive risks in loan management. At the same time firms will respond by building-up their liquid reserves and cutting-back on their spending plans.

In the event, the downturn ensues, caused by the financial and real restrictions imposed by banks and firms. The conclusion reached by Sinai is that "Financial instability is an endogenous process, rooted in the cyclical evolution of risky balance sheet positions for various decision-making units" (Sinai, 1977). In the paper co-authored with Eckstein, these writers emphasized that the credit "crunch is at the heart of the business cycle mechanism, particularly the upper turning point" (Eckstein and Sinai, 1986, p. 53).

## The Semmler-Sieveking model's link with Minsky

My objective consists in presenting the model's structure, produce the simulations that follow from its conclusions and finally establish the links with Minsky's general approach to the analysis of financial fragility and cycles. The Semmler and Sieveking's model (1988), "Nonlinear Liquidity-Growth Dynamics with Bankruptcy Risk" formalized the effects of changes in the external credit financing of business activity once the perception of lenders' risk reaches a critical threshold. In their model, Semmler and Sieveking developed Minsky's notion that over-extension of credit in the boom phase of the business cycle will precipitate sharp reversals in capital outlays, leading to growth fluctuations and the possibility of sharp downturns.

The historical antecedents of Semmler and Sieviking's model reach back to Hilferding's *Finance Capital* originally published in 1910. In that book, Hilferding regarded firms' decisions to expand output as being tied up with their ability to borrow from the banks. A period of prosperity is one in which business growth has been financed by new bank loans. As the boom matures, rising borrowing will reduce banks' reserves and loan interest rates will increase. As the peak of the upswing comes within sight the prolonged depletion of bank reserves calls for drastic measures. Obviously Hilferding did not believe that banks could procure additional reserves from the central bank and the public, or if they did, not in a magnitude proportional to the demand for loans. The upshot of a boom phase is a credit cut-off. Near the peak of the expansion "not only has the interest rate risen to its maximum, but it is impossible to obtain credit at all" (Hilferding, 1981, p. 273).

In the 1988 Semmler-Sieveking model firms using bank credit finance experience wider fluctuations in business activity than they would relying exclusively on internal funds. In this model rising borrowing leads to higher growth rates in output and a bigger need for more future credit. Optimistic expectations become self-fulfilling prophecies and the banks are willing enablers of the firms' rising expenditures. The underlying assumption in this model, also found in Minsky's writings, is that the debt build-up as such exerts no inhibiting pressure on borrowers or lenders. It is only when an unexpected shock occurs that banks take notice of the debt-burden facing their clients and take corrective action.

Once banks lose confidence in the resilience of the expansion, they will respond with credit tightening measures. Their policy change will dampen the upswing's euphoria only if the shock is powerful enough to justify a credit crunch. The nature of the response by banks will depend on the scope of the perceived perturbation. Shocks that do not meet the existing alarm threshold will not create appreciable dislocations. The boom will turn into a bust only if credit lines are entirely cut-off as fears of default mount. The imposed credit crunch will then exacerbate whatever financial problems confront the heavily indebted firms and so hasten their demise. Just as the euphoria of the upswing fed on itself as well as on the easy credit provided by the banks, the push towards recession will draw strength from their credit withdrawal. Thus, the initial concern with possible defaults that led banks to alter their lending policy becomes another self-fulfilling prophecy.

The 1988 Semmler-Sieveking model did not specify the kind of unexpected shocks that may bedevil a business expansion turning it into a bust. Its focus, however, centers on the decline in profitability. By contrast, Minsky was explicit on this point, as he focused on interest rate hikes:

> A break in the boom occurs whenever short and long-term interest rates rise enough so that alternatives and reversals in present-value relations take place. Often this occurs after the increase in demand financed by speculative finance has raised interest rates, wages of labor, and prices of materials so that profit margins and thus the stability to validate the past are eroded (Minsky, 1986, p. 220).

For their part, Semmler and Sieviking wished to formulate their non-linear growth and cycles' model focusing on two state variables, financial liquidity and productive assets. In addition, Semmler and Sieviking look at the differentiated impact of changes in financial flows taking place in the various phases of the cycle. They argue that these changes in financial flows have a stronger drag on real variables in a downturn than they do in the boom phase. They quote Bernanke's view that:

> Bankruptcy imposes net social costs, so that all agents have an interest in avoiding it. Consumers and firms do this by being careful to retain sufficient liquid assets to meet fixed expenses, banks and other lenders, by being selective in choosing borrowers and limiting the size of loans. The onset of recession strains the system by reducing the flow of income available to meet current obligations and by increasing uncertainty about future liquidity. There is a general attempt to insure solvency which leads to a reduced demand for consumer and producer variables—which may in turn generate further income reductions (Bernanke, 1981, pp. 155-159).

As the economy expands, business net worth rises and credit lenders respond favorably. On the other hand in a recession the negative effects of falling sales and declining profits are exacerbated by the attendant credit constraints that follow, depriving business of compensatory working capital flows. At such times, firms themselves will hoard their funds as a precaution against the threat of insolvency. Semmler and Sieviking set the foundations for their model by specifying three balance sheets, namely those of the Central Bank, the commercial banks and businesses.

## The capital stock

By definition, business sales equal capital outlays plus consumption out of profits, $S = C + c$. Capital outlays, C, include wage payments, materials and fixed investment. The expression $c = c_{\Pi}qS$ represents consumption out of profits (q is the profit margin on sales as in Foley's model). In Foley's tradition, the model distinguishes between productive and money capital. Capital outlays include wages, purchase of materials and net investment, leading to the growth of the capital stock. There are no savings out of wages.

Profits minus consumption spending out of profits provide the wherewithal for the expansion of the capital stock, $K= C + c - S(1-q) - c$:

$$\dot{K} = qS - c \tag{4.1}$$

Government deficits produce the increase in base money that expands by a multiple all deposits in commercial banks. These deposits in turn will provide banks with the reserves necessary, R, to finance the growth of capital outlays: $kR = D = R + L_f$ (where k is the credit multiplier).

**Business liquidity revisited**

Business financial liquidity, required to fulfill short-term commitments, consists of current assets, CA, plus inventories, Inv. Available total business liquidity, $L = L^B + CL + L^R$ include $L^B$ current assets net of inventories, (CA – Inv), available credit lines, CL (borrowing capacity) and liquid reserves $L^R$.

Note that if $L^R$ is a fixed fraction of $L^B$ and we label $b = \frac{L^R}{L^B}$, we can write the total available business liquidity as $L = (1+b)L^B + CL$. Finally, its time rate of change will be, $\dot{L} = (1-b)\dot{L}^B + \dot{CL}$. From the standpoint of its sources, the growth rate of total liquidity $g_l = g_m + g_n$ is the sum of the growth *rate* for the autonomous portion of liquidity $g_m = (1-b)\frac{\dot{L}^B}{L}$ plus the endogenous component. This growth of autonomous liquidity is linked to the growth of base money (bank reserves), R, and is assumed constant, along with the share of current assets net of inventories, $\frac{\dot{L}^B}{L}$. Then the growth path of the endogenous portion, $g_n L = \dot{CL}$, being related to the available credit lines, is given by:

$$\dot{L} = g_m L + g_n L \qquad (4.2)$$

For a measure of business liquidity, Semmler and Sieviking's model focuses on the financial liquidity/capital stock ratio, $\lambda = L/K$. The growth rate of this ratio will be:

$$\hat{\lambda} = \hat{L} - \hat{K} \qquad (4.3)$$

As indicated the growth rate of total business liquidity, g, is $= m + n$ and is linked to profitability. By definition, the rate of profit, $r = \Pi/K$, so that its growth rate:

$$\hat{r} = \hat{\Pi} - \hat{K} \qquad (4.4)$$

Semmler and Sieviking then assumed that the growth rate of capital outlays, C, will depend on the liquidity/capital stock ratio and the rate of profit. We have seen that profits, $\Pi = qS$, and sales, $S = C + c_{\Pi} qS$, so that rearranging the expression for capital outlays we have, $C = S(1 - c_{\Pi}q)$. Now since we assume that consumption out of profits, $c_{\Pi}$ and the profit margin, q are constants it follows that the growth rates of sales, $\hat{S} = \hat{C}$. Moreover, note that the growth rate of profits is, $\hat{\Pi} = \hat{S}$ and so it follows that $\hat{\Pi} = \hat{S} = \hat{C}$ and the growth rate of the profit rate will be given by $\hat{r} = \hat{C} - \hat{K}$. The growth rate of capital outlays then is a function of the profit rate and business liquidity plus a constant $\beta_2$:

$$\hat{C} = \hat{c}(r, \lambda, \beta_2) \tag{4.5}$$

The growth of the capital stock is linked to fixed capital investment, which is also determined by the profit rate, the growth of the business liquidity/asset ratio plus a constant $\beta_1$ representing the autonomous growth of capital:

$$\hat{K} = \hat{c}(r, \lambda, \beta_1) \tag{4.6}$$

Combining these expressions to derive the growth rate of the profit rate, that is the growth of profits minus the growth of the capital stock, we have:

$$\hat{r} = \beta_2 + \delta_1 \lambda + \mu_1 r - (\beta_1 + \gamma_1 + \varepsilon\lambda) \tag{4.7}$$

The model further assumes that the growth rate of endogenous finance also depends on the rate of profit plus total liquidity, that is, $g_n(r, \lambda) = \tau_1 r + \tau_2 \lambda$. Hence the growth rate of total liquidity will be:

$$\hat{\lambda} = g_m + \tau_1 r + \tau_2 \lambda - (\beta_1 + \gamma_1 r + \varepsilon\lambda) \tag{4.8}$$

In this differential equation, $\tau_1 r$ stands for the response of investment to the movement of the rate of profit and $\varepsilon\lambda$ for the response of investment to the liquidity asset/ratio. The expression can be simplified as follows: make $g_m - \beta_1 = \alpha$; $\tau_2 - \varepsilon = \varepsilon_1$ and $\tau_1 - \gamma_1 = \beta$. Then the growth rate of the liquidity/asset ratio will take the form:

$$\hat{\lambda}=\alpha+\beta r-\varepsilon_1\lambda \tag{4.9}$$

Similarly a number of terms in the expression for the growth of the profit rate can be consolidated, thus $\beta_2$-$\beta_1$ = $\gamma$; $\delta_1$-$\varepsilon$ = $\delta$; $\mu_1$-$\gamma_1$=$\varepsilon_2$. Semmler and Sieviking then indicate that $\beta_2 < \beta_1$; $\delta_1 > \varepsilon$; $\mu_1 < \gamma_1$. Finally, the growth rate of the profit rate will be, $\hat{r}=-\gamma+\delta\lambda-\varepsilon_2 r$ and substituting, we arrive at the two non-linear differential equations of the system:

$$\dot{\lambda}=(\alpha-\beta r-\varepsilon_1\lambda)\lambda \tag{4.10}$$

$$\dot{r}=(-\tau+\delta\lambda-\varepsilon_2 r)r \tag{4.11}$$

The simulation of this system applying small perturbation values ($\varepsilon_1$ and $\varepsilon_2$ are the only perturbation terms allowed to disrupt the system) produces a convergent dynamics in which the profit rate and the liquidity/assets ratio asymptotically approach their equilibrium values ($\lambda^* > 0$, $r^* > 0$). Figure 4.1 shows the results.

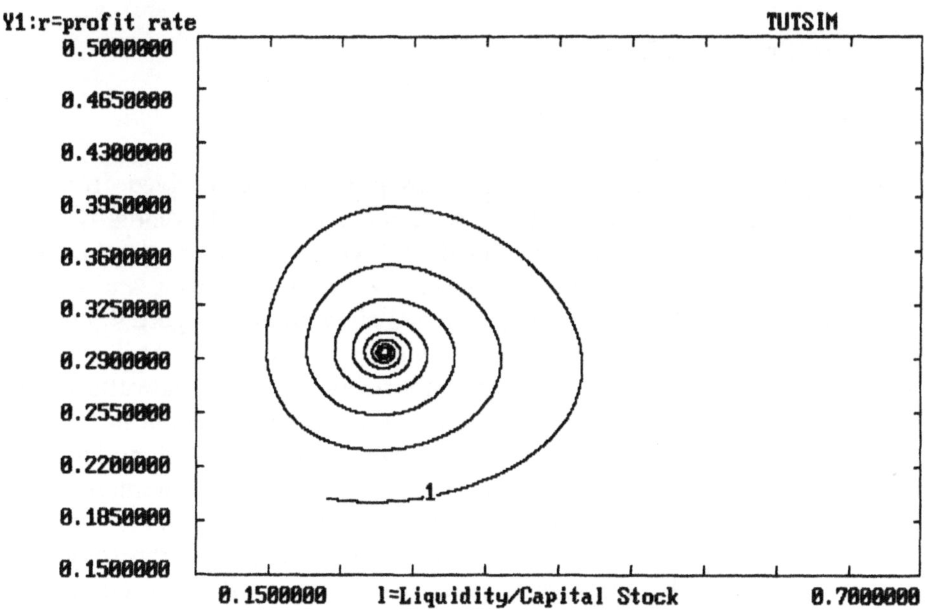


**Figure 4.1 Semmler's model diagram in liquidity profit rate space**

Semmler and Sieviking then extended their model to consider a situation in which the credit lines normally available to business suddenly close. They assume that the credit lines that banks make available to firms are contingent on their perception regarding a normal risk threshold. In a downturn the growth of business failures sends a signal that raises the risk involved in approving new loans. Firms themselves facing uncertain cash flows may become reluctant to maintain their capital outlays, choosing instead to expand their holdings of liquid reserves. In other words, aggregate business liquidity falls precipitously due to the closing of credit lines as banks respond to a heightened risk of defaults linked to smaller sales, as well as by the contraction of capital outlays themselves.

This chain of events starts with a decline in profitability below acceptable levels, $\phi$ (so that $r < \phi$) followed by a drop in liquidity below some conventional ratio, $\mu$ (when $\lambda < \mu$) and the sharp contraction in capital outlays. The idea of a credit and liquidity squeeze leads to a more complex dynamics controlled by the addition of a new term, h, in the model's structure of differential equations.

In this new system, h embodies the combined reaction of banks and firms to the decline in profitability and the liquidity asset ratio below acceptable levels.

$$\hat{\lambda} = \alpha + \beta r - \varepsilon_1 \lambda - h(\lambda, r)$$

$$\hat{r} = -\gamma + \delta\lambda - \varepsilon_2 r$$

When capital outlays are subject to substantial shocks derived from the liquidity squeeze, the system displays wide fluctuations that eventually move towards the inner limit cycle depicted in Figure 4.2. When the business response to vanishing liquidity is perversely strong, however, and capital outlays are drastically reduced, the system's simulation in Figure 4.3 shows the resulting collapse for both profitability and liquidity ratios. This outcome is strongly reminiscent of the effects that a rising capital-output ratio would impart on the otherwise stable Goodwin-model cycles presented in Chapter 3. In that model both employment and wage shares would collapse as profitability falls. While Goodwin's model precludes this alternative, the actual experience in the Spanish economy requires its inclusion.

As long as the perturbations do not cross a given amplitude threshold, the system remains stable, although it never reaches an equilibrium point. The possibility of a major depression is not excluded, nonetheless, once the strength of the shocks proves unmanageable. Such events, at any rate, are considered abnormal in this model.

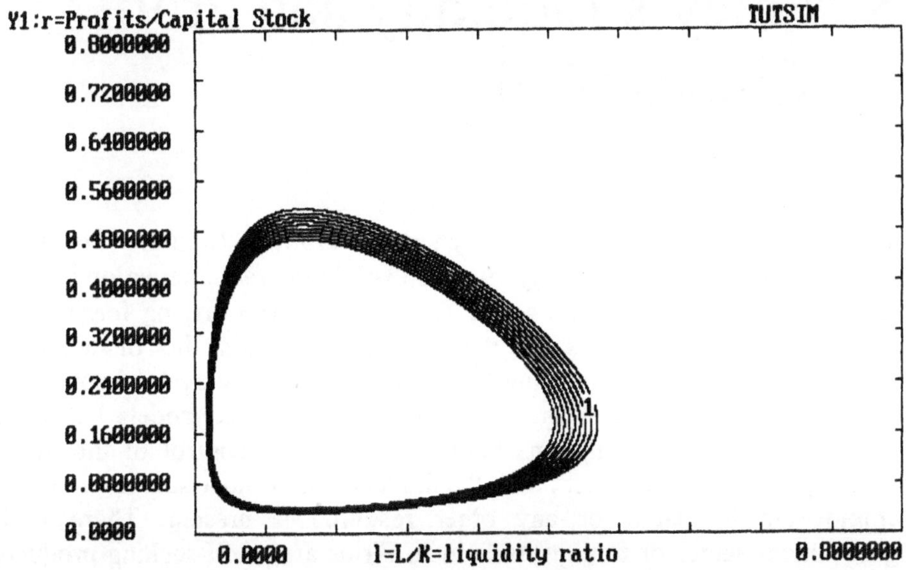


**Figure 4.2 Semmler's model diagram in liquidity and profit rate space with normal shocks: model's simulation**

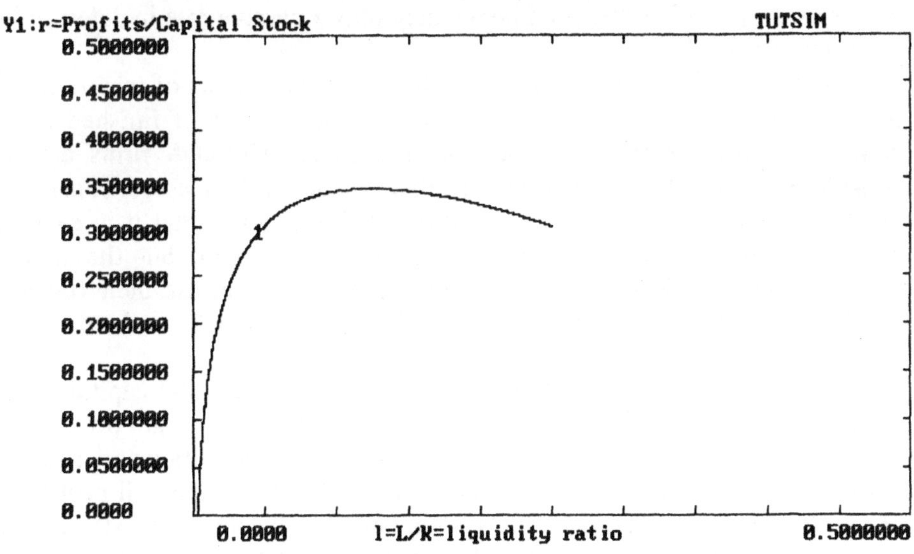


**Figure 4.3 Semmler's model diagram in liquidity and profit rate space with abnormal shocks: model's simulation**

# 5 Foley's Liquidity and Profit Cycles Model

The general purpose of Duncan Foley's model (1987a) "Liquidity-Profit Rate Cycles in a Capitalist Economy" was to explain the real interaction between capitalist firms and their economic environment. The driving force in this model's dynamics centers on the feedback between the financial and production decisions confronting firms. Strikingly, Foley's model conceptual structure is rather unique as an example of heterodox models because it retains monetarist assumptions behind the external control of the money supply growth. On the other hand, the model contains no assumption that full employment of labor or any other resource is present. There is no government sector or foreign trade in it. Firms are profit-seeking producers of goods for sale. Their profit margin on sales, q, determines the size of their profits. There are no saving leakages. Firms' capital spending, including wage payments, determines aggregate demand for their goods. Their total outlays set the volume of aggregate sales. Households spend all of their wages as they receive them and hence they play a passive role in determining aggregate demand.

Total business assets include circulating capital, stocks of materials and semi-finished goods, as well as fixed capital and stocks of finished goods held as a buffer between production and sales. Although firms are not considered primarily as portfolio speculators, part of their assets consists of cash reserves, securities and debt liabilities. Foley notes that it is easy for business firms to turn financial into productive capital, but the reverse change cannot be performed at will. Similarly, firms can use their financial assets to reduce their debt, but cannot increase their debt without market validation.

Balanced growth requires that the distribution of the total capital reflect the pattern of aggregate demand, as well as maintaining the right proportions between productive and financial capital. When these conditions are satisfied market and financial activities complement each other. Since all profits are reinvested in this model, once the system achieves balanced growth, capital-spending growth must be equal to the profit rate. Foley warns, however, that in fact capitalist growth does not proceed along such a balanced path.

## Liquidity and the interest rate

Firms in a modern economy use credit as a convenient means to bridge the time gap between their outlays on wages and materials and their sales revenues. The question is whether access to external credit simply provides firms with greater flexibility in their timing of recurrent expenditures or instead opens the way to periodic booms and busts. Borrowing increases as productive capital grows. Credit finances rising spending and therefore raises aggregate demand, resulting in higher capacity utilization and profitability.

In neoclassical economics, the savings and investment schedules determine the interest rate. On the other hand, the Keynesian tradition dwells on the distinction between money and productive capital, and the interest rate measures the price of liquidity. In a world without uncertainty regarding future sales, the rate of interest on bank loans would equal the firm's rate of profit. In Foley's model, money capital is not a perfect substitute for productive capital, and the interest rate clears the market for loanable funds. A rise in liquidity will drive the interest rate down in relation to the rate profit.

Firms rely on the banking system to create deposits, where they hold their money assets, M. The Central Bank controls the ability of banks to issue deposits by requiring them to hold reserves. The growth of these reserves depends on the purchase by the Central Bank of firms' debt and the willingness of banks to hold them as reserve assets. Firms can also extend credit to one another in commercial paper markets. Firms use money chiefly as a means of purchasing each other goods as well as paying wages. Thus, assuming credit markets are competitive, banks acquire firms' liabilities and their actions create new deposits. The central bank determines the growth of bank deposits through its controls of banking reserves.

## The model's nomenclature

In Foley's model, D refers to business debt. F stands for the firms' holding of others' debt, that is, financial assets. The sum of the money stock M + F equals total enterprise debt. E will be the firms' net worth. When firms undertake capital outlays, C they transform their money assets, M into productive capital X. The replacement cost will measure the stock of productive capital, and does not reflect the flow of expected profits on sales. S represents sales revenues, and q the profit margin. Sales bring in more money assets to the firms but reduce their productive capital by an amount equal to S(1-q).

Consider first that a rise in capital outlays and sales raises the profit rate, borrowing and the growth rate of the system. The decision to increase borrowing, B, increases the firms' money assets as it expands their debt liability. Lending decreases firms' money but increases their financial assets. Both borrowing and lending naturally involve interest payments. At the micro level the individual firm needs to know the amount of financial capital, F, available, how much productive capital, X, exists and the stock of financial liabilities, D, it carries. The change in financial capital available to each firm will be given by:

$$\dot{M} = i_F F' - i_D D' + S' + B' - L' - C'$$
$$\dot{F} = L'$$

Where S refers to the firm's sales (S' to its change), D' is the change in its debt, B stands for funds borrowed, (D'=B) and C its capital outlays on intermediate goods, wage payments and investment goods. Given the profit margin on sales, q = Π/S the change in the stock of productive capital available will be:

$$\dot{X} = C - S(1 - q)$$
$$\dot{D} = B'$$

Firms have control over C, B, L (and possibly q) but do not set the sales level, S and the rate of interest, i. Given the profit margin, q the profit rate on productive capital will be, $r = \frac{qS}{X}$ and since the profit margin, q, reflects the total growth of capital relative to the initial capital:

$$q = \frac{\dot{F} + X}{F + X} = \frac{qS}{F + X} + b(p) = r + b(p)$$

The firm's profits, however, depend on sales, which are out of its control. Hence, capital expenditures will be constraint by the stock of money and financial assets available. Taking the profit margin, q, as a constant, the firm's decision to borrow funds will depend on the difference between its rate of profit and the interest rate, p = r - i, so that:

$$\frac{\dot{C}}{C} = a(f)q \quad \text{and} \quad \frac{B}{F + X} = b(p) = b(r - i) \text{ and } b' > 0$$

Business capital outlays dependon firms total holdings of liquid assets, that is, e = m + f, including their stock of money and financial assets relative to their productive capital: f= F/X and m= M/X.

It follows from all of this that the higher the liquidity ratio achieved by firms, the stronger the capital outlays forthcoming and the borrowing involved. When firms expand their capital outlays in response to the increase in the sales to productive capital ratio, the expansion accelerates. The growth rate of their profit rate is the difference achieved between the growth rate of sales and the growth rate of the total capital outlays. Typically the higher the realized sales, the bigger the boom will be. The same thing happens if borrowing expands because the rate of interest has fallen below the profit rate due to a high liquidity ratio. At the opposite end, when liquidity is low the firms reactions will trigger the downturn. Assuming rational expectations, if the response of *all* firms to the growth of demand is identical, each one could believe that its expansion creates new markets and finance for all others.

The resulting growth cycles are the effect of fluctuations in the relationship between finance and productive capital expenditures. The growth in profitability will be:

$$\dot{r} = \frac{\dot{S}}{S} - \frac{(\dot{F} + X)}{F + X} = \frac{\dot{C}}{C} - \frac{(\dot{F} + X)}{F + X}$$

$$\dot{r} = a(f)q - q = [a(f) - 1]q$$

The rate of change in financial capital, relative to the growth of total capital is given by:

$$\dot{f} = \frac{\dot{F}}{F} - \frac{(\dot{F} + X)}{F + X} = b(p)\frac{1}{F} - q$$

In D. Foley's model, credit-financed spending acts as a non-linear accelerator of aggregate demand. The equilibrium growth rate equals the growth rate of the money supply, g. The profit rate will adjust to g through changes in the inventory to sales ratio and capacity utilization. When the profit rate is lower than g the interest rate will be falling. Liquidity measured by m = M/X increases because the growth of the money supply is higher than the profit rate. A falling interest rate leads to higher borrowing and new financial assets for the lending firms, f = F/X. Capital spending and aggregate sales relative to productive capital will also rise and so will profitability. The interest rate will now fall further below the profit rate. Eventually this rising liquidity induces a growth of capital outlays that exceeds the growth of the money supply. The rise in capital outlays, C, leads to the growth of aggregate demand and sales. Sales growth, decline in inventories, and higher rates of capacity utilization push the profit rate further up. Finally, as profitability rises above the growth of the money supply, m starts falling.

If borrowing and spending grows faster than the money supplied by the Central Bank, the interest rate will rise and profitability net of interest will fall. As the interest rate begins to rise faster than the profit rate, the gap between the two narrows and the incentive to accumulate weakens. This will give rise to a decline in borrowing relative to productive capital, B/X. The stage is set for a downturn leading to lower borrowing, spending, declining aggregate demand and lower capacity utilization. As liquidity declines in the mature phase of the cycle, the shortage of finance begins to dampen the growth of capital outlays. At some point, their growth will fall below their profit rates.

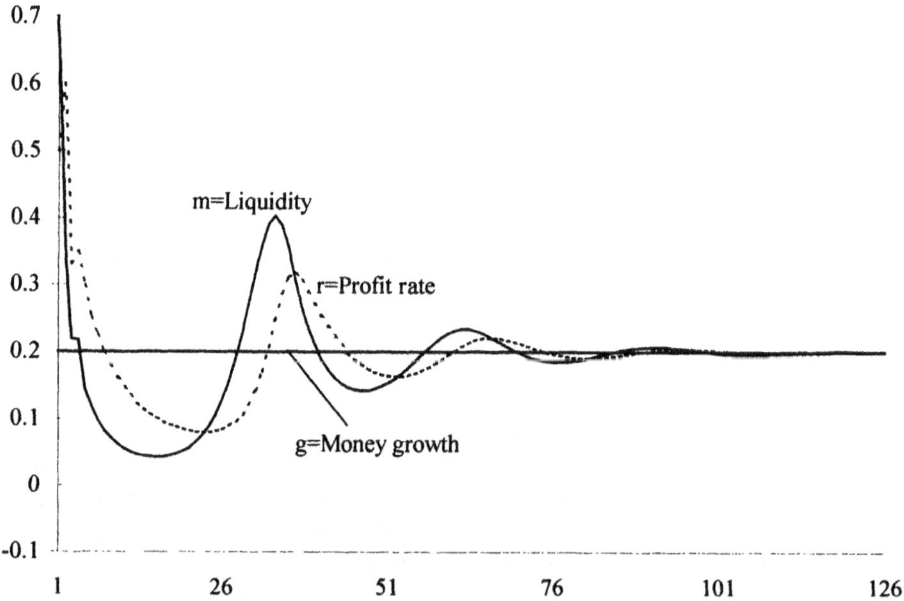


**Figure 5.1 Convergence of profit rate and money supply growth without financial accelerator: Foley's model simulation**

In Foley's model, the expansion phase is cut short due to the insufficient growth of the money supply, not by the excessive growth of the wage-share as in Goodwin's model. Weakening sales, rising inventories and lower capacity utilization of the capital stock combine to lower the profit rate. In the phase transition, the interest rate will fall less rapidly than the profit rate, thus choking the incentive to borrow and spend. At some point, however, profitability will have fallen below the growth rate of money and liquidity will start building up again.

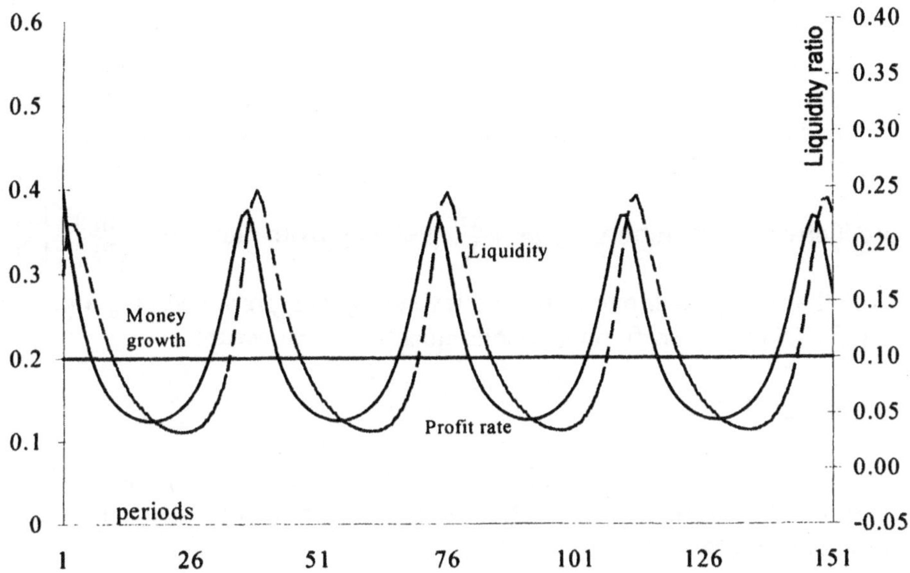


**Figure 5.2 Limit cycles with financial accelerator: Foley's model**

In conclusion, the growth of capital outlays requires a corresponding growth of liquidity. Borrowing depends on the profit and interest rates differential. As the boom progresses this gap is likely to narrow due to the insufficient growth of the money supply (controlled by the monetary authority) and this shortfall lays the ground for the boom's reversal:

> A rise in capital outlays and sales raises the profit rate, which tends to increase borrowing and the rate of expansion. There is however, a budget constraint in the form of the dependence of capital outlays on the liquidity of the system. This budget constraint links these two unstable systems so that they contain each other through a cyclical movement (Foley, 1987a, p. 374).

## The aggregate model in detail

All firms enjoy the same profit margin, as well as an identical propensity to increase capital outlays relative to their total liquidity. All profits, including those of the banking system, are re-invested: aggregate sales equal capital outlays, including wages and intermediate materials. Since aggregate financial assets equal aggregate debts, i(F - D) = 0, the difference between the interest rate and the (uniform) profit rate, p = r - i, depends only on the ratio of the money stock to productive capital, m = M/X. As the liquidity ratio grows, the interest rate relative to the profit rate declines because lending funds are more abundant, p= p(m) and p' > 0.

The changing relationships between the profit rate, r and finance relative to productive capital ratio, m and f, determine the growth path for the system. Figure 5.3 presents the simulation of the relationship between profitability and the ratio of borrowing to productive capital. We saw that the money to productive capital ratio was, $m = \frac{M}{X}$ and its growth rate $= \hat{m} = \left(\frac{\dot{m}}{m}\right) - \left(\frac{\dot{X}}{X}\right)$.

Note that the growth rate of the money supply is represented by g and recall that (X'/X) is the profit rate, r. Consequently we can write:

$$\hat{m} = g - r \tag{7.1}$$

We saw earlier that the incentive to accumulate depends on p, the difference between the profit and the interest rate. The ratio of financial assets to productive capital was:

$$f = \frac{F}{X}, \text{ and its growth rate, } \hat{f} = \frac{\dot{F}}{X} - \left(\frac{\dot{X}}{X}\right)\left(\frac{F}{X}\right)$$

The growth rate of financial assets therefore will be given by the expression, $\dot{F} = \dot{D} - \dot{M} = B - gM = b[p]$ and so B= b(p)X, therefore:

$$\hat{f} = b[p(m)] - gm - rf \tag{7.2}$$

In Figure 5.3 falling profitability forces firms to increase their borrowing relative to their productive capital assets. As borrowing and spending rises the rate of profit will recover and when this happens the borrowing ratio will start falling. This adjustment will continue until profitability reaches its peak and once again declines.

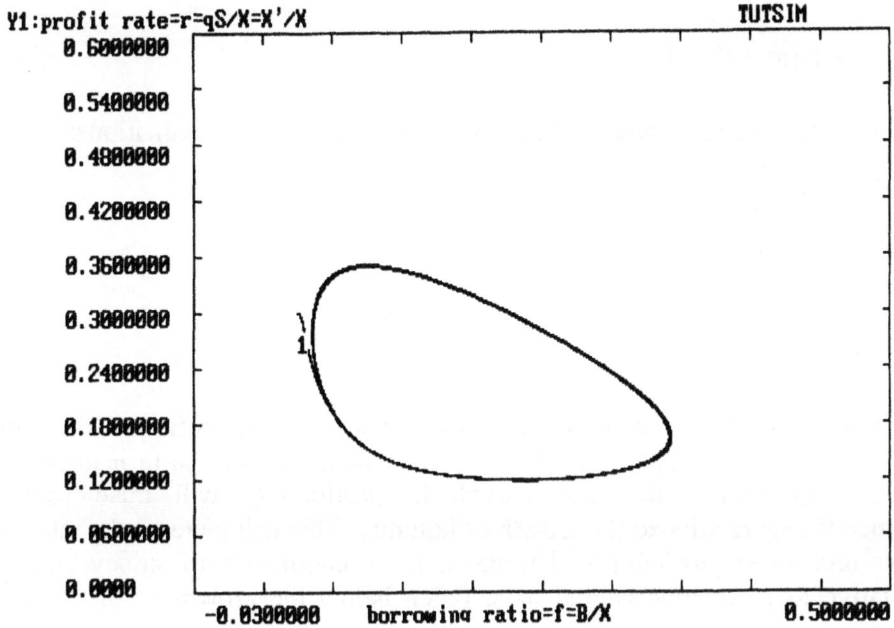


**Figure 5.3 Borrowing and profitability: Foley's model**

Since sales, S = capital outlays, C and the profit rate, $r = \frac{q\,s}{X} = \frac{q\,c}{X}$ =, it follows then that the profit rate's growth rate would be:

$$\hat{r} = q\left(\frac{\dot{C}}{C}\right)\left(\frac{C}{X}\right) - \left(\frac{\dot{X}}{X}\right)\left(q\frac{C}{X}\right) = \hat{\Pi} - \hat{X}$$

Now we should recall that the growth rate of capital, $\hat{X} = g = r$ and in addition, as we saw earlier, that the growth rate of capital outlays was a function of the rate of profit and the liquidity ratio. Finally, consider that total profits X' is defined as the profit margin times sales, or the profit rate times the stock of productive capital, hence:

$$\frac{\dot{r}}{r} = a[(m + f)] - r$$

Thus, we reach the last differential equation of Foley's model:

$$\dot{r} = [a(m + f) - r]r \tag{7.3}$$

The system's steady state will consist of the following three equations:

$$\begin{cases} r^* = g \\ m^* + f^* = \dfrac{b[p(m^*)]}{g} \\ a[g, f^* + m^*] = g \end{cases}$$

Simulations 7.4 and 7.5 show the interaction between the profit rate, liquidity and the supply of money. In the expansion phase the rise in m leads to an increasing profit rate. The growth in profitability will raise capital expenditures relative to the growth of liquidity. This will increase the interest rate and lower profitability. The decline will continue until money outlays relative to productive capital have fallen below the growth of the money supply.

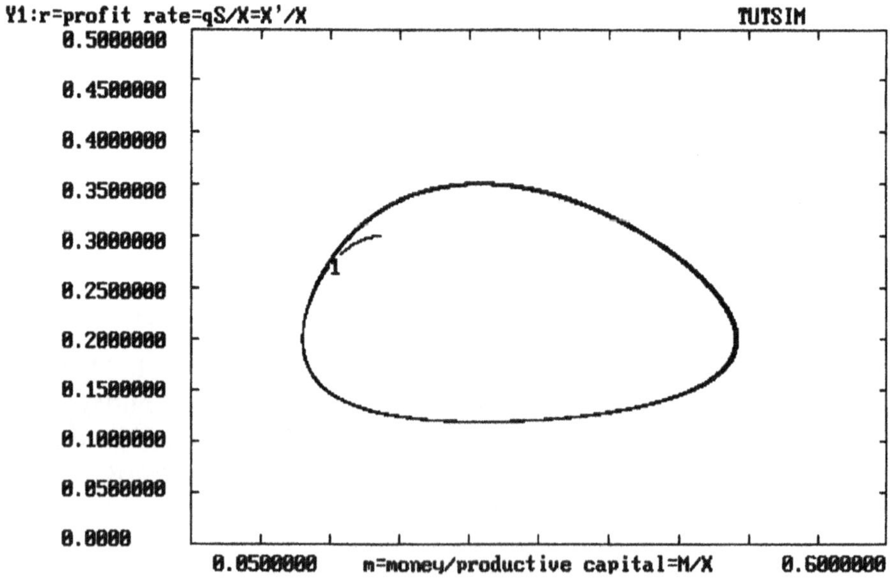


**Figure 5.4 Foley's phase diagram in profitability and liquidity space**

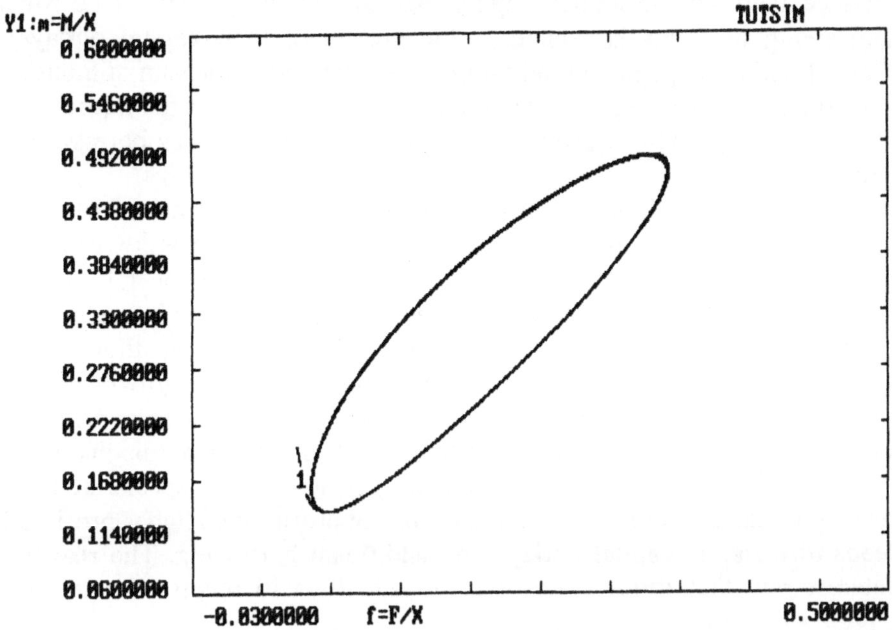


**Figure 5.5 Foley's phase diagram in f =F/X, and m= M/X**

## Model's summary

Foley's model sought to integrate the dynamics of finance with the cyclical growth of productive capital. Firms own productive capital, X, as well as financial assets, F. By assumption, all profits are reinvested and therefore the growth of productive capital is equal to the profit rate. Business profits and borrowing are the sources of business finance for capital growth. In the absence of the accelerator effect, the profit rate and the growth rate of capital will converge with the growth rate of the money supply.

Figure 5.6 below shows the empirical support found in Spain for the model's conclusions, represented in Figure 5.3, regarding the relationship between f, that is, credit finance relative to real assets (the capital stock) and r, average aggregate profitability. I believe that the evidence confirms the presence of a recurrent cycle from 1975 through 1998, involving borrowing and profitability, much as Foley's model postulated.

The basic dynamic assumptions of the model are as follows. The difference between the rate of profit, r, and the rate of interest, i, will determine the level of borrowing. Changes in the interest rate reflect the balance between the money supply growth and the growth of borrowing. Borrowing by firms is related to the growth of their capital outlays, C. Capital outlays depend on total liquidity, m, defined as the sum of money, M, plus financial assets, F, relative to productive capital X. As the liquidity ratio increases the growth of productive capital rises and so does borrowing and profitability.

In Foleys model, the profit margin and the growth of the money supply are exogenous and constant. Suppose that the profit rate is lower than the growth of the money supply. Then the interest rate will be falling and at some point the widening gap between the profit rate and the interest rate will induce firms to expand their borrowing. When they do so their liquidity (M/X) will be rising and capital outlays will expand. The growth in capital outlays will raise effective demand and sales. The growth of sales will reduce inventories and increase capacity utilization. It follows from this that the rate of profit will rise. When liquidity is rising, capital outlays accelerate and the growth of sales reinforces the increase of the profit rate. Higher profitability leads to a rise in capital outlays and additional borrowing. The rise in the interest rate that follows, however, eventually will reverse the trend and trigger a downturn.

Higher profitability will accelerate the growth rate of capital outlays and borrowing. At some point, however, the growth rate of capital will exceed the growth of the money supply and the rate of interest will rise. This increase will lower business borrowing, liquidity and capital spending. The growth of effective demand and sales will decline leading to a rise in inventories and a fall in capacity utilization. Thus, inevitably the rate of profit will be falling.

Absent financial over-shooting the outcome of the combined dynamics would be that the growth of capital outlays would adjust itself to the growth of the money supply. In addition, the profit rate itself would cyclically converge with the exogenous growth of the money supply.

## Advance findings: the model's empirical strength

As Foley's model would have it, Figure 5.6 shows the cyclical dynamics of profitability and credit finance relative to fixed capital stocks from 1978 through 1998. From the early 1960 through the early 1970s, falling profitability was primarily caused by technical renewal and the remarkable rise in capital output ratios. The forced contraction in spending of the late 1970s worked to restore acceptable levels of business solvency and brought excess demand into negative territory. This first period of prolonged retrenchment in Spain followed the unsustainable phase of the early 1970s when business borrowing reached its peak. In the following phase of the recovery, the internal funds earmarked for repayment of debt reduced working capital expenditures.

Periods in which the decline in the credit supply to capital stock ratio was associated with lower profitability include 1978-1983 and 1989-90. Both ushered in major transition phases, 1980 being the trough of a steep contraction and 1989 the crest of a recovery boom that unraveled into the deep slump of 1993. The depression of the late 1970s, however, allowed for a reversal of the profits share. The trend in profit margins rose as the demand for labor collapsed and real wages declined. As profitability recovered from its lowest level in 1980, confidence was restored and spending increased.

Setting aside the abnormal business experience of the early 1970s requiring large infusions of credit despite the decline in profitability, the post 1980 phase witnessed a more positive link between the two. After 1980, as Foley's model would predict, periods of falling profitability in Spain typically led to a decline in business sector working capital borrowing relative to its stock of productive capital assets. A lower trend in the demand for credit would stretch for several years, eventually lowering interest rates and thus setting a floor to the fall in (pure) profit rates.

Nominal interest rates peaked in 1981 and fell for the next six years. In that decade profit rates net of interest rose, stimulating a rise in spending. A growing supply of bank credit (relative to the stock of productive assets) was required to finance the expansion of working capital. In turn, the higher level of spending strengthened aggregate demand and so contributed to buttressing the upturn in average profit rates from their previous low levels. The cyclical reversal of the profitability trend was sustained through the 1980s but the upturn of accumulation and its impact on real interest rates, spiked by the higher demand for credit, eventually petered out. Without any question, the boom period after the mid-1980s was linked to increases in credit demand and therefore the growth of business debt.

Nonetheless, the dominant effect of the accumulation expansion on wages lies outside the domain of Foley's model. Goodwin's dynamics of accumulation presented in Chapter 3 tied the fluctuations of the wage share to employment cycles and offered a structural framework for the persistence of medium-term endogenous cycles that, to my mind, elegantly fits the facts of the Spanish experience.

As Shaikh's first model showed in Chapter 2, the positive excess demand associated with the boom phase pushed profitability up, but servicing the debt imparted the opposite effect. Profitability was also subject to short-term fluctuations due to endogenous changes in the ratio of output to input prices as the expansion phase matured. In short, as the full sway of an excess demand recovery reached its peak profit margins decreased. Perception of that decline would serve as a timely signal to the banks for lowering the growth of lending, hence reducing the growth of working capital and spending by the business sector.

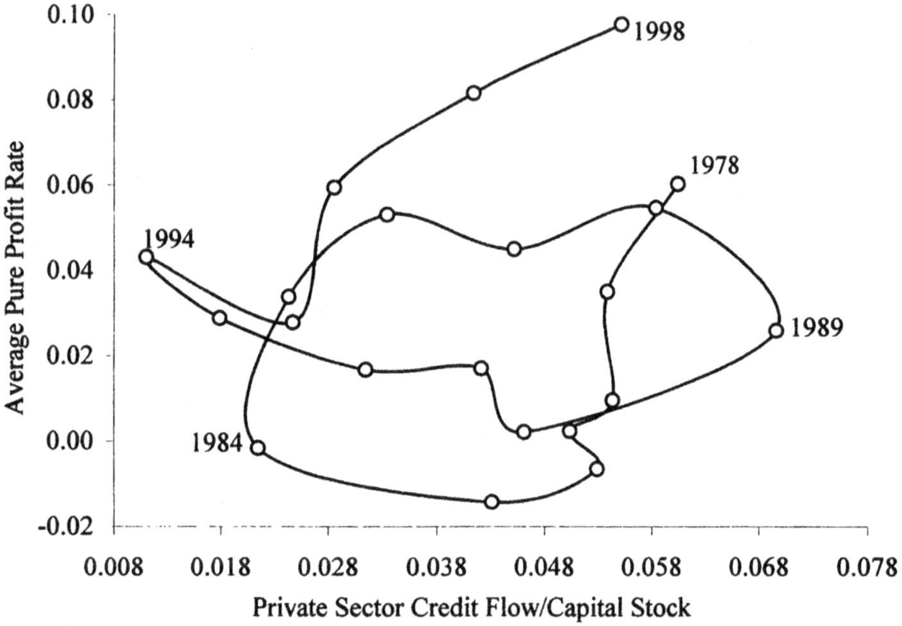


**Figure 5.6 Profitability and business credit/capital stock in Spain**

*Sources:* Series 832000; OECD Historical Statistics and Economic Outlook 66.

## Foley's model, real interest rates and external finance

It is worth noting, as Figure 5.7 shows, that despite the rapid increases in real interest rates of the early 1980s, the differential between Spain's real interest rates and the world's was not positive in those years. Indeed the early 1980s witnessed a recovery from the global slump of the previous decade in the U.S. and Europe. Credit growth accelerated in the mid-1980s once again, caused in great measure by the growth of public deficits. In contrast with the early years of that decade, after the mid-1980s the real interest differential experienced a remarkable increase, as official policy switched directions in favor of attracting foreign capital to finance growing public deficits. The scheme floundered as the exchange rate appreciated and the loss of competitiveness contributed to the spread of deficits from domestic public budgets to international trade.

The expansion geared the system's dynamics for its cyclical turning points once again. At the end of that decade the income distribution effect of expanding employment on wages lowered the profit share, deficit financing pushed real interest rates to unprecedented heights, the boom unraveled and by 1993 business activity collapsed. The period's euphoria was initially kindled by the unbridled expectations attached to Spain's joining the European Union. The expansion of the Spanish economy after the mid-1990s, however, as in other periods of its eventful past, was organically linked with the economic boom of the U.S. and Western Europe. Thus despite widespread reports prior to the year 2000 heralding the end of cycles, the Spanish economy lost its impetus shortly thereafter, as soon the U.S. economy faltered and the growth parameters of the core countries in the European Union shriveled.

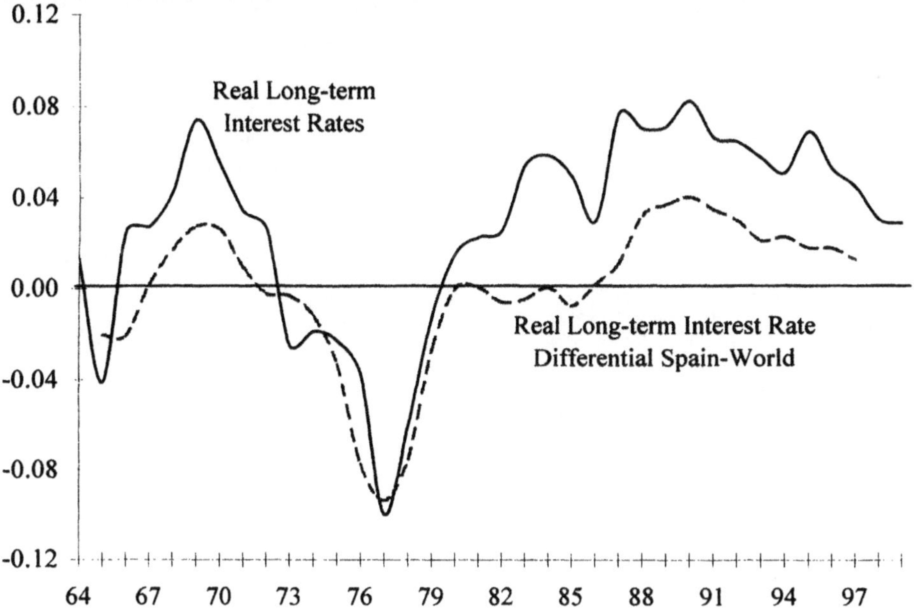


**Figure 5.7 Real long-term interest rates in Spain and real long-term interest rate differentials Spain-World**

*Sources:* Demo, RLP and L. Klein Institute, TLSP and TLINTE86.

# Part II: Overview of the Spanish Economy

# 6 The Spanish Economy in Transition

The years of turbulence experienced by the Spanish economy in the last half century can properly be grouped into distinct phases of a long development wave that peaked in the early 1970s and reached its lowest point in the early 1980s. One single question sets the stage for the unfolding saga of transition from the 1950s to the present. How did an economic fossil at odds with its European environment manage to gain new life and join its European neighbors in partnership? The travails involved in the dismantling of Spain's political and economic institutions of the 1940s and early 1950s provide the background for the dramatic events that followed.

## The take-off

In the aftermath of the Second World War, the material foundations of the Spanish economy were totally inadequate to withstand the social needs and economic challenges inherent in the reconstruction of Europe. Happily in the second half of the 1950s, among the salient features shaping the universe of choice confronting the business and political elites, the unsteady rise of profitability in Spain was decisive. This is not the occasion to bring out the (tortuous) causes behind this rise, but simply to take it as the launching pad for my investigation. The grounds were cleared to unleash the gales of creative destruction inherent in capitalist development. Policy makers reached the decision to expose the national economy to the winds of technical progress and foreign economic competition. The lure of capturing a share of the growing profits generated by a recovered European economy proved irresistible.

With the benefit of the hindsight gained in forty years dedicated to the relentless pursuit of structural changes favorable to capital accumulation, it is evident that policy makers saw increasing the share of profits in output as their over-riding objective. I propose to read the historical record of Spain's progress towards the consolidation of a modern capitalist economy as a turbulent sequence of stages, each solving some pressing problem while exhausting its curative powers as time went on. Indeed the characteristic feature of each stage was not only the discovery of new arrangements suitable to capital accumulation, but also unexpected obstacles and challenges to its stability.

## External sources of finance

While pursuing long-range policy objectives to boost internal business profitability through appropriate structural change, various transitional schemes were put in place for purposes of tapping easy sources of external finance for as long as they were available. Their implementation frequently stood in the way of the desired structural change, and on occasion undermined the modernization effort. It is instructive to note that the structural transformation of the economy was not successfully achieved by decree. Nonetheless, these schemes played a historic role in the overall development of the Spanish economy.

Examples of what I call external sources of finance follow. Somehow, each golden phase of easy access to hard currencies carried the seeds of its own destruction. I believe that each of these transitional phases was defined by some decisive characteristic, but all of them were motivated by the expanding economic horizons discovered when aggregate profitability started rising in the second half of the 1950s. It is instructive that in the 1940s and 50s, despite widespread economic penury, antiquated plant and equipment and low growth, average profitability was quite high by comparison with other countries as well as other subsequent periods, but the mass of profits remained relatively low and stagnant.

The rise of profitability brought with it expectations of a greater dynamism in accumulation, based on the advantages of technological renewal and modernization. It opened up the possibility of transforming a system of simple economic reproduction into one of expanded reproduction via the accumulation of growing profits and technological change. Various so-called development plans were hatched at the time, all of them enveloped in an atmosphere of irrevocable euphoria and total confidence in their sound forecasts. As a backward economy, Spain's advantage was that technological progress could be speedily imported in the guise of up-to-date capital goods and no expenditures on research and development were necessary. The renewal would involve no radical change in the political institutions supporting dictatorship and no substantial modification of the obsolete educational system. Foreign exchange was needed, of course, and precisely because the Spanish economy was so backward and relative business costs high (except labor costs), the potential for export growth providing the wherewithal for massive capital-goods imports was limited.

Technological change involving drastic reductions in the demand for labor would bring about, for example, the dramatic displacement of agricultural workers replaced by tractors. The rapid mechanization of agricultural production labors pushed hundreds of thousands off the land but technical change in industry offered no hope for their employment either. Indeed social unrest was a possibility looming behind the modernization plans of the policy makers. The formal schemes designed to tap external sources of finance needed to finance the modernization effort in agriculture and industry required receptive outlets for the expected massive displacement of labor caused by mechanization. The challenge facing these policy makers was unprecedented in Spanish history. On the one hand only when technical upgrading was available could Spanish firms compete successfully in the world market. On the other, the expressed commitment to modernization revealed in the official development plans highlighted the benefits of economic and technical change but eschewed acceptance of the social disruptions that were likely to occur. From the standpoint of policy makers, the solution to this conundrum was found in the promotion of mass emigration to Northern Europe.

## Mass emigration

Mass emigration of displaced workers to the growing economies of northern Europe would dampen social tensions in Spain while the counter flows of worker remittances that followed would provide ample supplies of foreign exchange needed for the modernization of plant and equipment. It is instructive to bear in mind that the search for access to large inflows of foreign exchange without the benefit of gut-wrenching moves to obtain export excellence (as for example the East Asian economies managed to achieve in the 1980s) is a distinguishing feature of the Spanish experience that repeats itself at various times. Reconstruction of the European economies provided welcomed opportunities for immigrants to earn a living and for Spanish businesses to capture significant amounts of foreign exchange. Indeed such finance proved decisive to implement the modernization of plant and equipment in the Spanish economy. In the crucial decade of the development phase spanning from the early 1960s through the early 1970s, emigrant remittances covered an increasing portion of the trade deficit. By 1971 they amounted to nearly 40% of the trade deficit.

The unexpected economic downturn affecting all advanced capitalist countries after 1973, however, witnessed the sharp reduction of such funds. The flow of remittances from emigrant workers dried up when the economic crises of the early 1970s spread unemployment throughout Europe and sent the guest workers home. After emigrant workers lost their jobs in the host countries, they were forced to cut short their sojourn abroad. In the 1970s, the growth in domestic unemployment in Spain was augmented by the inflow of former emigrants now returning as jobless workers.

As remittances dwindled in the 1970s and the world economic downturn took on the characteristics of an outright depression in Spain, massive tourist revenues from affluent Europeans came to the rescue placing a floor under the collapsing economy. From the early 1970s on to the present, tourist revenues filled the loss of emigrant remittances, as an indispensable (albeit volatile) flow of foreign exchange. Tourist revenues diminished when Spanish inflation outdistanced by far the European average and clouded the country's attraction as a vacation haven.

Finally in the 1980s, as large budget and trade deficits called for financing, policy changes enacted by an Administration confronting 25% unemployment rates, put in place a regime of high interest rates and over-appreciated exchange rates hoping to attract large flows of international capital. By 1993 these measures had instead throttled the mini-recovery from the depression trough, hurting both investment and export growth. High real interest rates and over-appreciated real exchange rates intended to attract foreign capital flows failed to prevent the economy from falling into the worst recession of a decade.

## Economic development and decline in profitability

As Figure 6.1 shows, profitability started falling in the early 1960s and continued to decrease steadily through 1980, enjoyed a reprieve in the second half of the 1980s but resumed its decline in the early 1990s. In the last seven years, it has recovered somewhat from the trough reached in 1993. The rate of fixed capital accumulation rose through the mid-1960s but eventually the impact of falling profitability pulled it down from its previous heights. It is noteworthy that the accumulation rate did not collapse before the mid-1970s although its subsequent decline outlasted the profitability downfall of that decade. The explanation for that delay must be sought in the behavior of the mass rather than the rate of profits. The growth in the mass of profits depends on changes in the rate of profits and the rate of accumulation.

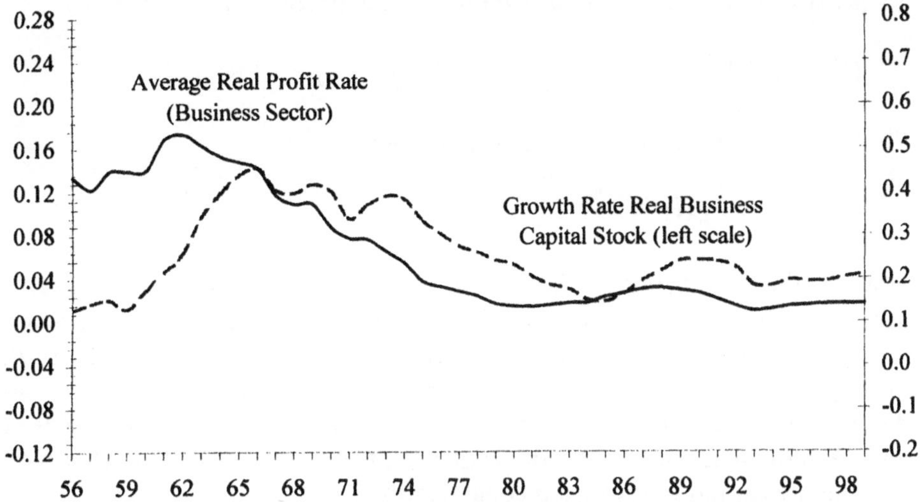


**Figure 6.1 Average profit rate and capital stock growth in Spain**

*Sources:* OECD Historical Statistics and Economic Outlook 66.

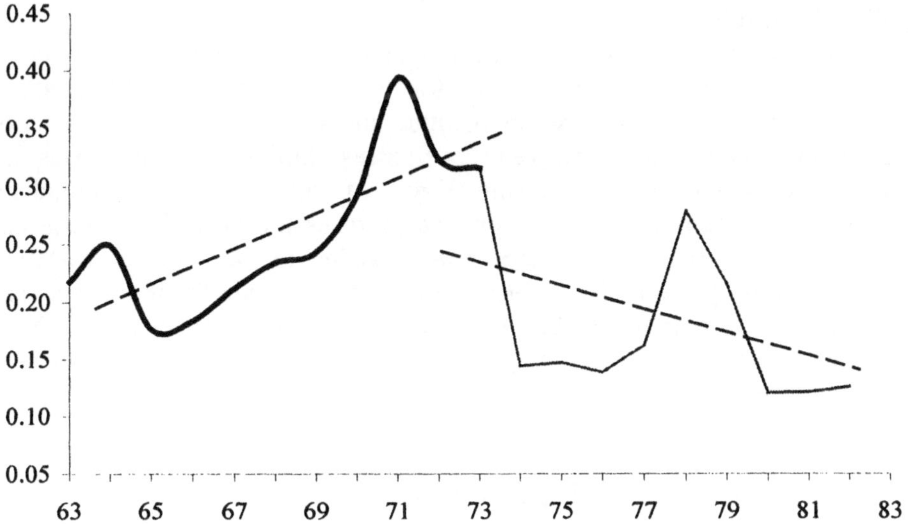


**Figure 6.2 Ratio of remittances to trade deficit**

*Sources:* Demo, TCDNRM; Series, 530954G and 540954G.

As previously indicated, the growth rate of the profits mass is given by:

$$\Pi^{\phi(t)} = r^{\alpha(t)} K^{\beta(t)}$$

So that the combined rates of change will be:

$$\phi(t) = \alpha(t) + \beta(t)$$

Now if the profit rate, r is falling at some rate, $-\alpha(t)$ but the rate of accumulation, $\beta$ is positive and larger than $-\alpha$ the mass of profits will increase. Eventually, however, if the rate of accumulation responds to the falling profit rate (because the incentive to accumulate weakens) and descends from its previous heights, the sum of both coefficients will cease to grow and the mass of profits will stagnate. Once this happens the incentive to accumulate capital will weaken considerably.

We may safely assume that the death of the Spanish Head of State was the subjective catalyst that after 1975 triggered the collapse in accumulation. Contemplating the state of future prospects for the recovery and advance of profitability, business confidence must have been seriously undermined by this fact as well as the recent upsurge in labor militancy demanding higher wages, all of them events contributing to the uncertainty of preserving political controls.

The destructive echoes of the accumulation collapse reverberated across every sector of the Spanish economy for the next ten years and beyond. A full-blown depression gathered momentum and swept away the remnants of traditional institutions. Insolvent businesses failed and the mass of unemployed labor scattered on the fringes of sinking industries found no outlet in emigration. Northern Europe was in recession as well. The return of former guest workers in northern Europe added to the social devastation brought about by the national depression. Yet, the seeds of future recovery were springing their roots deep into the soil of dashed expectations. How could economic development possibly fail to deliver the promised bonanza at the end of the road?

## Mechanization and the rising capital-output ratio

The previous question has a more prosaic counterpart, namely why did profitability decline so much in the 1960s, the development decade? The answer to this question divides economic theory into two camps. The neoclassical view sees accumulation without technical change as running into diminishing returns. In Solow's model of growth, the marginal product of capital will begin falling at some point and only technical change can lift the production function to a higher level. The Schumpeterian version attributes the decline in profitability to the spread of new methods or products among firms that played no role in their invention. These firms benefit from the breakthroughs introduced by innovating entrepreneurs, allowing them to expand production without the initial risks involved. The growing supply will reduce prices to the lowest possible level and consequently average profitability will be depressed for all. The appearance of new techniques will be required to lift the average profitability in each industry.

Now the experience in Spain points in the opposite direction. In order to make sense of it, a new interpretation of the aggressive nature of business competition (competition as a war for market share) is in order. A. Shaikh's work on competition and technical change provides a fitting framework for an alternative interpretation. The argument that follows is based on Shaikh's theoretical foundation. The possibility that technical change can lead to falling profitability because it raises the capital-output ratio is a daunting proposition. In this view, innovators will seek new methods of production as they strive to lower total unit costs on a sustainable basis. In this effort, they cannot choose their own profitability level. That will emerge from the unavoidable confrontation with similarly disposed and powerful opponents. Their efforts will be focused on the selection of techniques offering the lowest product unit costs. This will typically involve capital-deepening techniques. The rising capitalization of production will lower the total average cost, but firms must pay a price for this feat. The stock of capital per unit output will rise. A lower average total cost (achieved via a higher cost of fixed capital per unit output, compensated by a proportionately higher reduction in average variable costs) will then allow cutting-edge firms to lower their price below that of their competitors and so capture a larger market share. While their profitability may be lower after the event, it will still be higher than the profitability of retrenched businesses unable to match the lower price of the innovator.

Profitability was rising in the 1950s without the benefit of substantial technical change in the Spanish economy. Absent competitive pressures, the ability to extract a rising surplus from a politically controlled labor forced and a closed economy sufficed. Until rising mechanization spread throughout the national economy, the capital-output ratio did not increase. Once the Spanish economy opened its doors to the winds of technical progress in the early 1960s, however, profitability started falling. The capital-output ratio, reflecting the rising mechanization of advanced technology, went up substantially for over twenty years.

What is special in the Spanish experience is not only the fact that mechanization transformed the methods of production throughout the economy, but the rapid pace of the changes. Given the favorable financial flows of the 1960s, imports of industrial technology absorbed an increasing share of the international revenue transfers.

## Trends of the profits share

The share of profits in the business sector GDP decreased from the late 1960s through 1975. Was this trend reversal in the profits share responsible for the decline in average profitability as well, or were there other forces at play, such as the effects of capital deepening, behind its long-term decline? This question conflates the effects of mass emigration and the accumulation collapse that followed. Policy makers saw massive emigration in the 1960s as a social safety valve designed to muffle the outbreaks of social unrest caused by job losses. One of the unintended consequences of the large exodus of workers was the sharp reduction in the domestic labor force, thus strengthening somewhat its bargaining position. In the halcyon years of the early 1960s, after decades of suppressed wage expectations in an international environment of greater affluence, the movement for higher wages received its belated rewards. The rise in labor productivity during the decade cushioned the blow to employers and profitability did not fall sharply until the late 1960s. As Figure 6.3 shows, the aggregate profits-wages ratio fell sharply only from the late 1960s through the early 1970s, but for the next twenty-five years its overall trend went up. The cyclical movement of the profits-wage ratio underlay the rhythms of accumulation in this period.

As Figure 6.3 reveals the declining phase of the real profits-wage ratio (in 1980 pts) coincided with the turning point of the profits mass. In other words, the fall was itself a salient manifestation of the onset in the accumulation slump. The rise in the profits-wage ratio preceded the recovery of the profits mass trough in the late 1970s and in my view, reflects the weakening of the labor movement after years of growing unemployment. Unemployment continued to rise well after the mass of profits resumed its ascent. It could be argued that this reversal of trends in the profits-wages ratio was one of the major achievements of the slump, as workers learned under economic duress to moderate their wage demands or face unemployment.

Figure 6.4 explicitly shows the capital-labor ratio rising from the early 1960s through the early 1980s, as a reflection of the increasing mechanization of production and the evolution of the capital-output ratio exhibiting a long-term growth as well. Only in those periods in which technical modernization slowed down due to businesses tightening their budgets and spending plans, such as in the 1980s and late 1990s, was the trend rise in the capital-output ratio reduced.

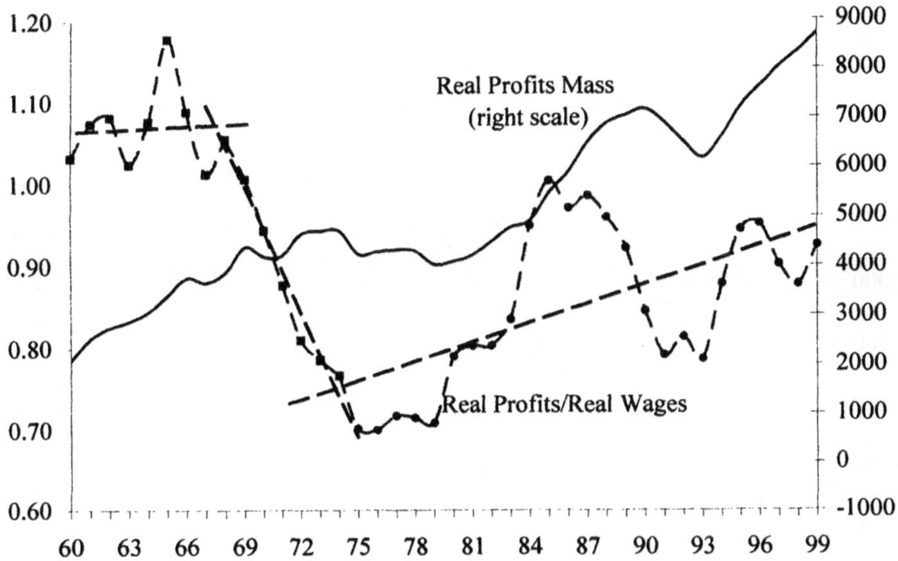


**Figure 6.3 Evolution of the profits-wages ratio and profits mass**

*Sources:* OECD Historical Statistics and Economic Outlook 66.

The restoration of business liquidity after years of deficit spending was achieved through the expansion of the profits share in business output, increases in business savings, and the reduction of investment expenditures. The financial gap between business capital spending and internal funds was sharply reduced at both ends of the equation. Indeed the period of economic recovery ushered in the early 1980s brought with it a sharp break with the trends of the capital-labor and capital-output ratios of the past fifteen years. First the rise in the capital-output ratio diminished markedly and then even fell briefly in the late 1980s. The steep reversal in the growth of the capital-labor ratio was directly linked to the fact that the restoration of profitability in the early 1980s brought the mechanization drive to a temporary halt in the

Spanish economy. Because of the slowdown in accumulation, however, the rate of unemployment reached unprecedented heights.

Despite modest recoveries in profitability and investment in the late 1980s and the second half of the 1990s, the rate of unemployment never again declined below 10% and in fact remained the highest of all countries comprising the European Union ever since. This is the still unresolved and daunting legacy of the depression years. It has now become a characteristic feature of the national economy.

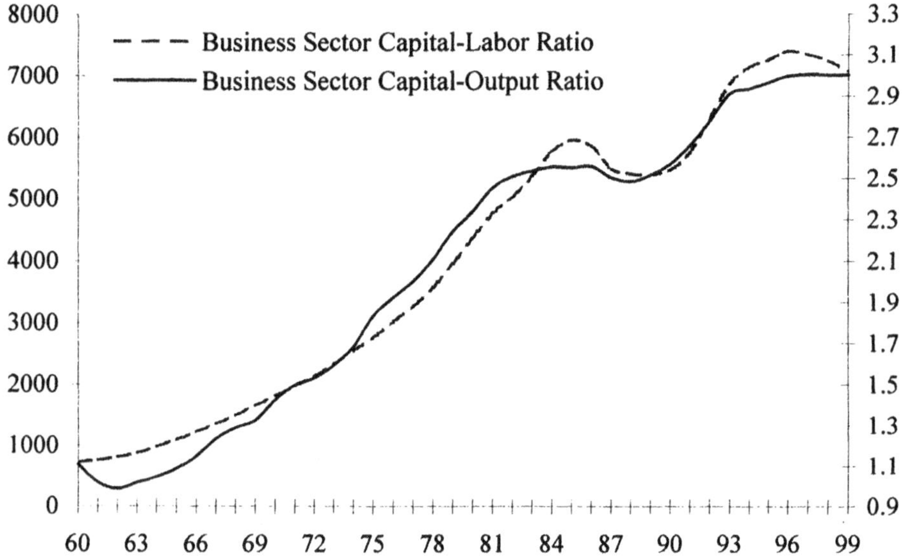


**Figure 6.4 Evolution of capital-labor and capital-output ratios**

*Sources:* OECD Historical Statistics and Economic Outlook 66.

## Unemployment, inflation and excess demand

After a prolonged historical hiatus, any country seeking to break out of its competitive backwardness through capital goods imports embodying the technical know-how and capital-intensity of the leading producers abroad has no choice in the selection of viable techniques. The break with the prevailing labor-intensive methods of production will be sharper the longer its isolation and therefore the more disruptive as far as labor employment is concerned. This is why mechanization in Spain brought about the displacement of labor in such massive scale and so suddenly. The pervasive introduction of tractors in agriculture alone added hundreds of thousands to the unemployed ranks. In the 1960s, many of these workers found jobs in Northern Europe (some estimates rise to over one million, that is about 10% of the labor force in the 1960s). Absent such outlets due to the global downturn of the 1970s, the reserve pool of labor reached dimensions that outranked all others in the OECD group of nations. In general the claim of conventional theory for mechanization is that replacing workers with machines will raise labor productivity and release the workers needed to sustain the expansion of production activities elsewhere. It is then assumed that accumulation will proceed apace because profitability will not be impaired in the event but rather improved. Contrary to these assumptions, the rate of capital accumulation in Spain was never high enough in the 1960s to compensate for the labor displaced by rapidly rising mechanization. Mechanization in Spain raised the capital-labor and capital-output ratios, caused the decline in profitability and the attendant accumulation of business debt and provoked a collapse of capital accumulation. Despite the upturn in the profits-wages ratio of the mid-1970s the rate of accumulation kept falling, and did not recover until the second half of the 1980s. Repayment of debts and caution took precedence over accumulation and further technical change.

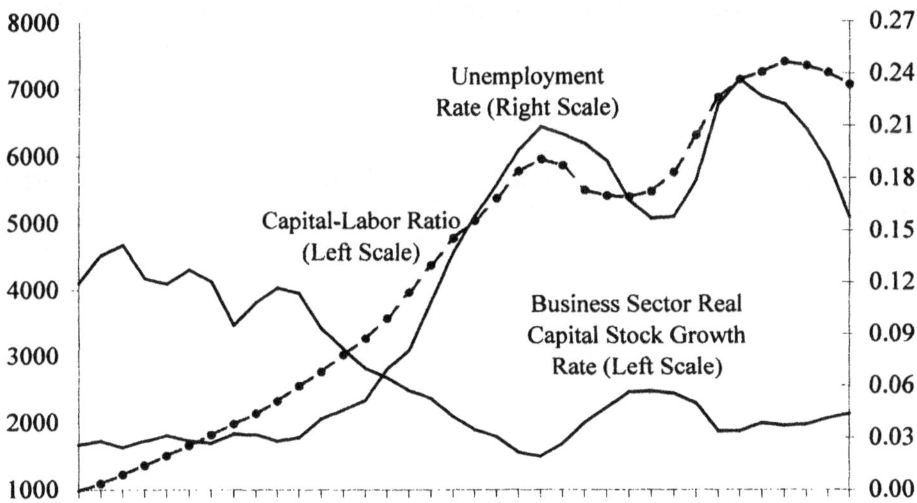


**Figure 6.5 Unemployment and accumulation rates**

*Sources:* OECD Historical Statistics and Economic Outlook 66.

In Figure 6.5 the evolution of the capital-labor ratio in constant 1980 pesetas, (used as a proxy for the dynamics of mechanization) set the stage for the inverse symmetry evident between the paths of unemployment and accumulation. As a matter of fact, and running contrary to the accepted stylized features of growth models such as Kaldor's, the steep rise in the Spanish capital-output ratio (registered for roughly two decades) tipped the scale between labor displacement and absorption. It also pushed profitability into a falling path and thus laid the grounds (after some delay) for the descent of the accumulation trend. While the emigration outlet in the 1960s delayed for a time the rise of the unemployed labor reserve within Spain, a decade later its growth reached unprecedented proportions.

The results of regressing the unemployment path on the capital-labor ratio and the capital stock growth time series from 1964 through 1999 shown in Table 6.1 confirm the theoretical conclusions derived from the Spanish case. There is indeed a close correlation between the trend rise in mechanization, the trend fall in accumulation and the evolution of unemployment. Cyclical movements around these trends are also reflected in the cyclical changes of the unemployment rate.

**Table 6.1 Unemployment, the capital-labor ratio and capital growth**

| Variable | Coefficient | Std. Error | t-Statistic | Prob. |
|---|---|---|---|---|
| C | 0.044 | 0.040 | 1.100 | 0.280 |
| Capital-labor ratio | 2.590 | 6.000 | 4.313 | 0.000 |
| Capital growth | -0.407 | 0.164 | -2.475 | 0.019 |
| Capital growth(-1) | -0.252 | 0.157 | -1.604 | 0.120 |
| AR(1) | 1.543 | 0.170 | 9.045 | 0.000 |
| AR(2) | -0.687 | 0.171 | -4.013 | 0.000 |

| | | | |
|---|---|---|---|
| $R^2$ | 0.990 | Schwarz criterion | -6.342 |
| Adjusted $R^2$ | 0.988 | F-statistic | 562.938 |
| Std. Error of regression | 0.008 | Prob(F-statistic) | 0.000 |
| Log likelihood | 115.145 | | |
| Durbin-Watson statistic | 1.844 | | |

In my view, policy makers in the 1960s acting on their desire to modernize the technical structure of production followed conventional theory and limited their efforts to the business of securing adequate sources of finance. In the 1960s, one such source was internally available stemming from the recent growth trend in business profits and the second was externally supplied by emigrant remittances. Despite the fact that both of them were not necessarily sustainable, the push for technical modernization was chosen with the gusto provided by conventional forecasts. This would explain not only the widespread revamping of plant and equipment that took place in agriculture and industry, but also the acceptance by policy-makers of the gut-wrenching social uprooting that followed. Unemployment reached a quarter of the labor force and the outbreak of high inflation in the 1970s revealed the structural tensions built-up in the 1960s. Finally, the blight of depression engulfed every sector of the national economy.

Depression is so rare and devastating that its denial remains entrenched in the Neo-classical critique of Keynesian economics. Moreover, even the name finds no acceptance in contemporary analysis of financial crises. The 1930s experience in the U.S. and other advanced capitalist countries remains fixed as a historical paradigm that denies legitimacy to all other versions of economic collapse. This is why the existence of depression in Spain was not acknowledged when it happened, and has been ignored ever since.

Contrary to conventional views, the rise in inflation did not occur as the economy approached full employment but exactly in the opposite conjuncture, that is, as the economy plunged into depression and unemployment grew very rapidly. It is interesting to note that the rise in inflation and the growth of unemployment were manifestations of one and the same thing, that is, the stagnation of the profits mass in the 1970s and the efforts to delay the collapse of accumulation through credit infusion. Aggregate profits stagnated in the 1970s, and many firms could not avoid bankruptcy. But despite the gathering momentum of the slump, the remaining firms in business and finance sought to weather the storm with the assistance of the banks, then and now the major repositories of credit finance in Spain.

The major effect of the profits crisis on labor was the growth of unemployment. The most telling impact of the profits crisis on those businesses that remained credit worthy in the long run was to make them more dependent than ever before on the credit assistance provided by the banks. In the interval between the first signs of the profits crisis and the delayed adjustment of accumulation plans, the share of credit finance for business investment rose markedly.

In fact this period of growing dependence on credit for the external financing of business investment plans stands in sharp contrast to the following phase of recovery and profits growth that began in the early 1980s. But this injection of external finance relative to stagnant aggregate real profits exerted mounting pressures on the average price level and resulted in rising inflation. One of the chief characteristics of Von Neuman's growth model is that the maximum growth of accumulation requires all profits to be reinvested. Shaikh has argued that the economic system will experience rising *throughput* tensions the higher the proportion of profits devoted to accumulation.

When all net business expenditures, including those on circulating and fixed capital investments plus the consumption of business entrepreneurs themselves are financed internally out of gross profit flows, aggregate demand expenditures equal aggregate supply and excess demand is zero. Once external credit finance is introduced, however, the possibility exists for aggregate expenditures to exceed internal funds and excess demand to emerge.

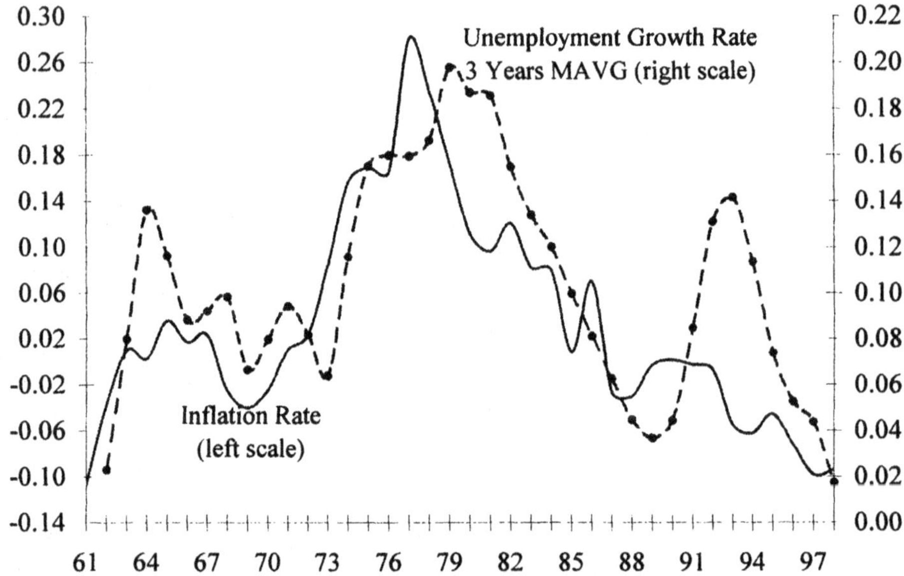


**Figure 6.6 Growth of unemployment and inflation rates**

*Sources:* OECD Historical Statistics and Economic Outlook 66.

## Summary of empirical findings

Empirically the path of excess demand in Spain fits very closely the movement of inflation. Periods in which bank credit financed business expenditures higher than the flows of gross profits would permit were also periods of rising inflation. Positive excess demand was present from the early 1960s through the early 1980s, but was particularly pronounced in the 1970s, reaching a peak in 1978. In the mid-1980s, business-sector excess demand turned negative, as the finance regime change in favor of internal funds, and concomitantly the share of profits rose. As expected inflation fell sharply in the 1980s, precisely the period in which the growth of unemployment declined.

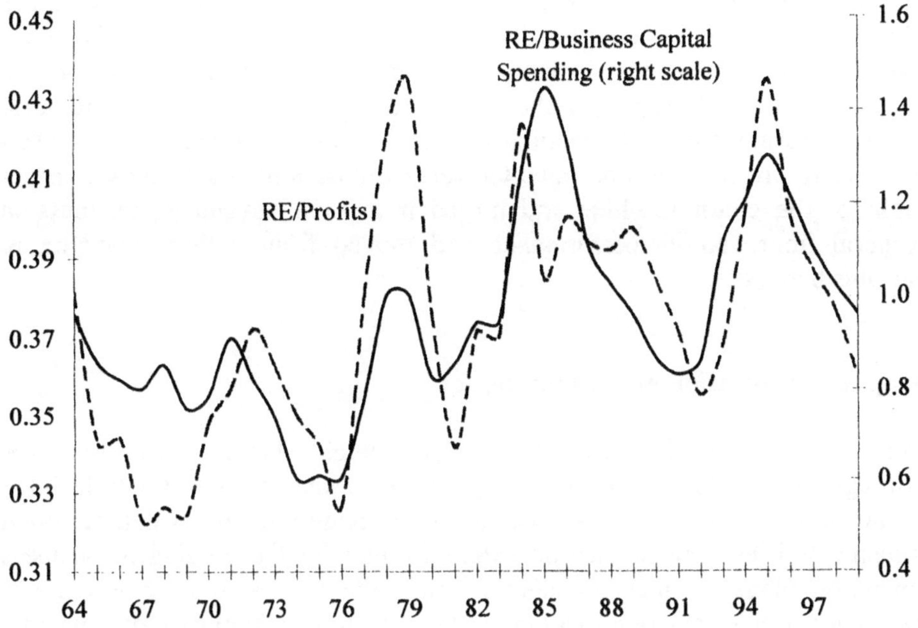


**Figure 6.7 Retained earnings relative to capital spending and profits**

*Source:* BBVA 2000 annual report.

## The recovery path

The recovery from depression troughs required a sharp turn around of previous practices in a number of key variables. The rise in real interest rates in the 1980s stands out prominently as one of the major reversals. Certainly, the necessitous borrowing of the 1970s was abetted by negative real interest rates that tumbled as official controls capped nominal rates and inflation rose to double digits. The rise in inflation severely affected the movement of real interest rates and therefore the income of the powerful banking system. Facing falling real interest rates, growing risk of loan defaults and an expanding credit demand, banks needed a change of the rules.

Jointly the deregulation of nominal interest rates and the successful containment of inflation created a new regime of high interest rates that encouraged firms to rely more heavily than they had in recent years on their internal funds when planning their investment spending.

After the second half of the 1970s Figure 6.7 shows the move to greater financial independence on the part of firms evidenced by the sharp increase in the proportion of capital spending covered by retained earnings, as well as the higher ratio of business profits internally retained. From the early 1980s on, the share of business investment financed out of retained earnings on average exceeded 90%. As the financial gap turned positive, the ratio retained earnings-capital spending rose and in fact, retained earnings itself relative to profits went-up. Since the early 1980s, while banks took a firmer hold of the credit machine and turned it to their advantage, business in general improved its performance and moved from deficit financing to surplus budgets.

## Capacity utilization and accumulation

As capacity utilization fell from its lofty heights before the early 1970s through the late 1980s, the share of gross fixed investment in GDP declined in tandem. This decline was a characteristic feature of the switch to sound finance and less dependence on external credit for the funding of business spending plans. In macroeconomic terms, the switch in finance regimes brought about a transition to a long phase driven by negative excess demand. The microeconomic improvement of balance sheets caused deflationary pressures on the economy that required massive public deficits in the late 1980s to stabilize.

Higher retained earnings but lower capital spending improved the balance sheets of business firms but lowered the economy's expansion growth well beyond its potential. The remarkable business recovery path from the 1970s depression was grounded in profound structural changes favorable to the practices of sound finance. In addition to the microeconomic improvement of balance sheets, the onset of depression in the business sector triggered concerted efforts to raise the trend of the real profits-wages share in real output, even before the mass of profits recovered.

It is remarkable then that despite the growth of public deficit spending in the late 1970s the growth of effective demand was insufficient to prevent a decline in capacity utilization and correspondingly a drag on capital accumulation. In addition, sound finance was no palliative for the growth of unemployment. With the safety valve of emigration unavailable, public spending was the only macroeconomic policy capable of assuaging the effects of unemployment in the midst of business recovery.

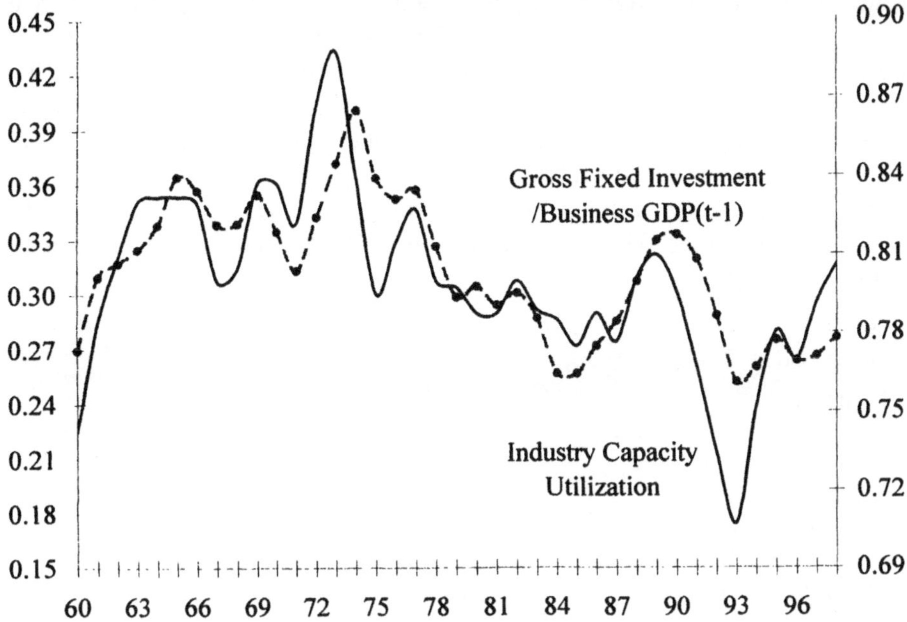


**Figure 6.8 Capacity utilization and capital accumulation in Spain**

*Sources:* Series, 321100, 972100T, and OECD Economic Outlook 66.

## Unemployment and the profits share

The recovery of profits as a share of the business sector GDP was a decisive aspect of the post-depression phase running from the early 1980s through the present. The precipitous decrease in the real profits-wages ratio that occurred in the early 1970s as a reflection of the stagnation in the profits mass led to a rising unemployment trend through the 1980s and early 1990s. As Figure 6.3 showed, the overall trend in the profits-wage ratio rose in the same period.

The dynamical link between the rise in these two ratios can be interpreted as evidence in support of a variant of the Goodwin dynamics. The decline in the profits share would lead to a fall in accumulation and a rise in unemployment. The unemployment growth would weaken the bargaining position of labor and lead to a lower wages share, which in turn would stimulate a rise in accumulation. The dynamical linkages would be established rather slowly because more than cyclical changes were involved. The rising trend set the critical path for the medium-term fluctuations in the profits share and unemployment. Thus, the sharp increase in the profits-wages ratio in the 1980s run into a steep, albeit temporary reversal in the early 1990s, ushering in the deep 1993 recession. The trough in the profits-wage ratio in 1993, however, was much higher than it was when the 1970s collapse hit bottom in 1980. These were not short-term inventory cycles caused by changes in excess demand, but rather slower fluctuations around a protracted structural trend raising the share of profits. Indeed the rising trend of the profits-wages ratio in the last twenty years was punctuated by two medium-term cycles. The first culminated in 1993 and the second one is still in progress at present.

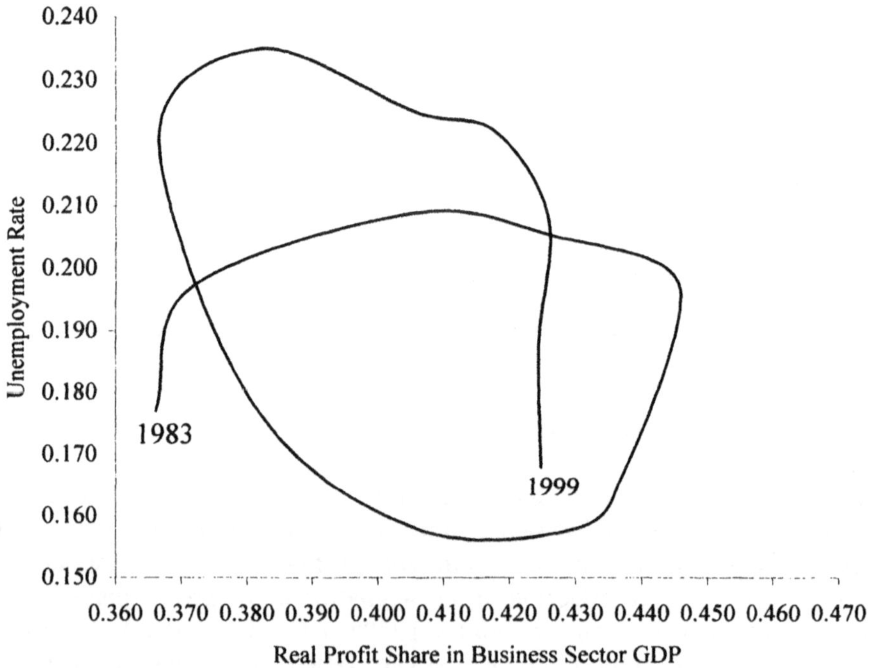


**Figure 6.9 Dynamics of the profits share and unemployment**

*Sources:* OECD Historical Statistics and Economic Outlook 66.

## Unemployment and public deficits

While business behavior became more "Classical", provoking a transition to negative excess demand, the public sector turned more Keynesian as it resorted to deficit spending to ward off the effects of declining capacity utilization and rising unemployment. After the mid-1970s, the trend to increasingly tie-up business spending to the availability of internal funds was sustained. As Figure 6.10 shows the balance sheets of the private business and public sectors moved in opposite directions. While business budgets moved from deficit spending to surplus, as indicated by the transition from negative to positive numbers in Figure 6.10, public deficits grew larger as a share of the business sector GDP through the mid-1980s. The reason for that must be traced to the opposite objectives pursued by business and government. The adjustment to practices of sound finance by the business sector, consisting of a move to retain a higher share of available profits and lowering the rate of capital accumulation, went apace and were dictated by the slump of the 1970s. The slowdown in accumulation was sufficiently pronounced, even when mechanization was halted, as to cause rising unemployment.

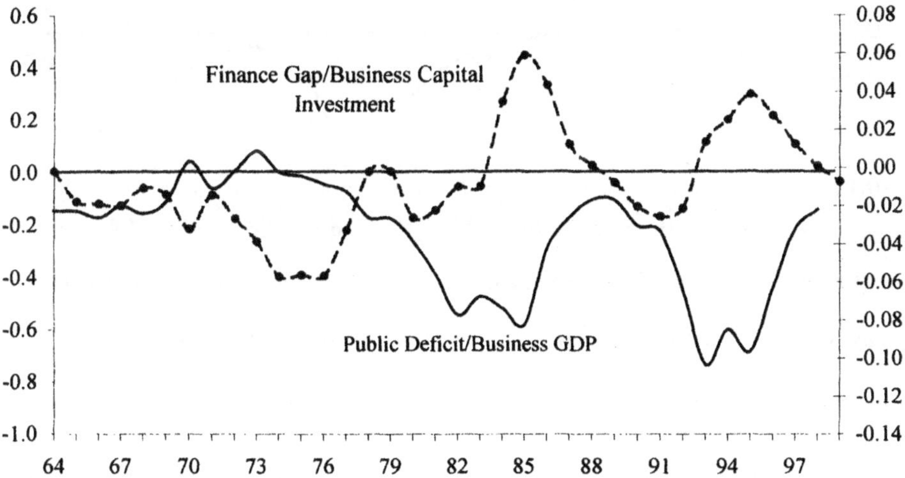


**Figure 6.10 Public deficits/GDP and business gap/investment**

*Sources:* BBVA annual report 2000 and OECD Economic Outlook 66.

The policy stand of the public sector, however, could not be motivated by narrow financial gains. While the lingering effects of the depression prompted a phase of austerity that led to high unemployment, public policy could not stand aloof in view of the deterioration in living standards following the transition to democracy. Public budgets moved from boasting modest surpluses in the early 1970s to deeper deficits in the mid-1980s and then again in the early 1990s. Keynesian policies came to the rescue of an effective demand weakened by the budget tightening of the business sector. There is no question of their effective impact on unemployment as well. Figure 6.11 shows the inverse symmetry of the unemployment path and the share of deficit spending in business sector GDP.

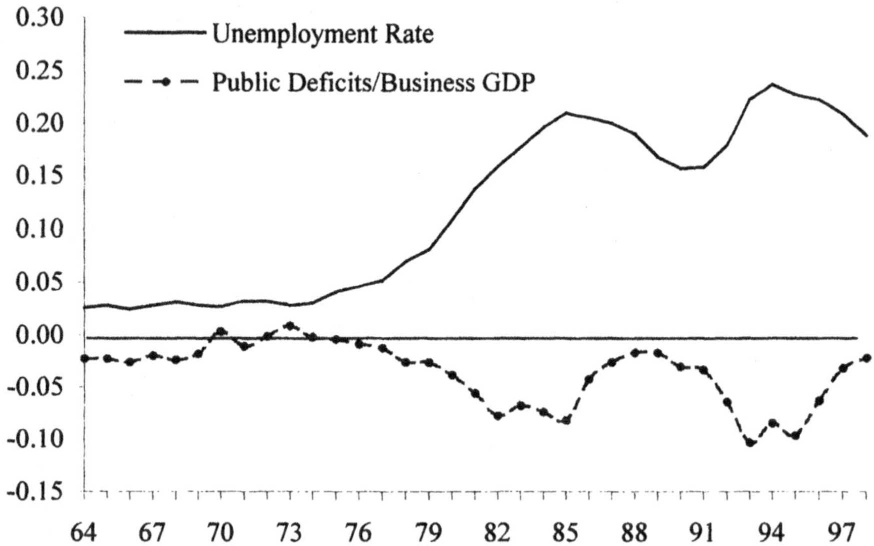


**Figure 6.11 Unemployment and public deficits/business sector GDP**

*Sources:* BBVA annual report 2000 and OECD Economic Outlook 66.

On the other hand, the policy of deficit spending, designed to cushion the unprecedented fall in employment taking place in the business sector, contributed to the slowdown of the rise in the profits-wages trend and even its transitional reversal in the late 1980s and early 1990s. The promotion of public sector employment strengthened the resolve of labor to reverse the erosion of wages. But doing so interfered with the relentless pursuit of sound finance exhibited by business since the early 1980s in the aftermath of depression.

In their recent treatise on economic growth and income distribution, Duncan Foley and Thomas Michl (Foley, 1999, p. 116) endeavor to highlight the contradiction detected by the Classical approach between accumulation and the growth of wages. They point out that since capital accumulation absorbs a portion of the net output and labor consumes the other, increases in wages will reduce the share of output allocated for capital expansion.

## From trade deficits to surpluses

After the curtain of isolation, protecting the Spanish economy from the raging storms of the world market was lifted in the 1960s, allowing for massive outflows of labor and equally large inflows of foreign exchange, the weight of foreign trade in the national income grew with time.

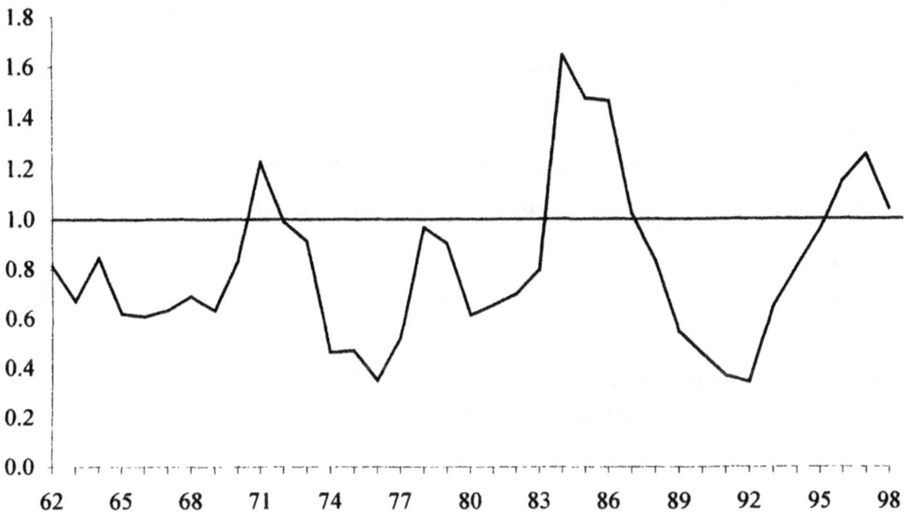


**Figure 6.12 Transfers and service balances/goods trade deficit**

*Sources:* Series, 508000G, 572200A and BBVA annual report 2000.

As previously stressed, the technological transformation of the Spanish economy could only come about via massive imports of capital goods. Emigrant remittances and revenues from tourist services largely financed the trade deficits of the development decade. As Figure 6.12 shows, by the end of the 1960s these combined flows of foreign exchange were more than adequate to cover the large imports of capital goods that exploded the trade deficit. When the flow of remittances dwindled in the early 1970s, tourist revenues filled in a good portion of the deficit in the goods trade balance. Sky rocketing inflation in the 1970s, however, took away much of the luster attached to Spain as a tourist destination. Tourist revenues recovered only after inflation was brought under control in the 1980s.

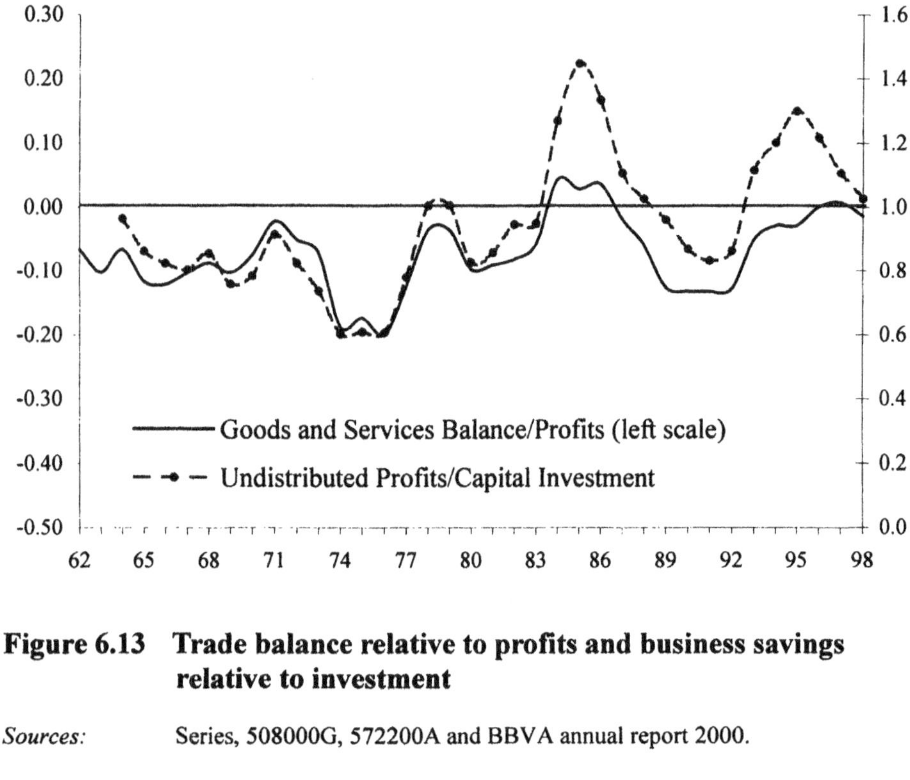


**Figure 6.13 Trade balance relative to profits and business savings relative to investment**

*Sources:* Series, 508000G, 572200A and BBVA annual report 2000.

As Figure 6.13 shows, the transition from business deficit spending to surplus budgets initiated in the late 1970s was organically linked with the improvement of the trade in goods and service balances. Lower imports made the difference. The evolution of the trade in goods and services balance, relative to profits very closely reflected the growth of business savings relative to capital spending. Let us recall that the business financial *gap* reflects the extent to which capital expenditures are financed out of business savings, so that a movement into positive space represents the growth of budget surpluses, business savings rising in excess of investment spending. It is worthwhile to ponder the idea that improvements in the balance of trade were accomplished because of this shift, that is the growth of business savings relative to investment spending.

Assisting these changes, bank policy was reversed and real interest rates shot-up after the late 1970s. Repayment of loans, restoration of business liquidity and the pursuit of budget surpluses replaced the previous financial regime associated with the development decade of the 1960s. Correspondingly, once the development drive receded and the demand for massive imports of capita-goods weakened, trade balances improved and especially so when invisible services (tourist revenues) are included in export growth. The Classical paradigm came into full bloom.

## Summary of institutional changes in the Spanish economy

Coming out of its isolation in the late 1950s the Spanish economy entered a decade of rapid economic development with the support of foreign technology and massive transfers of funds from its emigrant workers. By the mid-1970s the expectations of the development decade were dashed as mechanization wiped out employment for a growing portion of the labor force, profitability and accumulation collapsed and a full-fledged depression engulfed the nation. The banking system responded to the emergency with infusions of credit large enough for their best clients to weather the storm. Business deficit spending increased as aggregate profits and internal funds stagnated. The recovery from depression in the 1980s involved the expansion of the profits share in output, the growth of retained earnings to restore business liquidity and the curtailment of accumulation spending to allow for the repayment of the accumulated debts. The switch to sound business budgets, however, resulted in growing unemployment, and it is arguable that growing unemployment weakened higher wage claims. The persistence of mass unemployment in the late 1980s, however, conflicted with the inflated expectations nurtured by democratic institutions, and the public sector expanded deficit spending to create jobs. The reduction in the unemployment rate that followed (although never below double digit numbers) reversed the climbing of the profits share and the turn-around proceeded apace until 1993 when the economy suffered a major setback. Coming out of the new slump the resolve by businesses to increase its savings and expand exports matched the public sector commitment to reduce its deficits. Despite the boom of the second half of the 1990s, however, the fact was brought home once again that any spurts in accumulation with modern technology required higher capital-output ratios and as a result higher sustainable profitability remained ever so elusive.

# 7 Finance and Growth Cycles

I will be looking in this chapter at the role of finance in the propagation of business cycles in Spain. To that end, first I will distinguish between the short-term needs of business firms for working capital finance and credit borrowing to finance longer-term investment deficit spending. This kind of deficit spending involves investment expenditures requiring finance that exceed the internal funds available from previous periods. I will accept as a valid working hypothesis the Post-Keynesian view on these matters as expressed by Minsky:

> While the banking system does provide business with short-term financing, typically for activity based upon short-term expectations, the financing of investment and of capital asset ownership involves longer-term equity and debt instruments (Minsky, 1985, p. 35).

The real growth experience of a market economy never takes place without cyclical perturbations. Prominent Neo-Classical economists like Kenneth Arrow have recognized the fact that:

> Certainly since the extensive observations of Clement Juglar (1859) it has been accepted that there are fluctuations in economic activity, with positive but imperfect correlation of the different sectors of the economy, which show distinct persistence in time (Arrow, 1983, p. 279).

While some of these fluctuations occur because of random exogenous shocks, unpredictable perturbations stemming from all kinds of natural as well as unnatural events, others are inherent to accumulation itself. Droughts, wars and boycotts nearly always happen unexpectedly and impact the evolution of market forces. On the other hand, there are cyclical patterns that are internal to the growth dynamics of business enterprise as well.

Business expansion requires financing (Peek and Rosengren, 1995). The circuit of production and selling must be completed before revenues accrue. In the interval, costs must be incurred and means of payment must be available (Davidson, 1982, pp. 320-21). In this chapter, these are the questions under consideration. Short-term bank borrowing will bridge the working-capital time gap and short-term debts will be cleared once revenues begin to flow. Godley is very explicit on the significance of bank finance:

> One role of the financial system will be to provide the finance required for investment in fixed and working capital (in advance of sales taking place) if production and distribution are to proceed smoothly or at all. And it will also provide residual "buffer" finance for fluctuating inventories as short-term expectations are falsified (Godley, 1996, p. 4).

Firms are in business to make profits and grow. From that perspective, it is rational for them to take any action coherent with the fulfillment of their primary goal. Profit is the objective as well as the principal lever at their disposal to shape the future course of their growth. Profits provide the wherewithal for investment and the expansion of their capital stock affords them the most effective means to achieve economies of scale. Powerful means of production provide the arsenal necessary to gain market share and put their rivals out of commission. They can adopt many strategies to this end. What they cannot do from the start is thwart the thrust of all actual and potential rivals. The strength of that challenge will depend on the success already achieved by the opponents, relentlessly pushing for expansion of their market share. Market laws emerge out of the apparent clash of conflicting interests leading to unintended outcomes. When the dust clears, the path of aggregate profitability traversed by the leading firms will set the locus of possibilities for all the others, as well as the potential for capital accumulation of the system as a whole. There is no doubt that all market participants are subject to laws not of their own making. These laws become explicit only when freedom in the pursuit of each party's self-interest clashes against the constraints set by the actions of rivals.

## Excess demand and external finance

Before marshaling my empirical evidence in the final chapter, I will develop here my case linking the persistence of (positive/negative) excess demand to external finance. Briefly, I will argue that after 1960s, the fluctuations in the business sector excess demand spending caused the short and medium-term growth cycles in Spain. By this I mean that fluctuations in excess demand occurred after spending initially surpassed the sum of funds available from the previous growth period. These funds include undistributed profits plus depreciation funds. The external credit required for filling the *gap* between spending and business internal funds pumped new purchasing power into the system and raised business incomes all round. This is the occasion for the Keynesian multiplier story to make its appearance. From a Classical standpoint, however, the expanding firms acquired a debt obligation along with their excess spending power. Under the discipline imposed by budget constraints, the accumulation of such debt will set definite limits to the expenditures of the affected firm. Their plans must include a schedule for repayment and failure to comply with it will carry the loss of confidence on the part of creditors.

## The incremental profit rate and credit cycles

What exactly initiates the borrowing that feeds the growth of excess demand? A rising incremental profit rate is an essential feature of the cyclical upturn. Once this happens growing profit margins lay the grounds for optimism regarding future prospects to flourish. In a world of uncertain expectations, good omens are found in rising profitability of the latest investments. The waves of euphoria will justify credit expansion leading to the emergence of positive excess demand. Philip Arestis (Arestis, 1999) put it succinctly but without any loss of eloquence:

> Money thus allows entrepreneurs access to physical resources and labor required for production. In such an economy, money is the result of credit flows, where the leading role is essentially played by entrepreneurs. The ultimate determinant of the money supply is therefore, "animal spirits" (Arestis, 1999, p. 2).

As the upturn progresses, debt accumulates and profit margins generally cease growing. The growth of input costs outruns final output's prices. Tight materials and labor markets push unit costs higher and the growth in credit demand raises real interest rates. Absent interest rate hikes, borrowing in excess of internal funds cannot go on indefinitely unencumbered by the burden of repayment. The clearing of debts requires returning a larger sum than the money borrowed, the difference being set by the interest rate.

What ends the expansion phase of the cycle? How far can the business debt pile up before new credit flows are cut off? The answers given to these questions by Wesley Mitchell at the turn of this century (Mitchell, 1913, 1963) are as relevant today as they were then. At some point, the excess demand that gave rise to a cyclical boom ends up raising input costs faster than revenue flows. Profit margins begin to erode before the peak is reached. This is so because, in the mature phase of the expansion, competition for sales of a growing aggregate supply will restrain price increases at the same time that input markets are getting tighter. Once the deterioration in profit margins is underway, increasing risks of default spread caution among creditors. The provision of new credit need not be constraint as long as profit margins are rising. The situation is reversed, however, when profit margins stagnate (even more so when they begin to contract) and business debt is high. In this as in other matters, conventional rules will set the threshold beyond which a reversal in credit policy will occur. Firms will be required to lower their liabilities and restore their solvency.

Paying back past loans with interest eats up a growing share of internal funds, the size of which will depend on the extent of past borrowing. The legacy of such debt accumulation requires that the available funds for new spending in capital projects in the next phase of the cycle should be curtailed. Periods of positive excess demand will give way to their opposite, that is phases in which total spending for fixed and circulating capital will be less than the sum of the funds internally available. The surplus funds will be used for debt servicing. The initial expansion of incomes will be reversed. The multiplier effect now will contract the gains achieved during the expansion. At some point of the downturn, falling output growth will give rise to a surplus of labor and materials. After a period of slack, profit margins will be restored as the shrinking demand for labor, materials and finance lowers production and financial costs faster than goods prices (Mitchell, 1951).

## Data sources and empirical roadblocks

Starting in 1962, time series for the stock of credit supplied to private business as well as to the public sector are available in the Spanish Ministry for the Economy data bank called *Series*. I define the total stock of domestic credit as private plus public sector credit minus net foreign assets plus transfers.

A cursory look at this data brings home the fact that the stock of total credit relative to the nominal GDP rose steadily from the early 1960s through 1970 and kept on growing in waves up to the present. It is clear, however, that in the earlier period leading up to the mid-1970s the growth slow-downs did not involve actual contractions of the credit share in GDP. As the depression gathered momentum in the late 1970s, however, the fluctuations gave rise to phases of negative credit growth.

The massive debt accumulation built-up in the late 1970s was the result of special circumstances, namely the onset of a full-fledged depression, not a characteristic experience in business finance. It must be remembered that the existence of negative real interest rates prior to 1976 certainly contributed to the debt build-up.

As previously indicated, the growth of the credit/GDP ratio proved to be subject to persistent fluctuations. I will argue that the downward trend in this ratio that extended for a decade after 1976 was mandated by the unprecedented build-up of debt in the 1970s. A similar episode took place in the early 1990s. I will propose the hypothesis that in the second half of the 1970s the credit supply increased so much due to the profit crunch experienced by business firms and the attendant strength of their necessitous borrowing.

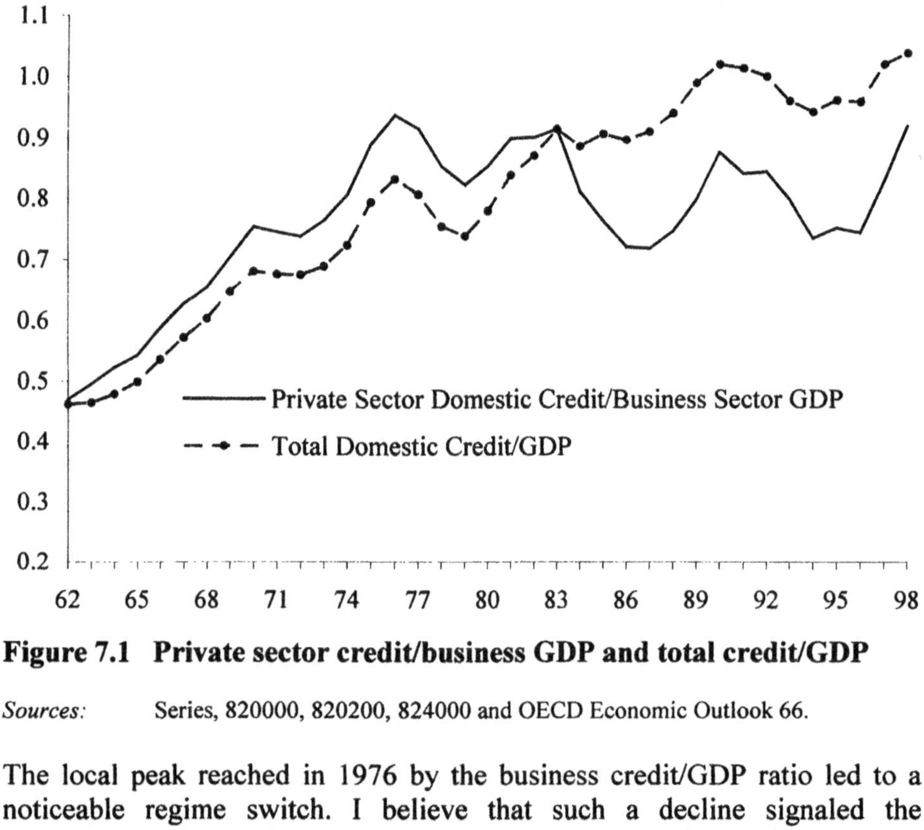


**Figure 7.1 Private sector credit/business GDP and total credit/GDP**

*Sources:* Series, 820000, 820200, 824000 and OECD Economic Outlook 66.

The local peak reached in 1976 by the business credit/GDP ratio led to a noticeable regime switch. I believe that such a decline signaled the introduction of a new financial regime based on lower deficit spending by the private and public sectors. If this is so, the prolonged slide in the credit/GDP growth of the 1990s could be interpreted as a byproduct of the rise in past financial liabilities as well as the harbinger of the deep recession felt in 1993. The finance needs for working capital and government deficits generally shaped the supply of credit by the banks, and Central Bank policy typically sought to prevent unnecessary dislocations. This is not to say that monetary policy appeared cast in a single mold for all times. Indeed the negative real interest rates prevailing in the 1970s gave way to very high positive ones in the 1980s. The Central Bank could not bring down interest rates at will because persistent public deficit in the depression phase and growing trade deficits in the recovery of the late 1980s required large doses of credit finance.

I will argue that monetary policy for the entire period tried to balance the financial needs of private and public borrowers with the lending practices honored by the banking system. I agree with Godley's assessment, "I am saying that (within strict limits, e.g. concerning credit-worthiness) banks respond passively to the needs of business for loans" (Godley, 1996, p. 20). I assume that the solvency of borrowers is always a central issue for all banks before loans are approved. I do not believe therefore that emphasizing the notion of 'credit rationing' by the banks on their own account or at the behest of the Central Bank contributed the decisive link to interpret credit restriction. Under normal circumstances, if the Central Bank is aware of excessive debt accumulation on the part of business, its policy will emphasize tighter discipline. Why focus on Central Bank policy to explain credit crunches when banks themselves would act the same in its absence? The interesting question is why banks increased their lending to insolvent firms in the 1970s and not why they restricted loans to overextended firms in the late 1980s and early 1990s.

The credit crunch would follow as a rational response to a perceived heightened risk of default. Risk aversion is a necessary feature of all market decisions precisely because agents are rational and understand the persistence of market uncertainty and risk.

## Working capital and investment finance

Credit finance refers to two different things. Business requires short-term credit to finance working capital expenditures before sale revenues are fully available. In addition, firms seek medium-term loans to finance investment plans not wholly covered by their retained earnings. Short-term credit is a revolving fund. Firms can borrow in anticipation of their revenues and pay their loans at more or less established intervals without their longer-term liquidity being impaired. This is the practice of credit-financed production, as Post-Keynesians rightly point out. I will adopt throughout this work the same post-Keynesian convention.

The foregoing implies that the *Series* data on the stock of bank credit (prepared by the Ministry for the Economy) issued to the private sector encompassed both types of needs. The loans were intended to finance short-term working capital, as well as longer-term commitments. In this data longer-term finance to carry out investment plans was also included. The post-Keynesian literature makes it clear that firms need short-term credit to finance all of their expenditures and my actual findings on expenditures and credit stock will bear this out. In Godley's dynamical model of finance and income determination, households "neither borrow nor invest" (Godley, 1996, p. 3). I will follow this convention. From my perspective of credit-financed production plans I will disregard consumer credit altogether without any harmful consequences. In addition, I will further assume that the *flow* of public credit financed the public deficit. Figure 7.1 showed the growth path in the stock of credit/GDP ratios for the Spanish economy as a whole, from the early 1960s through 1997. Figure 7.3 further down this chapter will present the longer-term business debt-retained earnings ratio path, reflecting the evolution of the financial *gap* (the difference between business capital spending and retained earnings) relative to retained earnings. Over the last thirty years, retained earnings on average financed about 90% of private fixed investment in plant and equipment. From the early 1960s through 1998, retained earnings averaged somewhat over 50% of pre-tax total profits, and its trend rose nearly 70%.

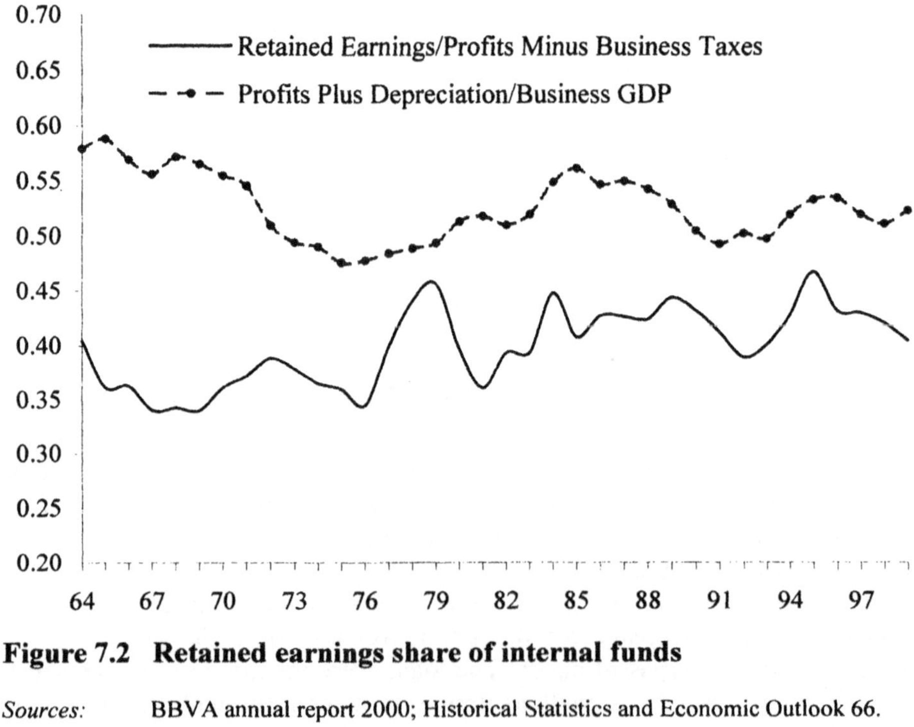


**Figure 7.2 Retained earnings share of internal funds**

*Sources:* BBVA annual report 2000; Historical Statistics and Economic Outlook 66.

Figure 7.2 shows the evolution of RE relative to profits net of business taxes. To avoid a further deterioration of their access to credit firms were obliged to cut back investment plans and prompted to increase their retained earnings out of net profits. It is noteworthy that firms typically fine-tuned their "savings" to the perceived needs for flexible finance dictated by the evolution of their internal sources of funds. In the early 1970s, the falling share of internal funds (profits plus depreciation) in the business sector GDP led to a sharp rise in retained earnings relative to profits. Once these funds recovered their previous levels, the share of retained earnings was brought-back closer to its long-term average, albeit subject now to a rising trend. The Demo data bank provided the time series for the period 1964-1970, and after 1970, the reliable BBVA annual economic report furnished the relevant data. It is noteworthy that after the mid-1970s, with the full weight of depression shattering expectations, both trends exhibited an upward trend.

After the early 1970s, periods of necessitous borrowing by distressed firms short of internal funds were followed by years of austerity, cutbacks required to restore internal finance levels compatible with the servicing of their accumulated debts. In the aftermath of the salvage operation mounted by the banks, the restoration of sound business budgeting and practices became an overriding concern for the surviving firms.

## Demand for working capital

All business spending is credit-dependent in the sense that credit finances expenditures in anticipation of future revenues. As Godley explains it:

> Firms require revolving finance from banks, not only because production and distribution take time while wages have to be paid in advance of sales being made, but also because they cannot know exactly what their sales are going to be and any shortfall requires a simultaneous addition to loans if the wage bill is to be met (Godley, 1998, p. 7).

Revenues received at regular and short intervals provide the wherewithal to service the acquired short-term debts on a continuous basis. Payments to the banks must include principal plus interest. Godley adds that:

> Banks automatically extinguish loans when cash or cheques are deposited by firms as sales are realized except to the extent that new loans, in an ongoing situation, will be needed to keep up the flow of production (Godley, 1998, p. 9).

As Figure 7.1 showed, the share of private-sector credit-financed expenditures rose significantly in Spain from the early 1960s through the mid-1970s. There is an apparent puzzle in reconciling the evolution of credit finance for working capital in the private sector as described by Post-Keynesian economists, and the actual story of investment being internally funded.

Taking into account the growing share of credit, relative to gross business income, received by the private sector through 1976 and then again in the years following the 1993 slump, it may seem paradoxical to note that for the entire period 1964-1999 the average yearly borrowing by business was only 3.9% of their investment in plant and equipment. Between 1964 and 1970, the average was 10.1%. As the depression gathered momentum from 1971 to 1979, the average yearly borrowing reached 21.2% and finally in the recovery phase from 1979 through 1999 the business sector had an average surplus of funds relative to capital investment amounting to 6.16%.

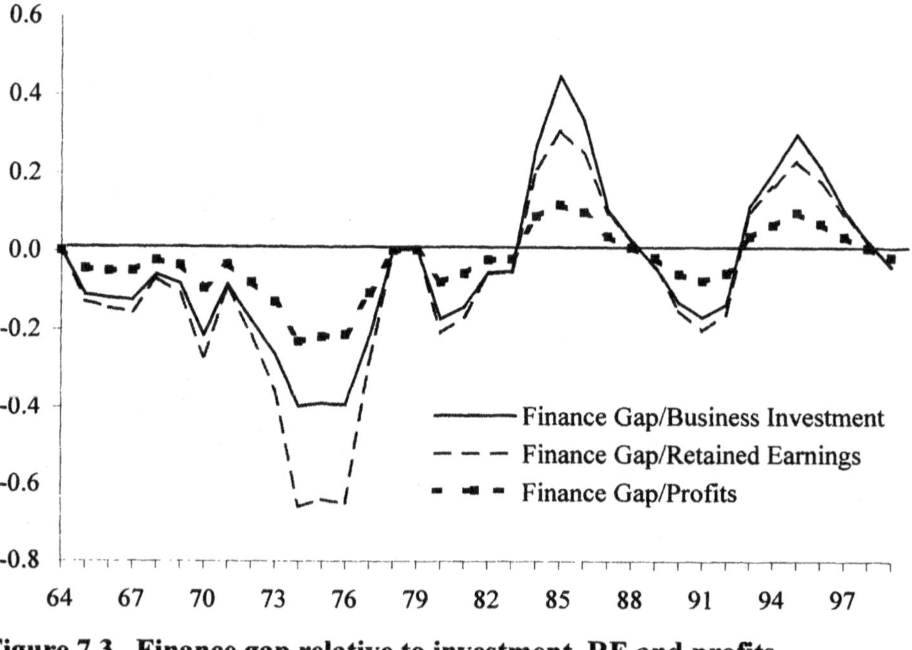


**Figure 7.3 Finance gap relative to investment, RE and profits**

*Sources:* BBVA annual report 2000; Historical Statistics and Economic Outlook 66.

Adding to this sum the depreciation funds, we have the amount matching the reported total expenditures for *gross* fixed capital investment. Gross fixed investment includes all spending on plant and equipment plus all construction spending (industrial as well as residential) plus the unintended changes in inventories. Business practice in Spain involved revolving short-term credit advances by the banks to cover working capital needs. Estimating the working capital finance supplied to cover business activity requires the subtraction of net foreign assets from the gross values. This modification then led to remarkable results. The flows of credit demand and supply to the private business sector, divided by the GDP, turned out to match each other closely. The results obtained provided confirmation for my original assumption, namely that the entire credit supply to the private sector could be understood as directed to business firms in response to their need for short-term working capital finance. This data must be distinguished from the time series on the financial *gap* for business firms, as reported in the L. Klein Institute's or the Banco Bilbao Vizcaya's (BBVA) annual data-bases. The *gap* series provides a better view of the financial conditions in which business operated after the early 1960s. This *gap* refers to the surplus or deficit finance outstanding each year in the business sector after subtracting from its investment spending the available retained earnings.

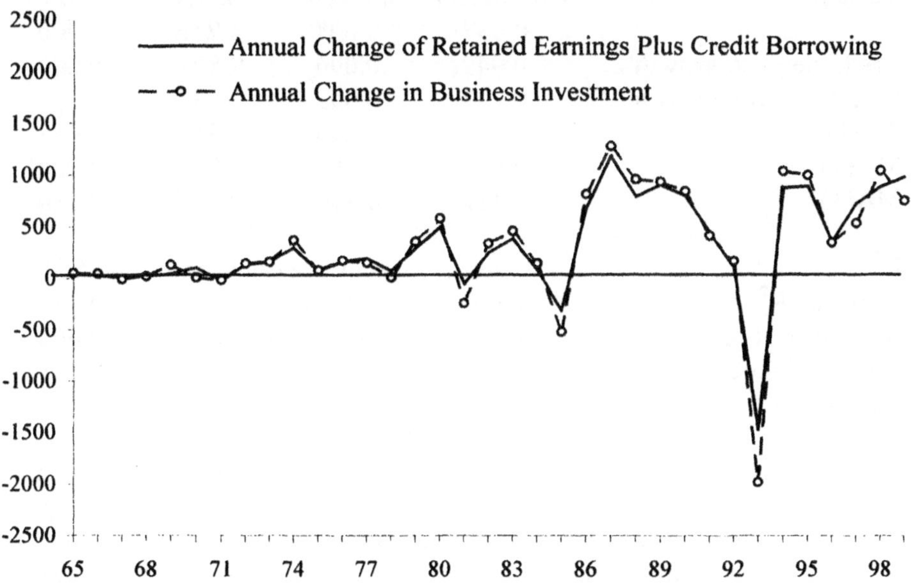


**Figure 7.4 Yearly fixed investment change and finance flow**

*Sources:* BBVA annual report 2000; Historical Statistics and Economic Outlook 66.

**Estimating working capital needs**

The arguments included in the best fit equation for the credit supply and the estimated (annual) needs of the private sector for working capital are as follows: 1. Private sector wages, $W^B$, (the difference between total wages, W and public sector wages, $W^P$); 2. Investment on plant and equipment, $I_K^B$; 3. Investment on residential housing, $I^H$; 4. Business sector depreciation, $Dep^B$; 5. Private sector estimated interest payments, $int^B$; 6. Business direct taxes, $T^B$; 7. Trade deficit, $Def^T$. Finally the credit demand equation for working capital will be:

$$Cr^D = (W - W^P) + I_K^B + I^H + Dep^B + int^B + T^B + Def^T$$

**Table 7.1 Regressing credit supply growth on credit demand growth**

Sample (adjusted): 1971 1998

| Variable | Coefficient | Std. Error | t-Statistic | Prob. |
|---|---|---|---|---|
| C | -0.037 | 0.008 | -4.256 | 0.000 |
| Credit demand growth | 0.949 | 0.096 | 9.822 | 0.000 |
| Credit demand growth(-2) | 0.233 | 0.092 | 2.537 | 0.017 |
| AR(1) | 0.439 | 0.229 | 1.910 | 0.067 |
| MA(1) | -0.543 | 0.184 | -2.947 | 0.006 |
| MA(1) | -0.421 | 0.190 | -2.207 | 0.036 |

| | | | |
|---|---|---|---|
| $R^2$ | 0.909 | Schwarz criterion | -4.584 |
| Adjusted $R^2$ | 0.890 | F-statistic | 49.945 |
| Std. Error of regression | 0.019 | Prob(F-statistic) | 0.000 |
| Log likelihood | 81.350 | | |
| Durbin-Watson statistic | 1.689 | | |

Table 7.1 shows the results of regressing this credit demand equation on the private sector credit supply. I believe that the high $R^2$ jointly with the high T-statistics and the low standard error of the sample, provide strong support for the good fit between the short-term credit demand and supply in the business sector each year. It is noteworthy, however, that the growth of short-term credit to finance working capital was inversely related to the evolution of the financial gap (longer-term finance for fixed capital investment) relative to retained earnings. Plotting the evolution of the (±) finance *gap* relative to

retained earnings and the domestic credit supply growth in the private sector reveals a significant negative correlation. The transition from the depression phase to recovery in the early 1980s witnessed the reversal from business deficit spending to budget surpluses. As this upward reversal occurred, the linear trend of the credit supply growth shifted downward.

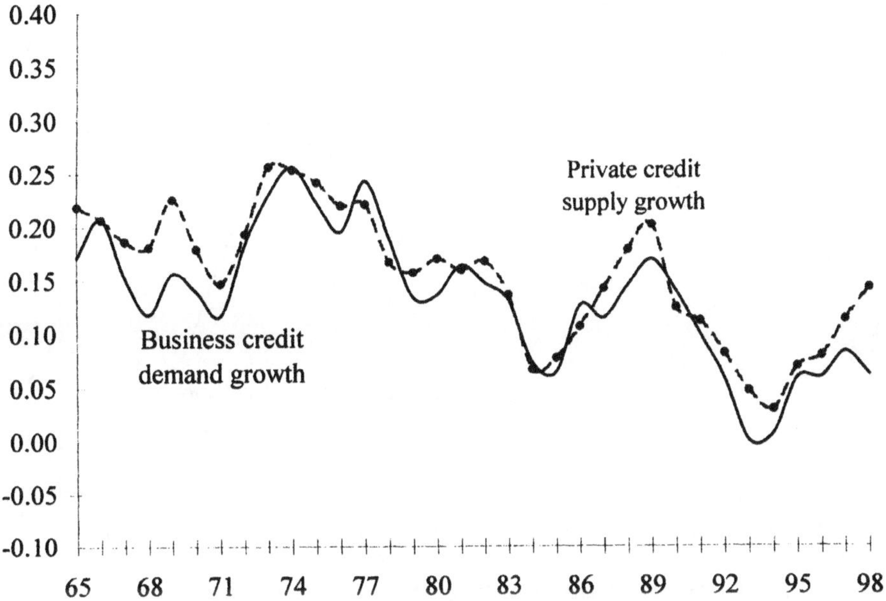


**Figure 7.5 Business credit demand and supply growth rates**

*Sources:* Series 83200 and Author's estimates.

Three factors explain why switching to surplus budgets from the deficit spending of the depression phase involved a lower credit growth to finance working capital. With regards to fixed investment budgets, whereas the overall linear trend of retained earnings out of profits increased and that of profit shares rose, the fixed capital accumulation trend declined and the overall growth rate never recovered the rhythms of the early 1970s. Despite the economic mini-boom of the second half of the 1980s, the growth trend of working capital requiring finance went down.

There is evidence to show that in the mid-970s firms were unwilling or unable to recognize immediately the severity and persistence of the downfall in profits. Having entered a phase of rapid growth in the 1960s it is perhaps understandable that the onset of depression was not readily recognized

(Sebastian, 1997). In conventional economic thinking, whether business or academic, the possibility of depression is simply ignored, being too disruptive of the accepted premises underlying those views.

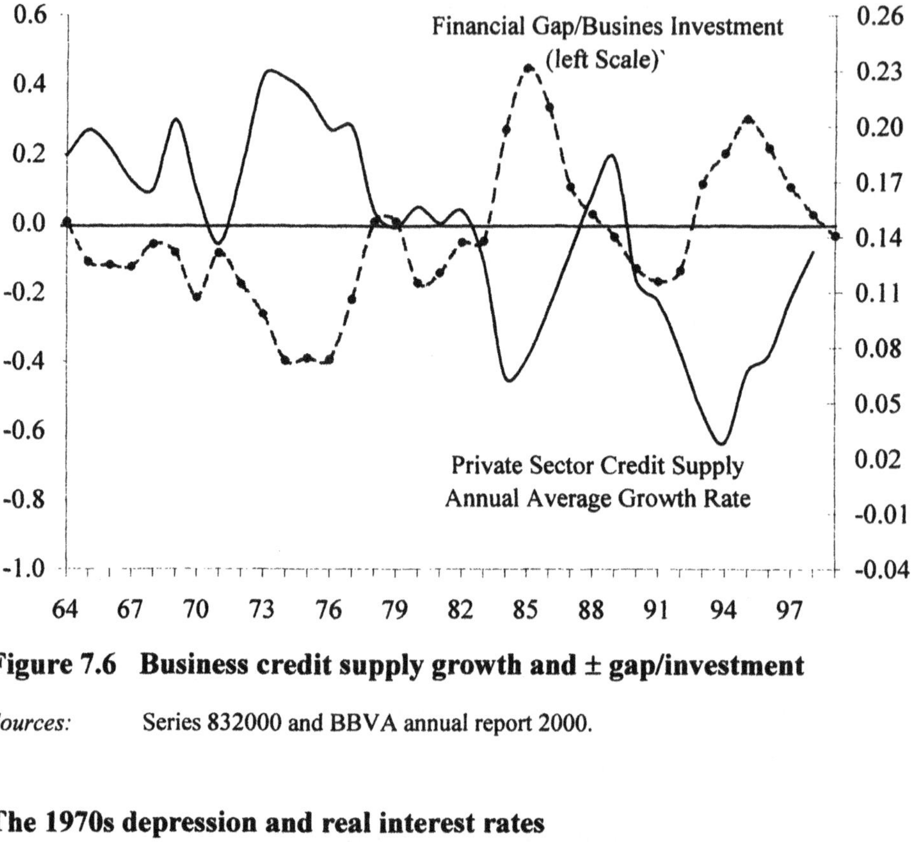


**Figure 7.6 Business credit supply growth and ± gap/investment**

*Sources:* Series 832000 and BBVA annual report 2000.

## The 1970s depression and real interest rates

The growth of credit in Spain declined *after* the economic recovery from the depression phase was under way. In fact, necessitous borrowing went up in Spain during the slump. Temin has argued that the decline in credit growth in the U.S. took place at the onset of the 1930s depression and the contraction originated on the demand side. He suggested a simple test to ascertain whether changes on the demand or the supply sides were the cause of the growth change in the credit stock. It is simply to look at the direction of the movement in real interest rates "on assets much like money" (Temin, 1976, p. 98). Real interest rates would rise if the observed change in credit growth went down due to the effective implementation of a restrictive policy by the monetary authorities (draining reserves from the banking system) with credit demand constant. On the other hand, real interest rates would be falling if the growth in credit demand by firms went down due to diminished profit expectations, with no change in banking policies. Of course, if both the credit demand and the credit supply growth rates were falling, a decline in real interest rates would indicate that the contraction on the demand side simply exceeded that of supply.

In the second half of the 1970s, the plunge in profits (net of interest) and sales shattered business expectations and forced firms to drastically curtail their spending. After the contraction in Spain provoked unmanageable structural bottlenecks, real interest rates declined not because the demand for credit fell but rather because high inflation rates exacerbated the effects of the slump. In the early 1970s both the capital-output ratio and real unit labor costs were rising. Output growth came to a halt. Fixed capital investment was not immediately curtailed after the mass of profits stagnated. Optimistic expectations carried on from the previous decade sustained the growth in spending and debt accumulation.

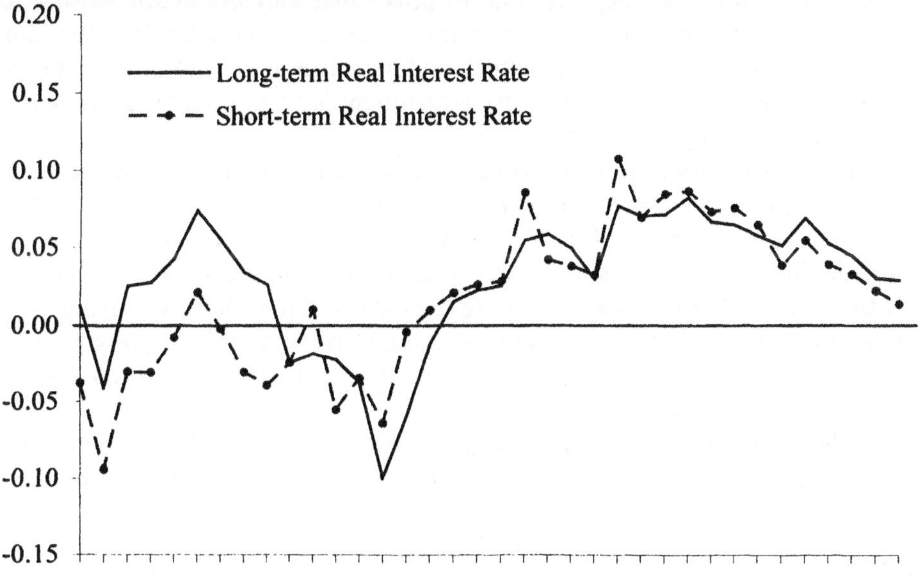


**Figure 7.7 Real long- and short-term interest rates**

*Sources:* Demo, RLP; L. Klein Institute, TLSP and OECD Historical Statistics.

High investment growth coupled with stagnant profits gave rise to accelerating inflation and falling real interest rates. As the depression bottomed out firms had to cut back spending because profitability collapsed and the debt burden reached unmanageable proportions. The accelerating inflation was the most visible symptom of the underlying rot. Negative real interest rates and the decline in bank profits brought home the message to the banking system. Drastic measures were required to restore profitability. Draconian changes were initiated to that effect and from the late 1970s on through the 1990s the rate of unemployment skyrocketed.

## Credit and GDP growth

In the Keynesian tradition, credit finances aggregate demand spending and output responds to the fluctuations in aggregate demand. The credit supply is dependent of the credit demand, in the sense that borrowers will not acquire new debt unless they need new purchasing power. Credit borrowing takes place as a prelude to spending. They will not have access to new purchasing power in turn unless they are able to prove that they are credit worthy. Of course cash reserves need be maintained by all businesses for the same reasons that they keep any other kind of reserves, stocks of materials, finished goods, labor etc. Inventory adjustment is an essential requirement of good management.

From my perspective, however, the solvency of the borrowing party, determined by any conventional measure in use, remains at the center of the decision to lend. The profitability of the borrowing firm and the extent of its indebtedness will be considered when banks make their decision to grant new loans. As long as business firms are deemed to enjoy the trust of the credit markets, they should able to borrow enough to meet their interest payment obligations. The ability to service interest payments on the acquired debt is a minimum requirement.

The GDP reflects the aggregate price of newly produced goods each year. Interest payments returned to the banks will reduce the purchasing power of the total credit issued by the banks each year. The aggregate interest payments due annually stem from private as well as public sector liabilities. Therefore, the relevant measure of the aggregate purchasing power for goods and services provided by the total domestic credit supply to business and government (excluding credit to finance foreign assets) will be a sum *net* of interest payments to the banks.

In order to account for changes in liquidity preference behind the build-up of cash reserves, I multiplied the net domestic credit flow, divided by the stock of credit issued annually, by the ratio of $M_3$ (liquid assets) to the GDP. The results are presented along with the nominal GDP growth path, in Figure

7.8. My analysis of the relationship between credit financing of working capital and the growth of economic activity led me to the following conclusions. The supply of short-term credit is a revolving fund responding to the finance needs of business for working capital. Firms will not expand their demand for credit without taking into account their expected sales.

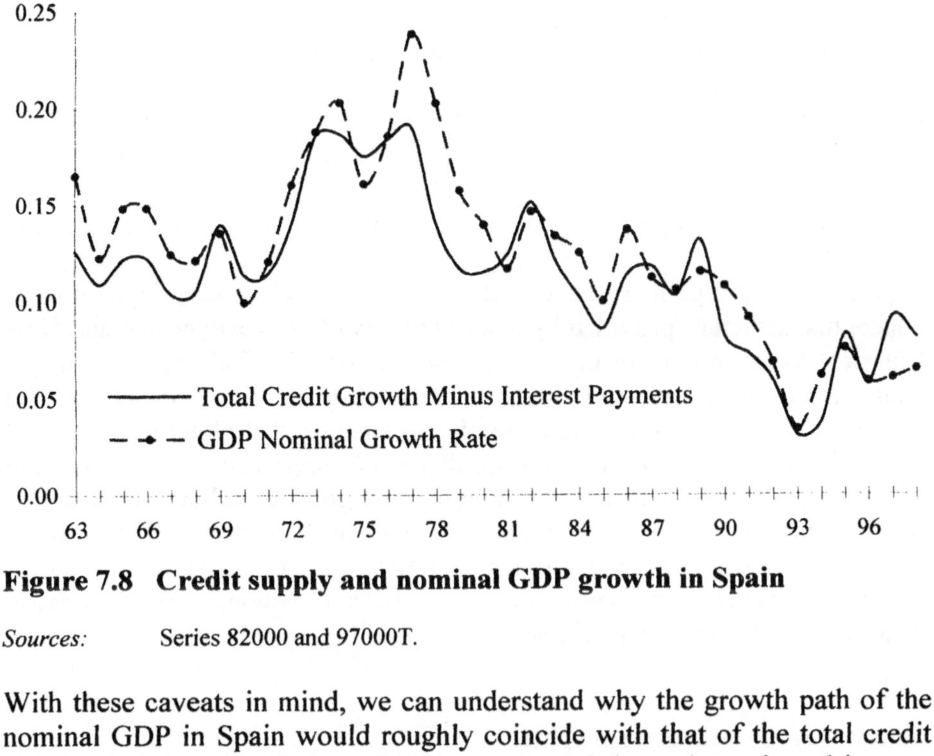


**Figure 7.8 Credit supply and nominal GDP growth in Spain**

*Sources:* Series 82000 and 97000T.

With these caveats in mind, we can understand why the growth path of the nominal GDP in Spain would roughly coincide with that of the total credit supply growth, excluding net foreign assets and the estimated total interest payments. The credit supply is not independent of the credit demand, not only because its growth implies an expansion of new business debts, but also because *normally* the decision by the banks to provide new credit is contingent upon their assessment of the likelihood that future business revenues will be adequate to repay new debt. Normally when a financial crisis breaks out and banks lose the required confidence in their client's ability to pull through the lean period, new credit will not be granted. Exceptionally, however, the rescue operation mounted by Spanish banks in the early 1970s was noteworthy for its consequences in the recovery phase. For such recovery witnessed a drastic change in the rules applicable to financing the budget supporting business spending.

# 8 Recessions and Shocks

Contrary to widespread belief, the National Bureau of Economic Research (Cambridge, Ma) “does not define a recession in terms of two consecutive quarters of decline in real GNP”. Moreover the NBER website specifically distinguishes between a recession and a growth recession: “A growth recession may encompass a recession, in which case the slowdown usually begins before the recession starts”. A recent study of fluctuations in the Spanish economy (Sebastian, 1998) nonetheless followed that definition and accordingly found three such episodes between 1971 and 1996. Prof. Sebastian’s book sought to lay out the theoretical grounds for the detection and analysis of the immediate changes in agents’ environment that triggered the recessions in Spain. The book achieved its goals while keeping within the conceptual structure provided by a selected mix of New Keynesian and New Classical assumptions. In my view, Prof. Sebastian’s findings are a major contribution to our understanding of the historical record on fluctuations, and particularly of those sudden and significant changes that altered the cyclical trend. In keeping with the “choice-theoretic” approach, Prof. Sebastian modeled the behavior of three representative agents, including non-financial sector firms, banks and consumers. All of them were assumed to respond with characteristic risk aversion to uncertainty and shocks. The behavior of firms and banks was interpreted as a rational response to asymmetric information present in capital markets.

### Shocks versus endogenous cycles

A man afflicted with heart disease may inadvertently step on a banana peel fall on his face, and die. Was his death caused by the mishap or his heart troubles? The man could very well have lived were it not for his weakened heart. His life could have conceivably gone on had he not ran across the fatal debris. Such dilemmas haunt all scientific efforts to explain the genesis of unique events, including recessions. At any rate, since cycles are macroeconomic phenomena, I am not convinced that the study of macroeconomic dynamics benefits from a primary focus on microeconomic practices. The notion that macroeconomic dynamics is merely a mechanical composite of individual behaviors needs to pass the test applicable to any fallacy of composition.

Because my perspective lies squarely within the traditions of Classical Political Economy, my search for evidence regarding the existence of endogenous cycles relegates stochastic shocks to the role of catalysts for underlying trends. Within this tradition, the availability of internal funds determines the tempo of accumulation, giving rise to side effects on employment and wages that produce the feedback loops behind the endogenous growth cycles formalized by R. Goodwin. Stochastic shocks are always present, creating the appearance of general disorder. What Marx calls "the anarchy of capitalist production" however is only the turbulent environment out of which the unintended order emerges. The dynamics of capital growth, intrinsically driven by profitability trends, (despite access to external finance) also provides the setting for medium-term endogenous cycles, as well as the context for the study of short-term recessions.

While shocks as the single most important source of fluctuations have received much attention by analysts wedded to the method and conclusions of general equilibrium economics, acceptance of the assumption has not been universal. Zarnowitz has expressed doubts regarding the explanatory powers attributed to exogenous shocks in the formation of business cycles. Benefiting from over forty years experience at the NBER, he pointed out a possible ideological interpretation for the popularity of the shocks approach. It was that "revival of the faith" in the business sector growth potential was itself a powerful consideration: were it not for shocks all would be well. In Spain's case, events have not always confirmed this article of faith. The exuberance of Spain's "economic miracle" (beginning in the 1960s) lasted but a decade. The anxiety caused by the slump that followed in the late 1970s lingered throughout the recovery phase of the 1980s and was aggravated by the downturn of the early 1990s.

Prof. Sebastian's analysis of fluctuations shows that erratic shocks impacting on a system riddled with structural rigidities and the responses of representative agents guided by risk aversion, caused the three recessions. Absent such perturbations and given the elimination of the system's rigidities, it is implied that the system's growth would have been steady and balanced. As a corollary of this, general equilibrium would result with full employment and no inflation. As it happened, powerful, stochastic shocks sometimes shifting aggregate supply and others aggregate demand knocked the system off its balance path. The existing structural rigidities then compounded the dislocations and the effects spread throughout the economy. For example, the oil price hikes of the early 1970s first disrupted factor costs, then upset product markets, and finally reduced labor employment and drained business of their funds. The disruptions led to recessions, sharp contractions in output and financial breakdowns, hence the rise of high and persistent unemployment of labor and productive capacity at the end of the decade.

It is likely that the "revival of the faith" in the growth potential of Spanish firms to achieve full employment, once the structural rigidities in the labor market are removed, needs frequent boosting. In any case, Zarnowitz's view was that:

> There is not much empirical validation that random shocks of all kinds play as large a role in business cycles as has been attributed to them in recent literature. The weight of exogenous policy factors, too, seems more often than not overstated. The theoretical interest in self-sustaining cycles, or elements thereof, declined in times when economic events and thought favored a revival of the faith in the private sector's capacity for stable growth (Zarnowitz, 1996, p. 75).

## New-Keynesian critiques

I believe that our appreciation of Prof. Sebastian's accomplishments could be enhanced by locating his approach within the framework of the New Keynesian critique. M. Dore has argued that for New Keynesian economists, focusing their analysis on shocks, misperceptions and the presence of structural rigidities allowed them to explain fluctuations without having to drop perfect competition and perfect knowledge as valid, albeit ideal constructs. Absent these rigidities cum shocks, perfectly competitive markets would bring about quick market clearing to cushion any sudden supply or demand shifts in product and factor markets. Keynesian economists theoretically anchored in the concept of perfect competition typically use the frictions of imperfect markets and the disruptions caused by stochastic shocks to bring legitimacy to their analysis of cycles (Dore, 1993, p. 102). As a critic of both neo-classical and New Keynesian economics, Dore has insisted that half-measures in Keynesian scholarship are not sufficient to recover Keynes' basic insight. As quoted by Mirowski, Keynes himself highlighted the differences between what he called the classical school, currently represented by New Classical and Real Business Cycles economists, and his own perspective:

> What is it that makes the cleavage which divides us? On the one side are those who believe that the existing economic system is, in the long- run, a self-adjusting system though with creaks and groans and jerks, outside interference and mistakes… On the other side of the gulf are those who reject the idea that

the existing economic system is, in any significant sense, self-adjusting (Mirowski, 1985, p. 46).

Blurring of the lines separating these two camps has alarmed those Keynesians that remain loyal to their master's message. Some of them have objected to the excessive baggage shared between Keynesian economists and the New Classical approach when they study aggregate product and labor markets. Among the leading New Keynesians, Stiglitz has proposed the need for the renewal of New Keynesian economics because the current paradigm leaves no room for the study of endogenous systemic fluctuations. This effort requires the assembly of a new set of building blocks. The first step involves replacing the emphasis on structural rigidities as the culprit *par excellence* with an understanding of how flexible prices and wages would in fact magnify the effects of small shocks. As an example, the impact of price deflation on nominal business debt could very well reverse any expected boosts to firms' spending (Greenwald and Stiglitz, 1993, pp. 23-44). Since most firms typically carry a certain amount of debt at nominal interest rates, price deflation may produce onerous burdens of real debt, crushing firms' ability to maintain spending plans.

Stiglitz's outlook found it unacceptable to assume that aggregate output fluctuations occurred only in response to stochastic shocks by optimizing agents endowed with imperfect information. He rejected modeling based on the assumption that all representative agents were alike because such an approach excluded the presence of asymmetric information and transaction costs. In addition, Stiglitz rejection of price stickiness as a general principle aiding and abetting the shock transmission mechanism sought to bring Keynesian economics back to its authentic track. The New Keynesian approach favored by Stiglitz should include three major blocks. They are: the behavioral characteristics of risk-averse firms; the central role of external finance in the framing of production plans; and finally the consequences derived from credit rationing by risk averse banks facing asymmetric information. Stiglitz rejected the view that since the aggregate supply of labor is independent of the labor demand schedule only erratic shifts in either one could explain employment cycles. Instead, he argued that labor market theories emphasizing efficiency and insider/outsider interpretations of wage determination should be integral components of the new Keynesian economics. In Stiglitz's view, these operational principles are required by Keynesian economists willing to challenge the single-minded preoccupation of equilibrium theorists with wage and price rigidities.

For example in the traditional vein of New Keynesian economics, Akerlof and Yelling (1985) have argued that if firms typically optimized their prices, the individual benefits derived from price adjustments might be relatively small and therefore not carried out, but the losses accruing to society as a whole might be quite large. Stiglitz dismissal of the Akerlof and Yellin conclusion was based on research carried out by Caplin and Spulber (1987) and his own empirical evidence contradicting their findings. In support of Stiglitz's rejection, Caplin and Spulber (1987) have systematically shown that some delay in price adjustments at the firm's level was perfectly consistent with full price flexibility in the aggregate. Greenwald and Stiglitz noticed, however, that as menu costs models were pressed into service in defense of sticky prices, their empirical relevance has steadily diminished due to technical progress:

> Indeed, these costs are small, and have become smaller as computer programs allow the printing of menus on a daily basis at a marginal cost of pennies (Snowdon and Vane, 1997, p. 563).

It can be argued that turning Keynesian economics into a shaky abode for sticky prices and rigid wages violates the breakthrough achieved by Keynes's General Theory. In light of the emphasis placed by conventional New Keynesians (or Post-Keynesians, for that matter) on wage hikes as the cause of inflation, it is surprising that the opposite effects of deflation are frequently ignored.

The gist of Keynes's main criticism of "classical" economics in Chapter 2 of the General Theory (Keynes, 1977) was that its explanation of how full employment might be restored was flawed. The "classical" theory of unemployment explained the appearance of excess labor supply due to above equilibrium real wage-rates. This imbalance, however, could only be transitional because its presence would push the nominal wage-rate down. The decline in wages that followed would then lower consumption demand and hence the prices of consumer goods. The real wage might perversely not fall at all, and indeed if consumer-good prices fell disproportionately relative to nominal wages, might even increase:

> Thus if money-wages change, one would have expected the classical school to argue that prices would change in almost the same proportion, leaving the real wage and the level of unemployment practically the same as before, any small gain or loss to labour being at the expense or profit of other elements of marginal cost which have been left unaltered (Keynes, 1977, p. 12).

No automatic mechanism, therefore, was available to bring about a return to full employment equilibrium. The system might settle in some intermediate position of income and employment, given the expected level of effective demand. It was precisely because prices were flexible that the necessary re-adjustment of the real wage rate could not be achieved.

## Aversion to risk

Turning to matters of risk, there is no question that Keynes's concept of "lender's risk" covered the banking side of credit, that is, "the involuntary default due to the disappointment of expectation" (Keynes, 1977, p. 144). Since the lending banks are not immune to the consequences of such failures, they will strive to avoid them. Certainly, the significance of risk was central to Kalecki's analysis of the determinants of firms' expansion, as far back as the 1930s (Kalecki, 1971, p. 105). One of the factors that according to him lent it "decisive importance" in establishing firms' size was the scale of entrepreneurial capital available, that is, the amount of capital owned by the firm. While firms could tap capital markets for growth, in general firms will not engage in large financial operations there because of aversion to "increasing risk". Entrepreneurs are aware of the fact that borrowing to expand in the face of uncertainty runs the risk of failure, the more so the larger the borrowed sum. They face "a net loss which, if it continues long enough, must drive his business out of existence" (Kalecki, 1971, p. 106).

Once you replace the framework of neo-classical perfect competition with that of classical "free competition", business risk naturally falls into place along with uncertain expectations and turbulent environments. It is in fact a structural feature of the classical approach.

## Medium-term cycles and recessions in Spain

Using quarterly data for the real GDP provided by the *Series* data bank, Prof. Sebastian proceeded to obtain the quarterly growth rate for the GDP. I have added the Hodrick-Prescott trend (using a parameter value of 100) to the quarterly growth data to replicate what Prof. Sebastian calls a cyclical trend. It turns out that the filter's parameter value was crucial to obtain the contours needed to identify official recessions. Then in keeping with the guidelines set by the NBER, Prof. Sebastian was able to pinpoint the quarters whose characteristics conformed to the NBER definition of recession. This definition requires at least two consecutive quarters exhibiting negative growth rates. He found four such episodes of recession occurring in 1975.1-1975.3; 1978.3-1979.3; 1980.4-1981.3 and 1992.2-1993.4. By default, all other periods were treated as growth quarters of an expanding economy. Figures 8.1 and 8.2 display the evidence presented by Prof. Sebastian to reach these conclusions.

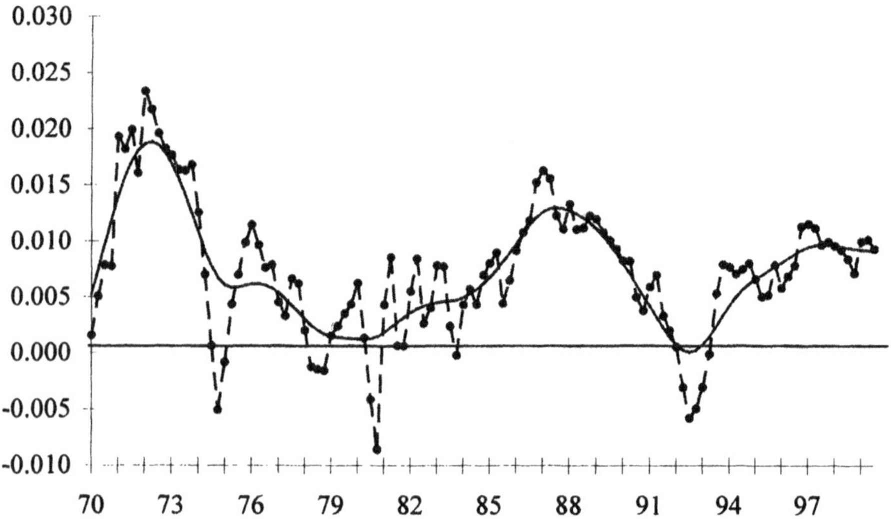


**Figure 8.1 GDP quarterly fluctuations and Hodrick-Prescott trend**

*Sources:* Series 920000T and Author's calculation.

Clearly many of the recorded fluctuations in the last thirty years were transient disturbances. Prof. Sebastian used his cyclical trend to rub out any such perturbations not meeting his stated criteria, while keeping the local minima associated with recessions. Once the unqualified quarterly fluctuations were removed, the cyclical trend revealed the appropriate results. After making his warranted selection, the analysis proceeded to sort out the plausible causes behind each of the four recessions.

Looking at the whole period 1970-1998, it is worth noting that each successive peak and trough was lower than the previous one. This pattern suggests the presence of still another longer-term cyclical growth trend, which I have depicted as a third-power polynomial path. Presenting the whole second cycle 1981.4-1992.1 as one of unqualified "expansion" obfuscates the broader cyclical patterns in which the official recessions occurred.

I believe that Prof. Sebastian marshaled an impressive body of data and succeeded in his endeavor to develop a story "put together from a specific theoretical perspective and capable of fitting a wide array of data". His stated goals were:

> To detect crucial changes in the evolution of relevant macroeconomic variables, deploying graphic analysis when it was useful to do so and more sophisticated and powerful statistical methods when the availability of data made it possible (Sebastian, 1997, p. 153).

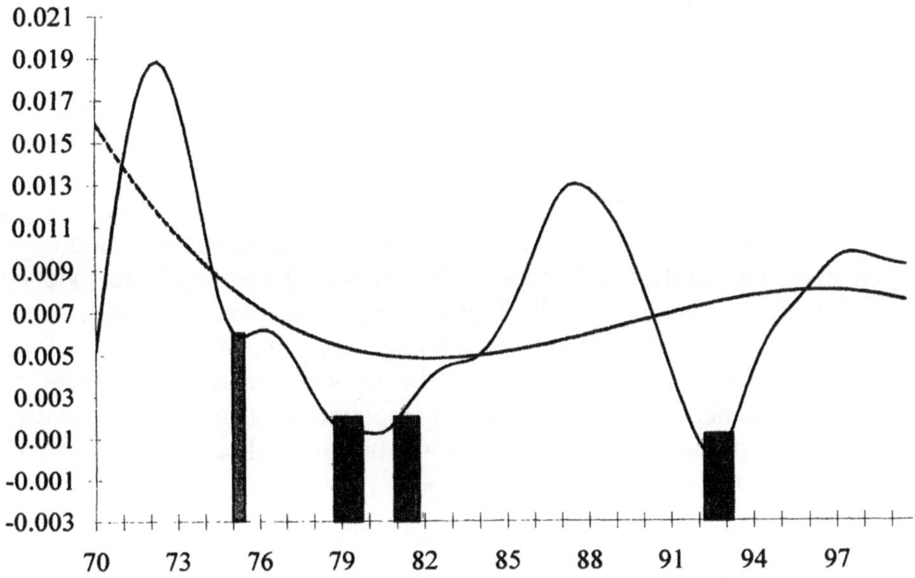


**Figure 8.2 Medium- and long-term cyclical trends**

*Sources:* Series 920000T and Author's calculation.

I believe, however, that Prof. Sebastian's story of the way in which erratic shocks and dislocations impacted on the rigid structure of the economic system could gain explanatory powers if placed within a broader framework. The overall cyclical growth patterns of the economic system were by no means limited to the short-term dynamics of the business cycle, including the occasional recession episode. There is no question that the choice of the appropriate object to study remains a controversial matter. In his broad investigation of *The Long Wave*, J. J. van Duijn pointed out that:

> Nevertheless, the term "cycle" as in the American "business cycle" and the English "trade cycle" may be misleading, and it is interesting to note that not all languages use this expression to refer to economic fluctuations. In continental

> Europe the term "conjuncture" is used...The conjuncture is the interplay of movements that together make up the direction in which the economy is going (van Duijn, 1983, p. 5).

Schumpeter (1939) acknowledged the existence of so-called Juglar fixed equipment cycles 7-11 years in length and structure cycles lasting 15-25 years (Kuznets, 1967). Casual inspection of Figure 8.2 confirms the presence of a longer-term cyclical growth trend within which the short-term recessions occurred. Two such complete cycles are evident, one starting in 1970 and ending in 1980 and the second in 1981 and running through mid-1992. A third, not yet completed growth trend cycle, is also visible. The upward phase of this cycle initiated after 1994.1 may have reached its peak in mid 1999. Possibly this date may ultimately prove to be the turning point for the third GDP growth trend cycle.

After presenting Prof. Sebastian's detailed argument explaining the genesis of the four recessions, I will take-up the unresolved question of the cyclical trend itself. I will present in Chapter 9 the available evidence showing that Goodwin's cyclical growth dynamics was applicable in the Spanish economy after 1970. The findings confirm the existence of two medium-term cycles, relating changes in the wage share (and thereby the profit share in net output) to changes in employment shares. It is noteworthy that their origin and transmission requires no initial shock, although such a shock may in fact occur.

## The extended downswing: supply shocks

According to Prof. Sebastian, the three recessions that punctuated the 1974-1981 downswing were caused chiefly by powerful supply shocks impacting an economic system burdened with structural rigidities. A catalogue of the main possible sources of shocks altering the state of confidence affecting agents would include factor price volatility; sudden changes in monetary aggregates or the exchange rate; sudden changes in productivity; unpredictable political changes. In addition, the strength of the response to any such change by firms will depend on the value of their assets, and by households on their net financial worth (Novales and Sebastian, 1999, p. 571).

During these seven years, obsolete economic and political institutions were unable to dampen the resulting imbalances. The elusive path of steady growth was permanently lost. Prof. Sebastian's comprehensive story of the events surrounding this loss was built on the assumption that the growth fluctuations exhibited by the real GDP and other macroeconomic variables were caused by random "supply factors". These were both of external and internal origins. The most notable of the external perturbations was the oil price-hikes. The internal shock destabilizing balanced growth was traced to the "excessive" and recurrent real wage-rate boosts of the 1970s.

Firms responded to the unprecedented hikes in variable input prices, including energy and labor, with output cuts. The rise in firms' uncertainty regarding the persistence of the shocks, combined with the attendant fall in the productivity of capital, lowered precipitously their propensity to invest. In 1974 oil prices rose by 166% and wage increases outstripping productivity gains continued through 1981. The rise in energy and other materials inputs pushed up the cost of doing business, while the steady growth of wages boosted consumption demand. The overall effect spilled into a double-digit inflation.

Misperceptions plagued the behavior of labor and business. Rapid growth and technological change experienced in the 1960s led workers to believe that similar wage-hikes could be sustained indefinitely. Firms made good on labor's claims because they misjudged the longevity of the slump and thought that wage increases would not last. Prof. Sebastian thinks that the 1975 recession was caused by the joint effect of supply shocks (the oil price hikes plus the inordinate wage boosts) and the ensuing deflationary demand shock, linked to the transfer of real income abroad. He considers it likely, however, that the wage boosts granted by yearend 1973 were sufficient to account for the decline in the system's growth, even if the oil price shocks had never happened (Sebastian, 1997, p. 61). Rising waves of layoffs after 1978 signaled the end of uncertainty for firms, a correction that by 1985 had produced 16% of unemployment. From 1974 through 1985 total employment fell by over 2.2 millions (ibid, p. 131).

Accepting Prof. Sebastian's evidence on the inflationary effects of wages growth, the post-1977 collapse in aggregate demand shock could only occur if aggregate profit losses outranked wages gains. Aggregate profits here must encompass those of the banking sector, as real interest rates remained negative throughout most of the 1970s. When taking account of the other side of the "substantial loss of profitability caused by these imbalances" (ibid, p. 83) we find the unprecedented rise in non-financial business debt.

Once real interest rates turned positive in the early 1980s the solvency of many indebted firms collapsed and the banks tightened their credit rationing. The disturbing impact of the second supply shock applied to the Spanish economy in 1980-1981 via new oil price hikes, was aggravated by continuing wage hikes, rising interest rates well into positive territory plus credit rationing. This was indeed the *coup-de-grace* for the ailing economy (ibid, p.

84). Loose monetary policy in effect during the 1970s contributed to the insolvency tide that sunk so many firms and finally provoked the severe credit rationing of the late 1980s. The increase in real interest rates after 1982 led to unprecedented hikes in the real exchange rate and the expansion of the trade deficit (ibid, pp. 99-100).

## Restructuring and cyclical recovery

Facing credit rationing in the 1980s and motivated by the severity of the slump, firms opted for radical (labor) cost-cutting measures as a way to expand their internal funds. Their efforts showed a measure of success as early as 1984 leading to the consolidation of their internal funds in the second-half of the 1980s. Prof. Sebastian noted:

> The existence of large quantities of resources created by firms that allow them not only to restore their financial health, but also the financing of huge investment plans, despite high real interest rates caused by a tight monetary policy plus a strong credit demand stemming from the public sector (ibid, pp. 88-89).

The improvement could not be sustained. By 1989, investment spending collapsed under the weight of new interest rate increases (from 11% in 1988 to 15% in 1989) and the lofty appreciation of the real exchange rate.

Prof. Sebastian argues that the investment collapse of 1989, a "permanent decline" in both equipment and construction spending, could not have served as the basis for the restrictive measures imposed by the Bank of Spain on commercial banks. Instead, credit tightening had to be triggered by the high debt stocks accumulated by households. Consumer misperceptions forced the hand of the Central Bank. In Prof. Sebastian's view, the 1990 Gulf War initially had a negative impact on consumer confidence. Once the war ended, however, consumers imagined that peace in the Middle East was synonymous with a prolonged economic bonanza.

While firms managed to recover their solvency in the second-half of the 1980s, households blithely lost it. Motivated by the belief that their own prosperity was assured by the recovery of business profitability, households piled-up large debts despite prevailing high real interest rates. In early 1989, the Bank of Spain stepped in and imposed such major credit controls on commercial bank lending that the "deep recession" in 1992-1993 was all but predictable if not inevitable. Prof. Sebastian sees the supply of credit to the business sector as a function of the scale of production and investment desired by firms. It is tied primarily to firms' expectations as well as the interest rate (Novales and Sebastian, 1999, p. 566). In turn the strength of aggregate demand is related to the scale of business activity, that is, aggregate supply (and the derived credit demand), "both sides are interdependent since they are simultaneously moved in the same direction by various factors" (Sebastian, 1997, p. 113).

The business decisions that led to the fluctuations in economic activity were made in the context of radical uncertainty about future conditions and motivated by risk aversion. In Prof. Sebastian's approach, these were not firms or households endowed with perfect knowledge, or agents acting wisely with perfect foresight. Rather they were all stumbling along the uncharted path of a dark depression. Misperceptions were frequent and unintended consequences followed. The unpredictable response by agents to uncertainty might well be triggered by large changes in a small number of key variables, or by small changes in a large number of environmental factors. Any inordinate rise in volatility involving key variables of their decision-making would lower the threshold of their tolerance and thus inhibit their activities.

## Endogenous medium term cycles

Once the object of investigation is broadened to include the cyclical trend and not just its local minima, it is clear that something other than erratic shocks was involved. The two complete cycles ending in 1993 as well as the unfinished third one starting then obviously displayed bigger amplitudes than the recorded recessions. In this context, the 1975 recession appears as no more than a kink in the longer contraction. The next two in 1978.3 and 1980.4, emerge as tumbles of a weakening system within the range of its trough.

From my perspective, the first growth downswing from the 1972 peak to the trough of 1980 was longer and deeper than the second, running from 1987 through 1993, with each successive trough reaching lower than the previous one. Examination of the overall trend running through these medium-term cycles (the complete cycle extends from 1980-81 through 1993) reveals that each successive peak was lower than its predecessor, and the second trough was also lower than the first. In short, the long-term growth trend of the system appears to be falling.

These were obviously not "business cycles" in the contemporary sense of brief, shallow dips in a growth path. The officially designated recessions occurred as the growth downswing was underway or had reached its trough.

It makes sense to reason that as the system's driving force weakened in the 1970s (because the profits share was falling) any major erratic shock or cluster of small shocks could cause the negative growth of two consecutive quarters.

Figure 8.3 shows that it would be difficult to argue that the stagnation and then decline in aggregate profitability after 1973 was caused by rising real wages. The linear trend of the real wages share in the business sector GDP did not rise but fell instead, while the trend of the capital stock in the business sector relative to the GDP nearly tripled between 1964 and 1998. This is the basis for my contention that the long-run decline in aggregate average profitability was caused by the effect of increasing mechanization on the capital-output ratio. The share of real wages in output, however, modulated the trend in falling profitability.

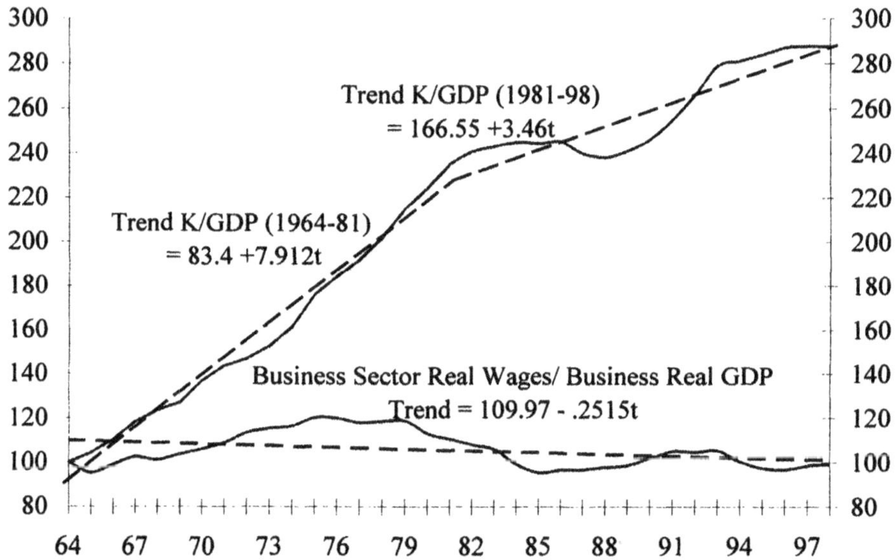


**Figure 8.3 Trends of real wages shares and capital-output ratios**

*Sources:* OECD Historical Statistics and Economic Outlook 66.

Assessing this evidence leads to the conclusion that the overall trend in profitability was preponderantly set by the sustained rise in the capital-(net) output ratio. In that light, I attribute the modulations in the movement of the profit rate to the cyclical behavior of the aggregate profit margin. Figure 8.3 shows the cyclical behavior of the real wages share rather than the real profits share. This is only to question the emphases placed on alleged trend increases in wages as the cause of all the system's problems, from inflation to unemployment.

Figures 8.4 and 8.5 show the close relationship holding between the deviations of the real profits (net of depreciation) share in the business sector GDP from its trend and the deviations of GDP growth rates from their annual trend.

Professor Sebastian's important contribution consists in identifying and measuring the probable strength of his shocks impacting on this endogenous cyclical trend. While Prof. Sebastian was concerned with determining the changes in behavior that provoked the four transient recessions, my focus instead encompassed the dynamics of the profits share and its impact on the growth of accumulation as the chief determinant of GDP growth rates.

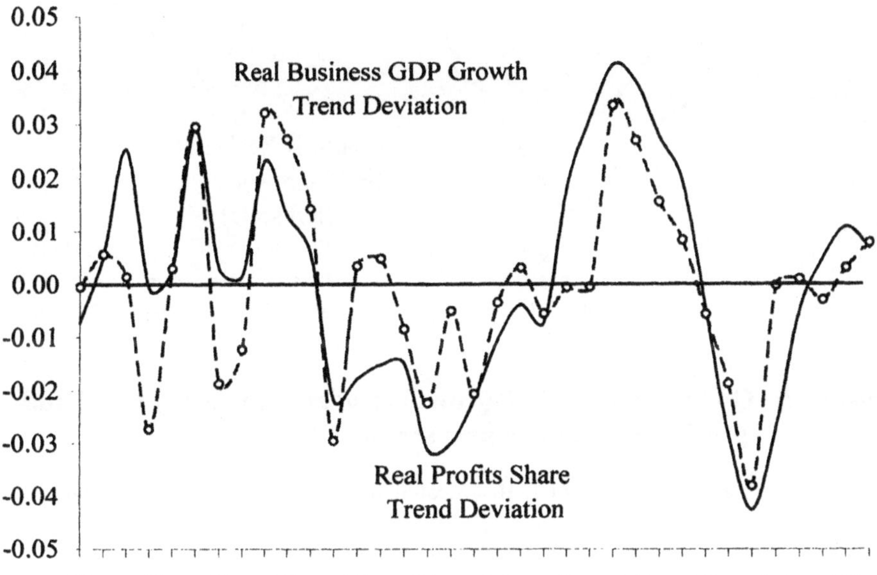


**Figure 8.4 Real annual GDP growth and real profits share**

*Sources:* OECD Historical Statistics and Economic Outlook 66.

My contention is that we need to acknowledge the existence of medium-term waves of capital accumulation caused by endogenous changes in the capital-output ratio and the profits share. Goodwin's model of cyclical growth provides an adequate framework to explain this dynamics. Profits are the object as well as the means to sustain accumulation. Since profits growth regulates the rhythms of economic activity, capital accumulation is subject to cyclical trends caused by technology and income distribution changes. In Spain the growth of profits was affected by the rise in the capital-output ratio and the fluctuations in employment related to the various phases of accumulation.

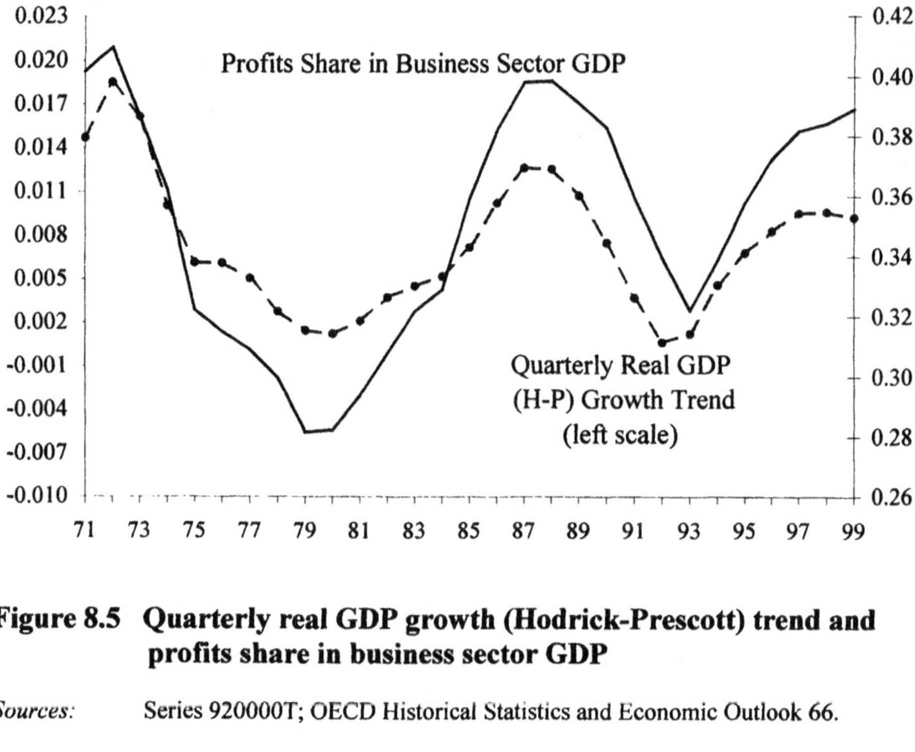


**Figure 8.5 Quarterly real GDP growth (Hodrick-Prescott) trend and profits share in business sector GDP**

*Sources:* Series 920000T; OECD Historical Statistics and Economic Outlook 66.

## Nonlinear growth dynamics of profits and wages

Figure 8.6 presents the phase diagram of real profits and wages growth (Hodrick-Prescott) trends, showing how periods in which both growth rates declined led to sharp downturns, such as 1970-1975 and 1989-1992. It is noteworthy that in both turning points 1975 and 1992, the growth rate of profits was negative, and the mass of profits fell.

From 1964 to 1970, the growth trend of profits declined, but after 1970 both profits and wages trends declined. In the case of profits after 1973 the mass of profits fell. These developments in aggregate incomes growth led the way to depression. After the initial contraction, reversal points occurred approximately at five years intervals. From 1975 to 1981 the rising trend in profits growth contrasted with wages dipping into negative growth rates. While in the early recovery phase of the 1980s both growth rates turned positive, in the second half of that decade, as employment gains were supported by public deficit spending, the growth of profits declined relative to that of wages. From 1989 through 1992, once again, both growth trends went down, and as it happened after 1975, accumulation suffered a new downturn in 1993.

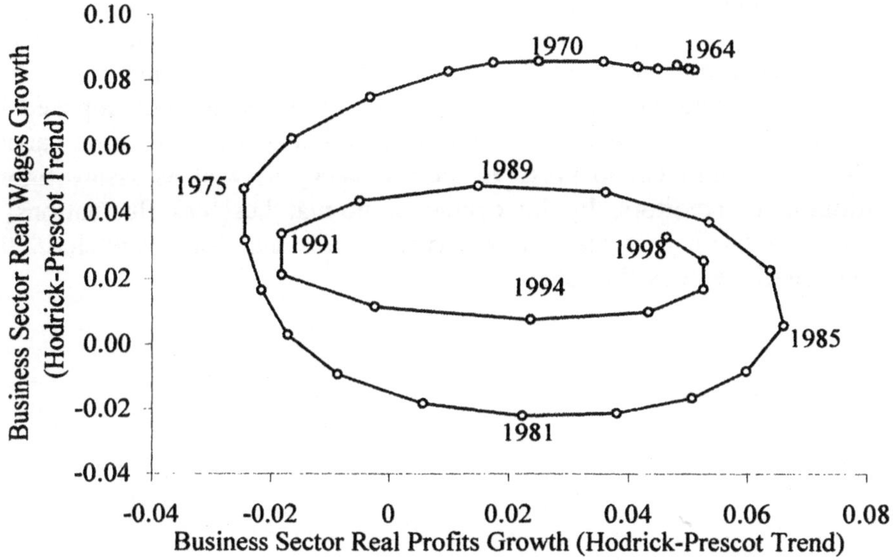


**Figure 8.6 Cycles in real profits and wages growth (Hodrick-Prescott) trends space in Spain**

*Sources:* OECD Historical Statistics and Economic Outlook 66.

## Summary of the classical view on fluctuations

The NBER recognizes that "A growth recession is a recurring period of slow growth in total output, income, employment, and trade, usually lasting a year or more. A growth recession may encompass a recession, in which case the slowdown usually begins before the recession starts, but ends at about the same time" (NBER website). The anti-Keynesian consensus prevalent among contemporary economists affirms the endogenous character of growth but relegates cycles to the vagaries of exogenous perturbations. The approach advocated in this book rejects the notion that the medium and short-term cycles traced by the growth path of the Spanish economy were the mere result of random shocks. It favors instead adopting the classical alternative, where the system is driven by endogenous growth mechanisms activated by equally endogenous cycles linked to income distribution. The evidence shows that in Spain fluctuations in the share of profits caused by changes in employment shares gave rise to accumulation cycles. The extraction and accumulation of profits was a necessary and sufficient condition for capital growth, but the credit markets were ready to boost that wherewithal when profit expectations energized the *animal spirits* of industry and banks. It is imperative to underlie, nonetheless, that the limits to growth imposed by profitability were not abrogated. The acquisition of debt by firms carried with it a commitment to preserve their solvency as well as assure timely restitution to creditors. In the course of normal business fluctuations, a reversal in profit margins trends served as a signal for a switch in the provision of credit by the banks.

# Part III: Evaluating the Models

# 9 Profitability and Accumulation

What is the relevant evidence in the Spanish experience linking profitability, finance and accumulation cycles? That is the question informing my empirical exploration in this chapter. Here and in the next chapter, I seek to evaluate the empirical support available to verify some of the main claims advanced by the models presented in Part I. In the Goodwin case, credit is not considered, accumulation finance being confined to internal sources, and Goodwin's cycles run longer than those produced in the other models. Differences aside, however, the models by Shaikh, Goodwin, Minsky and Foley place the dynamics of profitability at the center of the changes linking accumulation and finance.

I will anticipate here that my view of profitability as the central tendency of excess demand fluctuations developed in Shaikh's analysis appears to be empirically justified. My reading of the Spanish data supports the chief propositions derived from Shaikh's models linking the dynamics of profitability and fluctuations of excess demand. How can excess demand fluctuations be empirically identified? I will deploy the evidence garnered from the Spanish data in Chapter 10. Foley's model (1987a) explicitly linked the dynamics of the profit rate with the growth of bank credit giving rise to endogenous liquidity growth cycles. Here the empirical evidence is more elusive. The growth of his dynamical system, however, depends on the exogenous growth of the money supply, under the control of the monetary authorities. Indeed, in Foley's model, booms end due to liquidity deficiencies tied to a low money supply growth, while phases of low growth produce a surfeit of liquid funds. This approach is not helpful as a general guide to the historical record in Spain. The preservation of an exogenous money supply places Foley's model in a class by itself and separates it from both Shaikh's and Minsky's. On the other hand, despite the suggestive power of Minsky's approach to the analysis of financial crises the empirical evidence supporting it is not conclusive. I will present my findings at the end of this chapter.

## Working capital and accumulation

While the Goodwin model sidesteps the use of external finance, the other models under consideration include it. The production circuit must be funded before the product is sold. Under normal circumstances, the proceeds from sales will allow business to payback their (short-term) debt and make profits. Subtracting from gross profits the share paid as dividends to the shareholders, we arrive at business's retained earnings, RE. The evolution of business internal funds is central to the dynamics of credit cycles. Business short-term borrowing bridges the interval between present requirements for working capital and future revenues. I have assumed that this interval refers to the yearly circuit of business activity. Business investment in capital goods, on the other hand, is predominantly financed out of retained earnings. Bank borrowing to finance the share of capital investment not covered by internal funds is a small proportion of all outstanding debt. Investment deficit finance rose to near 10% of all private sector in 1974 only to fall precipitously after that year, turning into an increasingly larger surplus by the mid-1980s as profits recovered and investment plans were cutback.

The tendency in the average rate of profit to fall present in the Spanish economy after the early-1960s led to the stagnation of the mass of profits in the early 1970s and the decline in capital accumulation after 1975. Prior to the investment downturn, however, a sharp increase in bank credit filled the gap between investments plans and diminishing internal funds. The profit slump sapped the incentive to grow but business demand for credit expanded as a substitute for internal funds. Banks obliged because they recognized the need to avoid the impending collapse. They realized that a general breakdown of the system would seal their fate as well. Thus falling real output growth clashed with rising credit spending and the result, was growing inflation. Rising inflation coincided with falling real output and growing unemployment. The efforts on the part of banks to finance business deficit spending in excess of their real output growth based on profitability triggered inflation. Public deficit spending equally financed through credit borrowing blunted the decline in aggregate demand. Absent the recovery of profitability and investment growth, however, the expansion of government deficit finance caused the price inflation that came with the depression in real output to gain a new foothold at last.

As the gap between internal funds and business spending widened, the debt pile up reached unsustainable proportions. Businesses were forced to increase their share of retained profits and to curtail borrowing. The growth in business deficit spending of the 1970s was then replaced by public deficit finance in the 1980s. As business credit growth abated, government borrowing expanded. Government deficit spending, however, did not restore profitability, but instead added to the inflation pressures.

Ironically, for a study of the role of credit in the formation of business cycles it bears repeating once again that private business investment in plant and equipment was overwhelmingly financed out of retained earnings. The evolution of retained earnings is a crucial barometer of business capacity to borrow both short and long term. This rule applied even when a major slump unraveled the normal channels of financial reproduction. Following the reduced investment growth and improved profitability, credit borrowing declined, and by the mid-1980s, long-term deficit financing had turned into surplus budgets.

My intended course of action calls for a systematic evaluation of changes in retained earnings (undistributed profits) and external funds in relation to the time path of fixed capital expenditures. This requires showing that investment spending was closely correlated with internal funds.

## Internal funds versus external finance

The connection between (undistributed) profits and investment is the point from which I propose to explore the relationship between bank credit and growth cycles (Kiyotaki and West, 1996). I assume that normally firms use their internal funds, including undistributed profits plus depreciation, to cover a large share of their capital investments (Kopcke, and Howrey, 1994). This premise is also largely borne out by the empirical evidence available in Spain since the early 1960s. The financial health of non-financial firms may be deemed good when the *gap* between their investment spending and internal funds is relatively small. Generally, when firms enjoy a reputation of sound budgets, they will have access to external credit if a change in profit expectations warrants recourse to external sources of finance.

It is noteworthy that the share of retained earnings relative to aggregate profits net of depreciation funds rose cyclically from 1964 through 1998. The linear trend increase in the share of retained earnings out of profits net of business taxes was around 22% higher in 1998 than in 1964.

In line with these facts, Figure 9.6 shows that typically Spanish firms tailored their fixed investment spending to their available internal funds and that debt finance was but a small component of their capital spending. It is true albeit somewhat misleading to say that the overall average need for external financing of capital expenditures between 1964 and 1998 was minimal. I am referring here to the positive or negative *gap* between business capital expenditures and retained earnings. The available data for the years 1964-1998 shows that the ratio of external finance to business capital investment in the entire period under consideration amounted to somewhat less than 4%. This average, however, obscures the fact that a financial deficit of near 40% of investment spending in 1975 (the onset of depression), had turned into a surplus of 45% in 1985. Business budget deficits surfaced again only in the late 1980s for a total of three years. I believe that these surplus budgets of the early 1980s were necessary to service the debt accumulated in the 1970s. The sharp contraction in investment growth of the early 1980s was the result of accumulated debts in the previous decade, testifying to the iron discipline of debt servicing imposed by the banks. Indeed, excluding stock inventories, negative growth rates for gross fixed investment were recorded annually in the early 1980s. Investment growth fell, among other reasons, because funds were diverted to repay past debts and the wherewithal for accumulation shrunk.

## Measuring the capital stock

I am concerned here with the effect of technological change on the *evolution* of the capital-output ratio. Whether the ratio can be defined as the stock of fixed capital divided by gross or *net* output, either way its impact on long-term profitability is decisive. In the aggregate, the definition I used was the ratio of the business sector capital stock relative to the business sector GDP.

My concern with the long-term evolution of profitability centers on the *movement* of the capital-output ratio. Finding reliable measures of the capital stock and its changes was a crucial step in this quest. One available alternative to the estimates of the aggregate capital stock made by DEMO is the research conducted in the mid-1990s by Matilde Mas, Francisco Perez and Ezequiel Uriel for the BBV Foundation (connected to the BBV Bank) and available in diskettes. The DEMO data provided six aggregate categories for the capital stock, starting in 1954 and ending in 1988. The DEMO data offers the time series behind the official macro-model MOISEES, commissioned by the Ministry of the Economy and the Budget. They included value estimates in 1980 pesetas for the total (including residential) "capital" stock; the public (including residential) stock; the residential stock; the productive (private and public) capital (excluding residential) stock; the private productive (excluding residential) stock and the private capital (including residential) stock. While the BBV study presented the official time series for gross fixed investment beginning in 1954 (as DEMO does) including both private and public spending, its time series for the capital stock starts in 1964. The authors say that data for gross private fixed investment prior to 1964 is not reliable, but they fail to say why so. Thus, the results provided by the BBV study cover the period from 1964 to 1991 while those by DEMO cover the years 1954-1988.

Comparing the DEMO and the BBV data for the total capital stock (which includes residential as well as capital goods) it is clear that the general procedure used by both in their construction is similar. With regard to the total inputs, they both add annual investment flows to an initial stock, taking due account of its complex annual rate of depreciation, in order to arrive at the net annual accumulation.

A notable feature of the BBV study is that its data is highly disaggregated geographically. The major difference between the two studies of accumulation is the *level* of the initial stock and not its growth rate. Indeed, the growth rate of the total capital stock estimated in both research projects for the sample of years common to them is quite similar. Thus taking the first difference of the stock in both studies (after expressing both values in 1990 pesetas) reveals that the method of aggregation used by the BBV and DEMO researchers produces similar results: the annual flows are almost identical.

The estimated value for the total capital stock in 1954 presented by DEMO is lower than would be required to arrive at the 1964 level of the BBV study. Taking the rate of stock depreciation assumed by DEMO, the initial endowment necessary to arrive at the estimate for 1964 in the BBV study should be about twice the given value. The authors of the BBV study acknowledge that their initial stock evaluation was taken from the research on the wealth of the nation published in 1968 by Universidad de Deusto.

Since I am concerned with the evolution of profitability the crucial factor for my estimates of capital-output ratios is *not* the initial level of the capital stock as such but its growth path. While the BBV stock level is *higher* than DEMO's, the growth path is sufficiently close to blur any major methodological difference between the two.

Once we know the method of aggregation employed by DEMO and the BBV team, it is possible to extend the DEMO estimates through 1991 (to match the BBV sample range). Surprisingly, the BBV study completely avoids any reference to *Series macroeconomicas para el periodo 1954-1988: un intento de homogeneización* (Corrales, and Taguas, 1989). The BBV authors also avoid mentioning that this work was included in *La Economia Española, una perspectiva macroeconomica* (Molinas, Sebastian and Zabalza, 1991). The DEMO diskette included in this book contained the previously mentioned estimates for the six categories of the capital stock. I have no grounds, therefore, to accept the claim of unique and superior results made by the BBV team.

At any rate, in this book I have decided to avoid choosing between the DEMO and BBV estimates. Instead, I will use the capital stock data for the business sector offered in diskettes by the OECD Economic Outlook 66.

## Measuring profits

Since data on aggregate business profitability is not readily available, my procedure to eliminate it took as a point of departure the calculation of the annual flow of aggregate net profit-type income. The official wages time series refers to total payments made by businesses to their workers. Therefore, my relevant measure of profit-type income is the equivalent of what in Spanish conventional accounting is called "net business exploitation surplus", namely the residual after subtracting from the business GDP as given by the OECD Economic Outlook (on diskettes), wages and current stock depreciation. Net aggregate output is defined as the gross output, $Y^L$ produced in the business sector comprising both private and public enterprises, minus the depreciation of the capital stock. Aggregate profits will be defined as:

$$\Pi_t = Y^L_t - Dep_t - W_t$$

Computing the values for this equation required previous estimates for $Y^L_t$ the output of the business sector, as well as $Dep_t$ the depreciation of the capital stock. I have decided to use the OECD data for the business sector GDP because it is reliable and regularly updated. With regard to depreciation and the capital stock, I used the estimates under the heading of "private productive capital stock" provided by the data bank Demo (compiled in conjunction with the Ministry of the Economy macroeconomic model known as MOISEES) in my earlier book on the Spanish economy (Roman, 1997). I did so at the time because I assumed that they best represented the capital stock used in the business sector of the economy. My explicit goal then was to trace the evolution of profitability in the private sector of the economy. I now realize that the estimates presented by Demo for both private and public "productive" capital stock would have provided a better measure of capital accumulation and its effect on profitability, as both categories enter into the "business" sector employing wage-labor.

I also believe that there are no solid grounds to distinguish between private and public businesses that employ wage-labor. Both are subject to the law of profits governing the behavior of firms that produce goods and services for the market. I have chosen to include all such enterprises in the generic category of the "business sector" as a convenient device to unravel the dynamics of credit and profitability. In other words, my "business sector" will be the recipient of business credit. I will assume that the working-capital needs of businesses as a whole, without distinction of private and public firms determine the supply of short-run bank credit. Generally, credit flows to the public sector roughly covered government spending, including deficits.

In short, the difference between the supply of credit to the private sector and to the economy as a whole can be attributed to the changing fiscal policy of the public sector.

## The incremental profit rate and accumulation

I have assumed that the growth of profits produced by recent investments qualifies as the bellwether factor in shaping business future profit expectations. The simple rationale for this rule is that the vision of the future may be decidedly shaped by the current outcome of near past expenditures. Thus, planned investment growth will be strongly influenced by the evolution of profits relative to recent investments. Of course, the average profit rate plays a role in shaping investment decisions, but it does so precisely because changes in the average reflect the movement of the incremental profit-rate.

I define the incremental profit rate as the change in profits net of depreciation relative to investment with one-year lag. I take it that firms go into business in order to make the biggest possible profits. Expectations beget, if fulfilled, the necessary justification for past capital expenditures and lend confidence in the anticipation of future results for planned spending. Such prospects of (present value) future yields are strongly tainted by current profit levels derived from recent investments. The ratio of total profits flowing annually to the sum of fixed investments net of depreciation constituting the net stock of capital provides a measure of average profitability, the profit per unit of total capital advanced.

Expectations of future returns will be particularly sensitive to the evolution of profits related to past recent investments. Here is where the incremental profit rate comes into play. Its evolution is a harbinger for the movement of the average profit rate and a bellwether of future expectations driving investment growth. The movement of the investment growth path should then be a lagged function of the incremental profit rate.

Figure 9.1 plots the incremental real profit rate and the real investment growth path in the U.S. economy. I believe that Figure 9.1 showing my estimates for the U.S. economy and 9.2 for the Spanish data confirm that order of causation establishing the primacy of profitability relative to investment growth (not the other way around as Post-Keynesian would have it). In Spain the upward trend of the incremental profit rate started as the depression deepened, thus showing it to be one of the chief restorative functions of the slump, namely the reversal of the incremental profit rate trend. In the second half of the 1990s, the falling trend of the incremental profit rate on the other hand does not augur well for the future growth of accumulation. The fact that according to my calculations this measure of profitability declined in 1998, leads me to believe that investment growth (at least the plant and equipment component) will be falling in the near future, thus possibly leading the way for the first cyclical downturn since 1993.

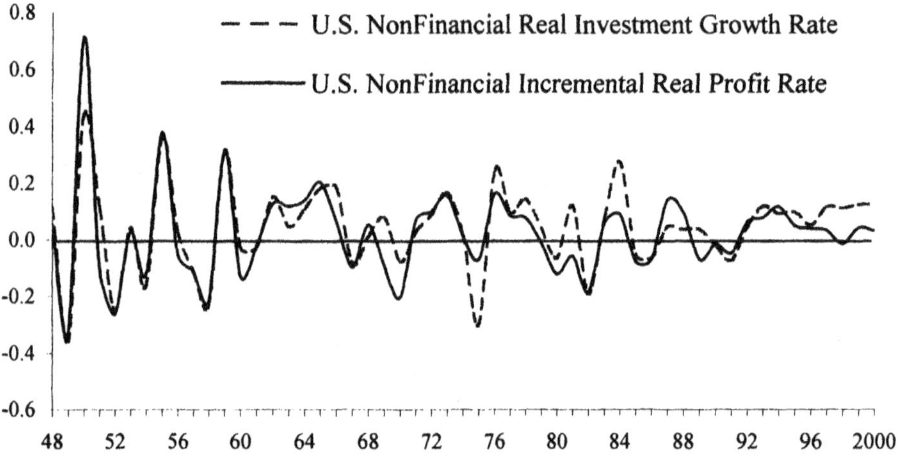


**Figure 9.1 Incremental profit rate and investment growth in the U.S.**

*Sources*: NIPA, Tables 1.16, 3, 7.1; Flow of Funds, F6 and F 101.

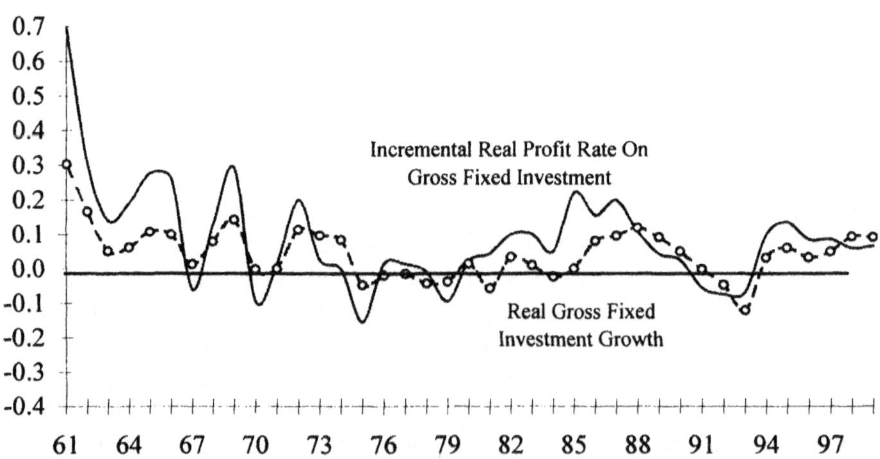


**Figure 9.2 Incremental profit rate and investment growth in Spain**

*Sources:* OECD Historical Statistics and Economic Outlook 66.

A falling incremental profit rate in Spain made it necessary to raise extended credit to finance on-going private investment plans for capital goods (negative numbers represent deficit spending and therefore debt expansion). Obviously, these plans were not immediately downsized, possibly because businesses misjudged the depth and breath of the economic slump.

I have defined the incremental profit rate as the addition to current total profits relative to the net increment of the capital stock caused by investment in the previous year:

$$\text{IcrPrf}_t = \frac{\Pi_t - \Pi_{t-1}}{I^f_{t-1}} = \frac{\Delta\Pi_t}{\Delta K_{t-1}}$$

And then the average profit rate will be the ratio of the gross annual profits flow to the sum of the net incremental changes registered by the capital stock from the base year to the present:

$$r_t = \frac{\Pi_t}{\sum_{t=1}^{t=n} \Delta K} = \frac{\Pi_t}{K_t}$$

We should expect that the movement of the incremental profit rate will anticipate that of the average and I believe that the empirical evidence confirms that assumption.

## Horizontalists versus profit constraints

I accept the fact that Post-Keynesian economists such as Basil Moore have successfully demonstrated how the supply of bank credit is driven by the financial needs of business firms and not by the policies pursued by the central bank (Moore, 1988, 1996). The central bank's main task is setting the interest rate. This is a fine correction to the monetarist belief that decisions taken by the central bank to increase or decrease the supply of money will automatically reach their intended goal.

An increase in bank reserves brought about through open market operations will not necessarily stimulate a higher demand for credit, even if interest rates have fallen. As Paul Davidson so eloquently put it, money enters the system as new debt, and firms do not necessarily seek additional debt without first raising their profit expectations.

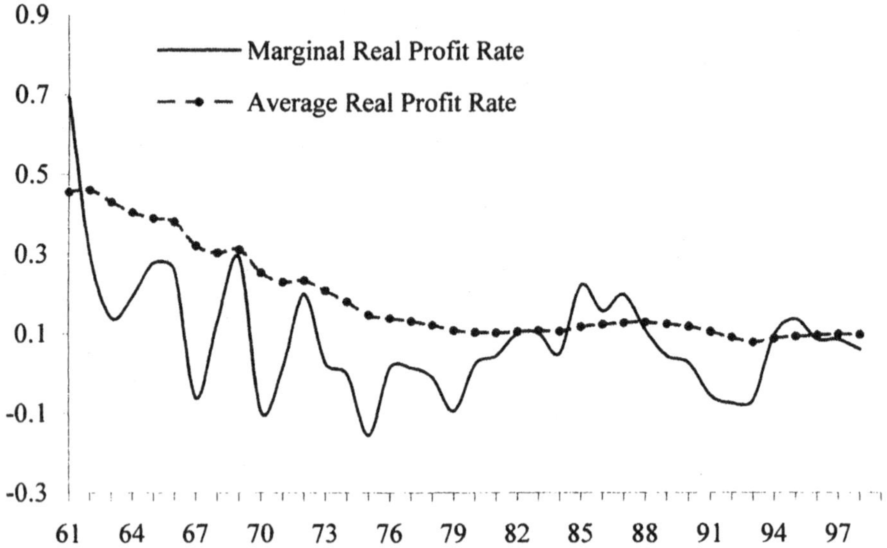


**Figure 9.3 Average and marginal profit rates in Spain**

*Sources*: OECD Historical Statistics and Economic Outlook 66.

On the other hand, it is my contention that the banks' assessments of the anticipated profitability of business enterprise weighs heavily in their decision to extend or curtail further lending. How this weight is evaluated depends on the strength of the expectations entertained by both sides regarding the future course of business profitability. Banks will find the means to attract reserves and supply additional credit as long as business expansion is justified by the expectation of growing internal funds.

I cannot assume, as Post-Keynesians "horizontalists" do, that the provision of bank credit was exclusively determined by the needs of industry without further qualification (Pollin, 1986). I will argue rather that the evolution of business profitability in Spain and the growth of business internal funds set the boundaries for the acquisition of debt liabilities by business firms. Such an assumption implies that before undertaking new borrowing firms will take into account their prospective ability to service debt, while still remaining solvent. Before granting new loans, banks will be expected to exhibit similar concerns as they evaluate their clients' ability to pay. To put it bluntly, I cannot accept the notion that the bank credit supply is independent of the perceived solvency and liquidity of borrowers.

The engine of capital accumulation runs on profits. Credit is the lubricant that allows for smooth, steady operations when the machine is powered. This oil is useful only as long as capitalist firms are running and connected to a live power source, the profits of enterprise. Business firms cannot go on borrowing beyond some limit set by the degree of confidence with which banks view the potential for the growth of internal funds. This generalization will hold true, however, only in the healthy phase of capital accumulation, that is, when internal funds are growing as fast as fixed capital spending. In times of financial hardship, banks will shift their orientation from short-term evaluation of their clients' prospective solvency to assisting their best customers with emergency finance. Avoiding the massive risk of general default appears to override the micro principles of sound finance.

The sum of retained earnings, depreciation and external finance (the *gap* between business capital expenditures and retained earnings) provided the total funding for gross fixed investment. The single major difference between the finance sources for business capital expenditures and gross fixed investment was the addition of depreciation funds to the latter.

Another complementary factor contributing to the contraction in the rate of accumulation (investment as a share of the business sector GDP) was the sharp decline in industrial capacity utilization that took place after the first-half of the 1970s. From a high of .89 in 1973, industrial capacity utilization dipped to .79 in 1980 and finally sunk to .70 in 1993. Why then should new capacity be added when the existing stock is underutilized?

## Profitability and credit-worthiness

In fact, both, in the case of the U.S. and that of Spain, there is overwhelming evidence that normally business firms do finance their fixed investment plans preponderantly out of their own retained earnings. This is why I believe that in the final analysis the evolution of profitability sets the trend around which fixed investment plans are built (Knox, 1952, pp. 269-297).

My empirical findings indeed lend support to the idea that the evolution of profitability established the center of gravity for the borrowing capacity of growing firms. Profitable firms elicit confidence from creditors. On the other hand, profitable firms are more prone to finance their investment spending out of their own internal funds. Hence, while they may have better access to credit, they may need it less than distressed firms. This is the basis for my argument that credit borrowing will cycle around the (nonlinear) profitability trend, giving rise to GDP growth cycles of a shorter time span.

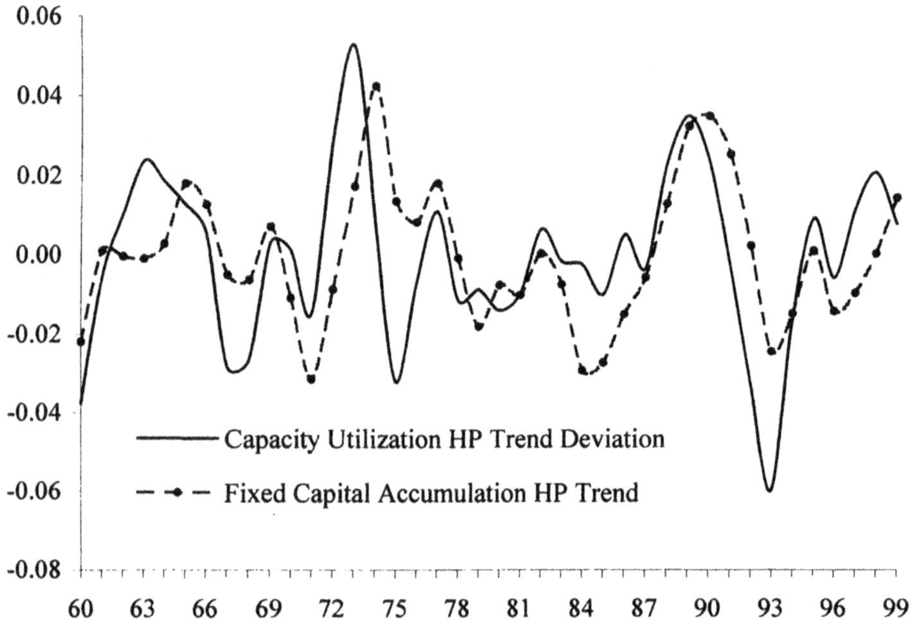


**Figure 9.4 Fixed investment and capacity utilization (Hodrick-Prescott) trend deviations in Spain**

*Sources:* Series 321100, 972100T and Author's calculations.

My perspective departs from Keynesian economics because I reject the notion that aggregate demand growth determines real output growth. This view will apply to the bank credit supply as well. This position does not imply accepting the opposite principle, namely that the bank credit supply necessarily creates its own market demand.

Such a practice was breached once the depression brought the question of financial distress to the doorsteps of both industry and the banks. As internal funds diminished in the late 1970s, the banks faced the dilemma of backing-up insolvent firms or standing by as their traditional clients went bankrupt and the ground slipped from under their feet. This dilemma was not confined only to Spanish banks and creditors. Japanese banks faced a similar quandary in the early 1990s. In a meticulous study of Japanese practices, J. Peck and E. S. Rosengren observed that in Japan:

> close lending relationships made it difficult for Japanese banks to reduce credit availability to their domestic customers. Even though Japan fell into a prolonged

recession in the early 1990s, domestic loan growth at Japanese banks continued throughout the period (Peck and Rosengren, 1999, p. 30).

Peck and Rosengren attribute the special role of banks as primary lenders to the existence of imperfect information in capital markets, certainly a feature characteristic of the Spanish economy. Indeed, in the early phase of the depression debacle starting in the early 1970s, the available data reveals the unprecedented growth of the financial *gap* between investment spending and internal funds. Historically the relationship between banks and their business clients in Spain underwent a sharp change when the system as a whole fell into a slump. In the second half of the 1980s, on the other hand, the share of retained earnings out of profits rose markedly presumably to redress the previous years of excessive dependency on bank finance.

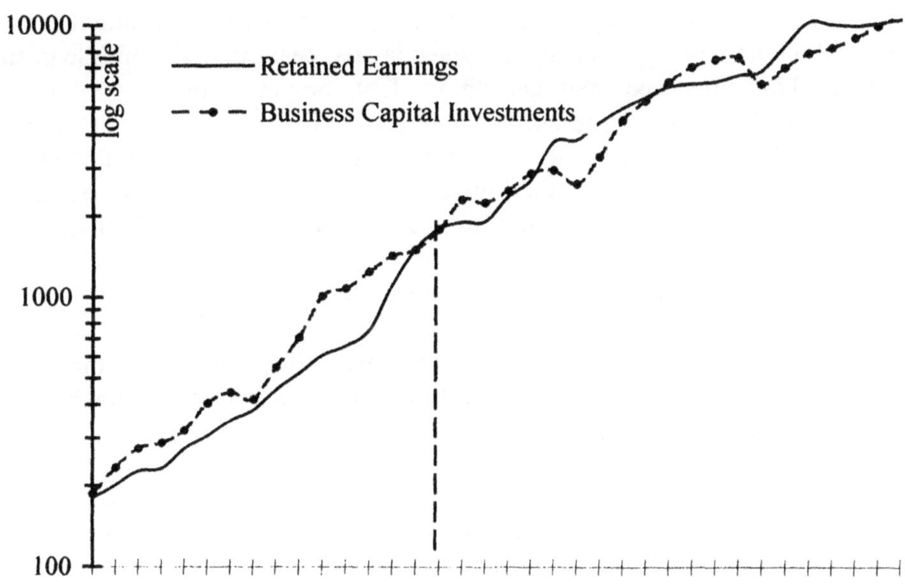


**Figure 9.5 Retained earnings and business capital investment**

*Source:* BBVA Annual Report 2000.

From 1964 through 1998, retained earnings, nonetheless, on average covered near 95% of capital expenditures for plant and equipment. The trend in the ratio retained earnings-business capital investment rose during this period so that in the mid-1990s, particularly after 1993, retained earnings exceeded business capital expenditures by a substantial amount.

The cyclical movement in these ratios crucially hinged on the evolution of internal funds, retained earnings to be precise, falling lower (deficit finance) or rising higher (surplus finance) than capital expenditures. I would argue that a significant switch in finance regimes took place in the early 1980s as the depression touched bottom. As Figure 9.5 reveals, investment plans after 1964 included a substantial, and after 1971 growing share of external finance.

## Distressed borrowing

As the depression of the 1970s deepened, drastically lowering profits (net of interest) without inducing the corresponding cutbacks in investment plans, necessitous borrowing reached its highest levels, peaking in the middle of the decade. This unprecedented growth in debt, however, brought with it a forceful reallocation of internal funds. First, a higher proportion of internal funds, including profits and depreciation allowances, were retained for business use. Secondly, after the initial shock, investment plans were sharply reduced in order to set aside the money necessary to repay the high debt accumulated in the early 1970s. Thus, we can conclude that the effects of the slump were cushioned in the earlier years, but the length and depth of the depression were augmented by the need to reserve surplus funds to settle acquired liabilities. In addition, after the early 1980s, including the boom years of the decade's second half, Spanish firms remained much more financially self-reliant than they ever were.

At critical times (i.e. the onset of depression) banks will overlook the insolvency of their best clients hoping that the slump be short-lived. M. Fry quotes Manuel Hinds' seminal study (Hinds, 1988) on why distress borrowing although not a characteristic form of bank lending may nonetheless happen:

> Faced with immediate bankruptcy, both bankers and their debtors give priority to their survival over other, longer-term objectives, including profitability. Debtors borrow at interest rates higher than the long-term profitability of their real assets, even if they have no clear idea of how they are going to repay their debts. Bankers refinance bad debtors because failing to do so would force them to increase their write-offs. Furthermore, bankers lend almost exclusively to bad debtors because, to remain liquid, they raise deposit interest rates to levels that the more solvent borrowers are not willing to pay (Fry, 1995, p. 383).

This is exactly what happened in the Spanish economy in the first half of the 1970s. After having fallen deep into negative numbers throughout the 1960s, real interest rates bounced back to lofty heights, reaching a positive value in the new decade and rising above 5% by the mid-970s. They were no doubt propelled by the situation described by Hinds, which in the Spanish case meant falling into a prolonged depression that brought havoc to the system as a whole.

As real output growth rose and full employment was approached in the 1960s, (with the help of massive emigration) real interest rates fell precipitously and inflation was tamed. Indeed, it was a decade of miraculous expansion. The onset of depression in the early 1970s however undermined the foundations for growth, as gross profits stagnated and pure (enterprise) profits plummeted. Real output growth in response to the stagnation of profits collapsed. The profits slump forced banks to overlook the insolvency of their clients (at least in the short-run), but real interest rates shot-up, as would be expected in such a case. In the mid-1970s, for instance, expenditures on plant and equipment exceeded retained earnings by about 45%. This was an unprecedented situation caused by the collapse of profits and the deepening depression. Business retained earnings stagnated in 1973, one year before planned investment growth declined.

The sharp increase in business long-term borrowing that took place in the first half of the 1970s however, was followed by an equally large reduction in deficit spending, as business brought its capital investment into line with retained earnings. Private investment in plant and equipment is a component of the larger gross fixed investment. Gross fixed investment includes residential construction, and financing comes largely out of retained earnings plus depreciation funds. The finance sources for gross fixed investment after 1964 include RE, plus 90% of depreciation funds plus the bank credit extended to fill the gap between planned private investment in plant and equipment and RE. Whereas borrowing to fill in the gap between planned investment in plant and equipment rose to 45% of fixed gross investment spending in the mid-1970s, budget deficits turned into surpluses by the mid-1980s. In 1985, internal funds exceeded fixed gross investment by over 40%.

## Empirical strength of Goodwin's growth cycles in the Spanish economy

I will begin now to deploy the empirical support found in the Spanish case for the main propositions of the Goodwin model of growth cycles, based on the effect of rising employment on the share of wages (hence the profits share) and its impact on accumulation.

Considering the empirical support for Goodwin's model provided by the Spanish economy, several of its central assumptions need modification. Chief among them is the stability of the capital-output ratio. Goodwin assumptions include the proviso that notwithstanding intensive capital deepening and steady technical progress, accumulation will take place with a constant capital-output ratio. It may be remembered that this is the ratio of capital to potential output (capacity). Indeed Goodwin's implicit assumption is that actual output is always equal to capacity output and so it follows that in his model capacity utilization remains constant despite persistent fluctuations in employment and output. Secondly, the wage share in output responded to the cyclical movement of the employment share as the model predicted, but an additional specification was required. This is so because the category "employed" labor force includes both wageworkers and self-employed people. My employment share refers to the ratio of wage workers employed relative to the total labor force. My special Phillips function specifies the relationship between this employment share for wageworkers and the growth of real wage rates. The empirical evidence for this specification is much stronger than for the employed labor as a whole.

Furthermore, the whole question of effective demand is bypassed. In its absence, one must conclude that the completion of the employment and wage cycles around their normal trend should take much longer than the typical span of business fluctuations. This hypothesis is in fact confirmed by the Spanish data.

If we allow the capital-output ratio in Goodwin's model, $b_l$ to rise, simulation of the outcome shows that both the employment and wage shares will implode. Goodwin's model was clearly not intended to reflect the transition to depression and its effects on employment and wages. The capital-output ratio in Spain more than doubled from 1964 to 1984 but the shares of employment and wages in Spain did not fall to zero as a result because its growth was interrupted in 1984. This is because the growth of the capital-output ratio was interrupted in 1984. As Figures 6.4 and 6.5 showed one of the chief effects of falling profitability in the 1970s was to lower the rate of accumulation. The introduction of technical change slowed down after the mid 1980s, and a two-year trend reversal of the capital-output ratio occurred in the late 1880s. In line with the slowdown in technical renewal, by the end of the 1970s the growth rate of real output had reached its lowest level since 1959. As a reflection of the lapse in technical change and the contraction of investment, the growth of labor productivity, linked to mechanization embodying technical change, registered its biggest decline.

With these caveats in mind the interpretation of Figure 9.6 is straightforward. There were two complete growth cycles in Spain from 1970 to

1998. The cycles were not symmetrical and reflected parameter changes, most prominently the higher upward trend of the capital-output ratio in the period 1970-1981. The first was longer and more turbulent than the second.

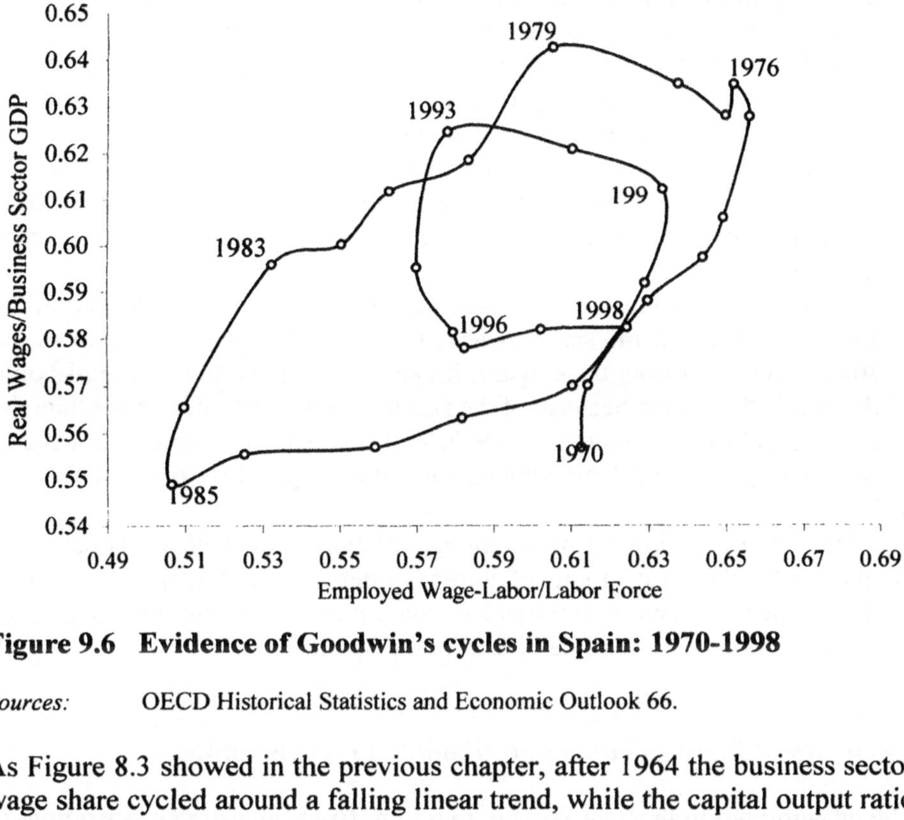


**Figure 9.6 Evidence of Goodwin's cycles in Spain: 1970-1998**

*Sources:* OECD Historical Statistics and Economic Outlook 66.

As Figure 8.3 showed in the previous chapter, after 1964 the business sector wage share cycled around a falling linear trend, while the capital output ratio trend in the same period nearly tripled, causing a significant fall in the profitability trend. I believe that this evidence supports the conclusion derived in that chapter that the cyclical behavior of the wage share modulated the trend in profitability but its overall trend was set by the secular rise in the capital-output ratio. The apparent implosion of both employment and wage shares from 1976 through 1985 was the result of rising capital-output ratios and falling profitability. Recovery from the full-fledged depression had to wait for the second-half of the 1980s. The growth in employment that ensued, however, laid the grounds for a rise in the share of wages in the business sector GDP and through its negative impact on the profits share provoked the sharp slump of 1993. The recession in turn eroded the share of wages and opened the way for the upturn in activity.

## Evaluating Minsky's view of rising interest rates and downturns

The empirical evidence linking the movement of real interest rates to the turning points of business cycles is not entirely conclusive. In Spain, profitability net of interest fell steadily in the 1970s while inflation was on the rise and real interest rates plummeted into negative numbers.

On the other hand, in the early 1980s the rise in real interest rates may have prolonged the decline in pure profitability while the downward turn in real interest rates after 1983 may have eased the profitability surge. It is not clear, however, why the collapse of profitability at the end of that decade could be attributed to an unexpected spike in real interest rates. Other factors such as the rise in capital-output ratios and the transitional dip of the profits share were at work.

The fact of the matter is that profitability gross of interest peaked at the end of the 1980s and the same underlying forces that pulled it down in the 1970s exerted their drag once again. It cannot be argued that the mini-boom of the late 1980s ended because of the rise in real interest rates rather than the fall in profitability. In fact, after 1987, real interest rates trended down and after one single reversal maintained their downward drift through the late 1990s.

After 1980, the impact of declining inflation on real business debt was weakened by the rising trend of internal funds. Thus, Minsky's view that deflation carried with it unintended consequences raising the danger of financial defaults could not be upheld in the Spanish case.

## Summary of findings linking profitability to accumulation

Under normal circumstances, the trend in fixed investment spending is closely tied-up with the evolution of profitability, *via* the incremental profit rate, and more specifically with the share of retained earnings in gross profits. In a period of normal growth, the borrowing capacity for non-financial business will depend on their ability to produce and realize adequate profits. Recent findings on the determinants of investment add support to the link between profitability and accumulation (Gilchrist and Himmelberg, 1999), even if my measuring yardstick is different (i.e. their marginal product of capital versus my incremental profit rate).

In a critique of Gilchrist and Himmelberg's paper, Prof. David Gross expressed doubts that financial-market imperfections were the cause behind the minor role played by external finance in investment decisions, as the authors had argued.

**Figure 9.7 Real long-term interest rates and pure profitability**

*Sources:* L. Klein Institute, TLSP; Historical Statistics and Economic Outlook 66.

While acknowledging that "Unfortunately, the neoclassical model does not do a very good job in describing the empirical investment behavior of individual firms", Prof. Gordon subscribed to the authors' contention that:

> Improvements in economic fundamentals, such as the marginal product of capital (MPK), directly increase investment through the standard neoclassical channel while at the same time improving the firm's financial position. Hence even if financial markets are perfect, financial variables will be correlated with investment (Gross and Rotemberg, 1999, p. 262).

The use of external finance should not cloud the strength of profitability in setting the central tendency of accumulation. The historical record shows that periods of business deficit spending (positive excess demand) to finance a high rate of investment growth in Spain were followed by years in which such growth was curtailed (negative excess demand) in order to build-up a reserve of internal funds and so preserve the credit-worthiness required by creditors. Falling profits in the early 1970s triggered an explosion of debt, but its amplitude was limited to a few years. The prospects of wholesale ruin facing a bankrupt industrial sector forced banks to overlook the lack in credit-worthiness of their best clients and so indulge their necessitous borrowing. This atypical behavior could not be maintained beyond the depression phase. Following this period of debt-accumulation, firms struggling to survive with a heavy burden of debt were forced to reduce their fixed investment spending and instead build-up their liquid reserves. Even after the incremental profit rate bounced back up, credit borrowing to finance capital accumulation declined markedly, as firms sought to restore their solvency with a view to keep open their credit lines. Pressures to restore practices of sound finance were inevitable once business activity recovered from the slump.

# 10 A Classical Growth and Cycles Model

In order to provide the strongest possible conceptual support for my empirical investigation of excess demand fluctuations in Spain, I will begin this final chapter with a review of the foundations of Shaikh's classical growth and cycles models. Their basic structure derives from the fact that dynamical analysis deals with the deviations of growing variables from their trend. As a general approach, eschewing the notion of perfect knowledge, the growth of aggregate demand decisions need not match the growth in aggregate supply outcomes based on uncertain profit expectations. The emerging disparities, however, will not lead to explosive motions but instead give rise to further adjustments at both ends of the market system, sellers and buyers.

### The fast cycle: constant profit margins

In Shaikh's models excess demand, (±) E, is defined as the difference between aggregate demand, AD, and aggregate supply, AS. Within the Keynes-Kalecki tradition, excess demand is the difference between investment and savings: $E = AD - AS = I - S$. Therefore assuming that all savings comes out of profits net of interest, $\Pi$ (interest payments must be counted as business costs), aggregate savings, $S = s\Pi$. Aggregate investment, I, includes spending on circulating capital, $I_c$ inventory adjustments, $I_v$ and fixed capital, $I_f$. Hence excess demand will be written as:

$$E = I - S = I_c + I_v + I_f - s\Pi$$

If excess demand is zero, $E = 0$, the actual change in the inventory of finished goods will be identical to the desired adjustment. On the other hand, when $E \neq 0$, that is $AD \neq AS$, the change in inventories will differ from the desired amount. Changing inventories provide immediate signals of the divergence between aggregate demand and supply. In response to it firms will adjust their supply plans up or down hoping to realign their stockpiling with desired levels. Any change in inventories relative to the desired level will elicit a counter growth in circulating capital, $I_c$. Investment growth in circulating capital, $I_c$ will lead to a rise in the production scale and finally to a growing output. The desired change in supply, Q' inevitably will require a previous change in spending for labor and materials inputs.

On the other hand, investment in fixed capital, $I_f$ leads to the growth of the fixed capital stock $K_f'$, and so the growth of capacity output will be given by $N' = qK_f' = qI_f$.

A few definitions are necessary: capacity utilization is defined as $u = \frac{Q}{N}$ and excess capacity utilization, $\pm x = \frac{(Q-N)}{N}$. The schedule for average variable costs, k, associated with spending in circulating capital is given by $k = \frac{C}{Q}$; Consequently changes in output will result from changes in circulating capital investment, $Q' = \left(\frac{1}{k}\right)C' = \left(\frac{1}{k}\right)I_C$. Finally the (produced) profit margin on circulating capital, $m = \frac{\Pi}{C}$ and therefore:

$$\Pi' = mC' = m\,I_C \tag{10.1}$$

Now since $\Pi \equiv Q - C$, the profit margin is given by $m = \frac{1-k}{k}$. Shaikh generally assumes, albeit provisionally, both ratios, the unit costs, k, and the profit margin, m, are constant. In the new version of the model, however, the analysis adopts a more realistic view and the fluctuations in profit margins and unit costs will drive the dynamics that produces a limit cycle in excess demand space.

The next stage in this review consists in tracing the feedback loops between the evolution of excess demand and its effect on profits and the rate of accumulation in circulating capital. In the short-run, accumulation in fixed capital is assumed to be constant.

## Impact of excess demand on profits and accumulation

In the short-run it is reasonable to assume both categories $I_f$ and $I_v$ as constants, that is the change in desired inventories, $I_v = 0$, actual inventories match the desired level. The key is that positive or negative excess demand,

E will impact on produced profits, $\Pi$ by increasing or reducing realized profits, R$\Pi$. Only when excess demand = 0 will excess profits = 0 and realized profits = normally produced profits. It follows from this that changes in output, Q', are a function of excess demand, that is Q' = F(E). We saw that $Q' = \left(\frac{1}{k}\right)C' = \left(\frac{1}{k}\right)I_c$ and therefore $I_c = f(E)$.

Shaikh assumes that accumulation in circulating capital is a linear function of excess demand, so that $I_c = hE$ $(0 < h < 1)$ and $E = \frac{I_c}{h}$. In addition, the desired level of inventories, $I_v$ is assumed to be a linear function of the change in circulating capital, C', that is $I_v = vC' = vI_c$. Given these specifications, the next step requires writing the equation for excess demand as, $E = \frac{I_c}{h} = I_c + I_f - s\Pi$ and then, since $I_c = \frac{\Pi'}{m}$, the expression becomes $\frac{\Pi'}{mh} = \frac{\Pi'}{m} + I_f - s\Pi$. Finally the change in profits will be:

$$\Pi' = \left[\frac{smh}{1-h}\right]\left[\frac{I_f}{s} - \Pi\right]$$

Now because the constants s, m, and h have positive values, while h<1, the expression $\left[\frac{smh}{1-h}\right]$ will have a positive sign. Moreover the ratio $\left[\frac{I_f}{s}\right]$ is a constant, and therefore the driving force of the dynamical adjustments must be located elsewhere. Indeed, the change in produced profits, $\Pi'$ will be negative when $\Pi$ is larger than $\left[\frac{I_f}{s}\right]$ so that produced profits will decline, and vice versa when $\Pi$ is smaller than $\left[\frac{I_f}{s}\right]$.

## The dynamical approach

The next stage in the development of Shaikh's model requires transforming the conceptual structure into a real dynamic system, with adjustments taking place not in levels but in ratios of variables growing at differing rates. To this end all variables in the previous system need be measured relative to the level of produced profits, Π, that is, $e \equiv \frac{E}{\Pi}; a_c \equiv \frac{I_c}{\Pi}; a_v \equiv \frac{I_v}{\Pi}; a_f \equiv \frac{I_f}{\Pi}$; and after formulating this new dynamic approach, the equation for excess demand will be expressed in ratios:

$$e = a_c + a_v + a_f - s = a_c(1+v) + a_f - s \qquad (10.2)$$

Further development is now required: the previous function for a change in profits $\Pi' = mI_c$ should be written as $\frac{\Pi'}{\Pi} = m\frac{I_c}{\Pi} = ma_c$.

Changes in the rate of accumulation of circulating capital, $a_c$, are assumed to be a function of the excess profit margin, μ, that is, $a_c' = f\mu$, or more precisely, $a_c' = h\mu$ $(h > 0)$. But as previously noted $a_f$ represents a slow-moving ratio that for all practical reasons can be taken to be constant in the short-run. The same consideration applies to the propensity to save out of profits, s.

Thus, the change in the ratio of excess demand to profits will be, $e' = a_c'(1+v)$. Since $a_c' = h\mu$, we can go on to write the change in excess demand relative to profits, $e' = h\mu(1+v)$. If we call $h(1+v)=H$, we have $e' = H\mu$. Despite the fluctuations in excess demand, the mark-up, the ratio of prices to costs, is assumed constant. Then it follows that excess profit, μ, defined as E/C (excess demand relative to investment in circulating capital) should be proportional to our excess demand, because $\mu = \frac{E}{C} = \left(\frac{E}{\Pi}\right)\left(\frac{\Pi}{C}\right) = em$. The time change, finally, of the ratio excess demand to profits:

$$e' = Hme \qquad (10.3)$$

This is a first order differential equation establishing a short-run positive feedback between relative excess demand, e, and its rate of change e', that is, as relative excess demand becomes positive its rate of change becomes also positive.

In its first version as presented in Chapter 2, the change in the rate of accumulation was assumed to be a function of the excess profit margin, $ac' = h\mu$. The rise in excess demand, however, was contingent on the growth of business debt, acquired to finance the attendant deficit spending, and so business liquidity was temporarily impaired. The restoration of business liquidity required setting aside funds for repayment of debts. But doing so would therefore impose decreases in investment spending relative to profits, thus leading to a reversal of excess demand signs. In the short-run accumulation will converge with its balance trend, where excess demand = 0, and its growth rate will be constant as given by the profitability parameters. The balanced path growing at a constant rate follows from the assumption of a fixed profit margin. When random shocks are allowed, however, the system's growth turns into a stochastically sustained cycles around its critical path.

## Wesley Mitchell: changing profit margins

Changing the assumption of constant profit margins takes into account that once sales exceed the produced output, realized profits will be larger than produced profits. If in the course of a business upturn output prices rise faster than input costs, the profit margin will increase. Changes in the profit margin will crucially impact on the rate of accumulation and normally produce an endogenous cycle.

Wesley Mitchell's work pioneered in the meticulous investigation of the changes in the structural relations between input and output prices that produce endogenous business cycles. The guiding thread in Mitchell's stage analysis was that the various phases of the cycle are linked to each other by internal developments (Mitchell, 1951, 1963). Each phase in the evolution of business activity undergoes changes that prevent its continuation along the same path and create the basis for a reversal. For Mitchell the transformation of prosperity into a "crisis" was ultimately due to the deterioration in profit margins that is intrinsic to the cyclical growth of business activity.

I believe that Mitchell's work best describes the medium-term dynamics of fixed capital investment cycles. His use of the term *depression* and *crisis* should serve as a clue to the dimensions of the phenomena under investigation. These are no transient blips in the growth path of output. The depth and amplitude of Mitchell's *crises* qualify as exhibits in the showcase of Schumpeter's and Marx's slumps. They are clearly not examples of inventory adjustments.

While it is perfectly true that Mitchell excelled in his empirical investigation of medium-term business cycles, there is no question in my mind that he aimed at the construction of a unified theory of cycles. His goal would be achieved when:

> After tracing this process of cumulative change by which prosperity breeds crisis, crisis evolves into depression, and depression paves the way for a return

> of prosperity, the present theory of business cycles has reached its appointed end (Mitchell, 1963, p. 147).

In order to unravel the changes that bring about the downturn, Mitchell separates those responsible for halting the expansion from the catalysts that precipitate the contraction. He then identifies two distinct phases in the cyclical upturn. The early one results from a revival in business activity leading to higher rates of capacity utilization and falling real unit costs. It follows from this that sales and profits will rise.

As the boom gains momentum, however, input prices start rising faster than product prices, in other words firms experience "an increase in the cost of doing business-an increase that threatens to diminish profits" (Mitchell, 1963, p. 52). The rise in unit costs is not only or primarily confined to wages. As Mitchell points out materials costs are often twice as large as wages, and the materials bill frequently amounts to two-thirds of the total capital outlays. Because in the early stage of the expansion new firms enter business, the aggregate demand for materials, labor, equipment and finance will increase and their cost-prices will be bid up.

Taking into account that the input prices paid by one set of firms are the output prices of another, we face a quandary. Why is it that higher costs cannot be passed on as higher prices beyond a certain stage of the boom, why is it that a profit squeeze inevitably occurs? Mitchell's query takes this form:

> What prevents business enterprises from maintaining a profitable adjustment between the advance in two sets of prices, those which constitute costs and those which constitute returns? (Mitchell, 1963, p. 54).

With regard to labor Mitchell found that while the wage rate rises noticeably as the expansion proceeds, its average productivity declines. In the early stage, marginal firms bring into line their old productive assets (induced by the rising tide of prices and profits) while new firms add their capacity. The euphoria encourages an expansion of productive capacity that proves unsustainable as the boom reaches maturity. For as long as the expansion of industrial activity gives rise to an even larger capacity growth, the product growth rate will exceed that of prices. As far as capacity is concerned:

> The difficulty arises whenever the increase in the capacity of certain kinds of mines and factories...in certain districts proceeds fast enough to keep selling prices from rising as rapidly as costs (Mitchell, 1963, p. 58).

The real side of Mitchell's cycles is primarily linked to the dynamics of fixed capital accumulation. Initially investment in circulating capital, including labor and materials, increases the rate of capacity utilization. At some point, however, higher capacity utilization will call for a rise in fixed capital investment. Finance cycles, moreover, are an integral part of the complex dynamics. In the early phase of the upturn, as profits rise, the banks accommodate the growing need for credit. Profit growth encourages credit growth and a "pyramid of credits" emerges. Firms are willing to push to an "extreme limit" their borrowing capacity (Mitchell, 1963, p. 65). The debt build-up proceeds unabashedly to the brink, even though interest rates have been rising. The crisis matures in two stages. First, the expansion is halted by the increasing costs of doing business and the profits squeeze caused by excess capacity. Next, the forward motion is reversed when the accumulation of debt pushes the interest rates so high that business solvency dwindles and further borrowing is not allowed.

## Shaikh's formalization of Mitchell's observations

As previously indicated, excess demand, E, is the difference between real aggregate demand, D, and output, Q. Realized aggregate profits, $\Pi R$, is the difference between real aggregate sales and total costs, that is $D - pC$. C represents total inputs and p relative input costs, that is, inputs prices relative to output's. Relative input costs are *normal*, $p_n$ when excess demand, $E = 0$ and then produced profits, $\Pi \equiv Q - p_n C$.

The significance of this consideration is that positive excess demand could increase realized profits due to the expansion of sales above produced output, but the actual outcome depends on its impact on relative input prices and the profit margin. The idea that changing profit margins will have an impact on realized profits can be expressed as follows:

$$\Pi R = (D\text{-}Q) + (Q\text{-}p_nC) + (p_n\text{-}p)C = \Pi R = E + \Pi + (p_n - p)C$$

By definition the excess profit margin, $\mu$, involves the normal margin, m plus the difference between the normal and the actual relative input prices:

$$\mu \equiv \left(\frac{\Pi R - \Pi}{C}\right) = \left(\frac{E}{\Pi}\right)\left(\frac{\Pi}{C}\right) + (p_n - p) = em + (p_n - p)$$

Therefore from 10.3 the growth rate in the rate of accumulation in circulating capital, $a_c' = f(\mu) = h\mu = hme + h(p_n - p)$.

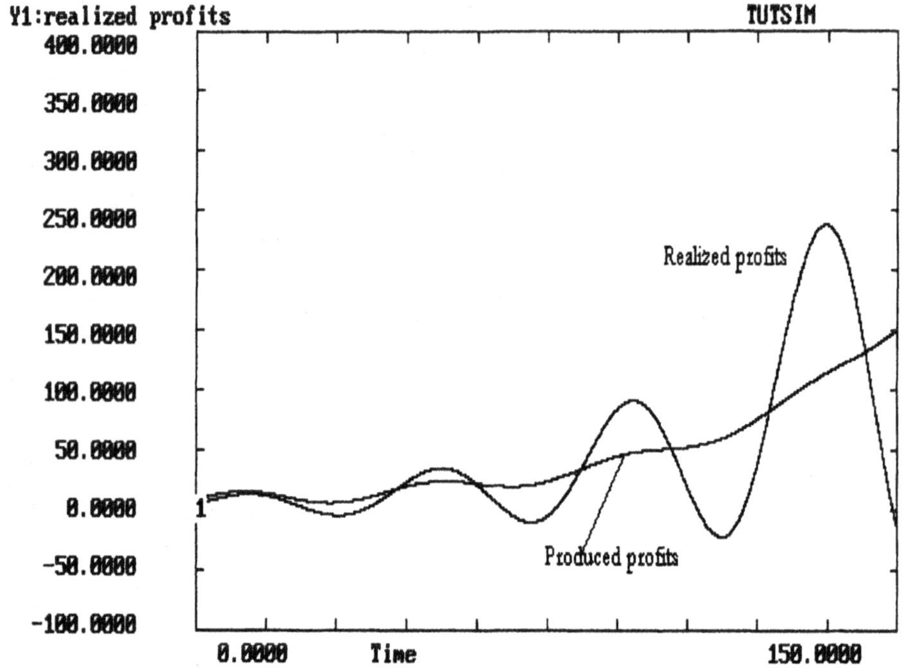


**Figure 10.1 Produced and realized profits: Shaikh's model**

### Relative costs and stylized cycles

As Figure 10.2 illustrates, the different phases of the cycle follow one another as relative excess demand, e, and its rate of change, e', rise and fall. As the boom phase moves from point A to B, relative input (to output) prices are falling, $p' < 0$ and while relative excess demand is negative, its growth rate, $e' > 0$. At point B excess demand = 0, which means that aggregate demand equals supply and $p' = 0$ because both input and output prices are rising at the same rate. Between the points identified as B and C, excess demand is positive but output prices, while still rising, are beginning to decelerate, hence profit margins are growing progressively smaller. After reaching the peak at point C, excess demand begins to fall because input costs are rising faster than prices and profit margins are falling.

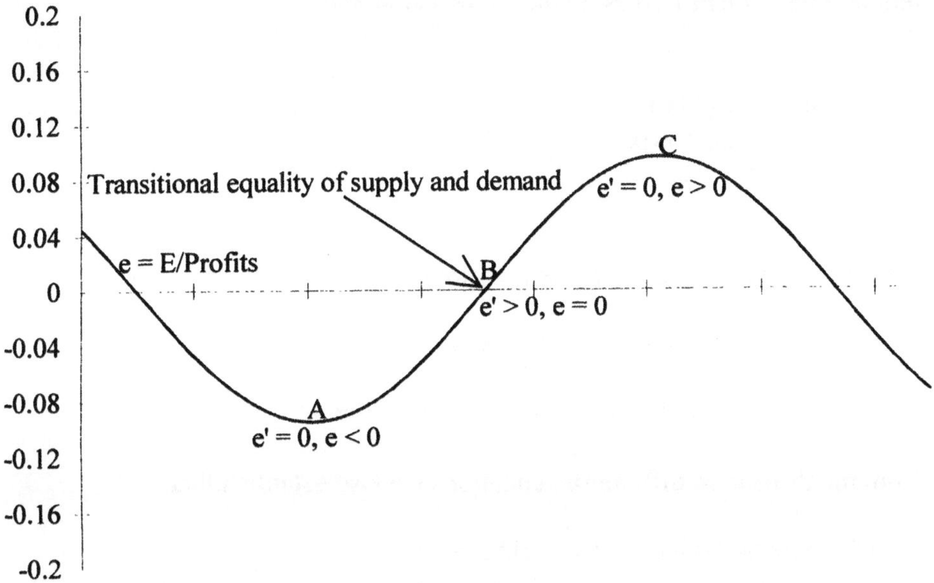


**Figure 10.2 Properties of the stylized cycle in excess demand**

In light of this evolutionary pattern Shaikh proposed a relative cost reaction function reflecting the different phases of both relative excess demand and its rate of change:

$$p' = f(e, e') \quad \left\{ \begin{array}{l} p' < 0 \text{ when } e < 0,\ e' > 0 \\ p' = 0 \text{ when } e = 0,\ e' > 0 \\ p' > 0 \text{ when } e > 0,\ e' = 0 \end{array} \right.$$

More specifically Shaikh selected the function:

$$p' = ae + b(e)\,e' \tag{10.4}$$

Where $b(e) = be^2$ stands for a good representation of the model's conceptual structure. In this function the coefficient b(e) gets larger depending on the size of relative excess demand e. Then the significance of its rate of change, e' will depend on the level of e, that is, when e is small the impact of e' will be also small, but when e is large the impact of e' will be correspondingly strong.

We now have three differential equations as the core of the dynamical version I have identified as Shaikh's second model:

$$\begin{cases} e' = a_c'(1+v) \\ a_c' = hme + h(p_n - p) \\ p' = ae + (be^2)e' \end{cases}$$

Substituting we can derive the expressions:

$$e' = h(1+v)me + h(1+v)p_n - h(1+v)p$$

$$p' = ae + h(1+v)mbe^3 + h(1+v)p_nbe^2 - h(1+v)pbe^2$$

From the three core differential equations we also establish that:

$$a_c'' = hme' - hp' = hme' - hae - (hbe^2)e'$$

$$e'' = a_c''(1+v)$$

Since $h(1+v) \equiv H$ and $e'' = H\mu' = H(me' - p') = Hme' - Hae - H(be^2)e'$ we arrive at the final form of the differential equation that captures the set of relationships previously established:

$$e'' + H(be^2 - m)e' + Hae = 0 \tag{10.5}$$

This turns out to be a second order non-linear differential equation named after the mathematician Lienard. It has one critical point when $e^* = 0$ and therefore relative costs, $p^* = 0$.

We can now establish the relationship between produced profits at any point and the critical path identified as the center of gravity, $e^* = 0$, where AD=AS. Recall first the equations for relative excess demand and then the expression for the growth rate of profits:

$$e = a_c(1 + v) + a_f - s$$

So that when $e^* = 0$ and provided that $s > a_f$ the accumulation rate in circulating capital will be:

$$a_c^* = \frac{s - a_f}{1 + v} > 0$$

Normally produced profits, Π* exist when e=0 and AD=AS. As long as the propensity to save out of profits, s, is larger that the rate of accumulation in fixed capital, $a_f$ the growth rate of normally produced profit is given by:

$$\frac{\Pi^{*\prime}}{\Pi^*} = ma_c = \frac{m(s - a_f)}{1 + v} > 0$$

**Conceptual structure behind slow cycles**

The growth of capacity output is a function of investment in fixed capital, that is $N' = qK_f' = qI_f$ where $q = \frac{N}{K_f}$ is assumed to be constant. By definition, capacity utilization is given by the ratio of actual to capacity output, $u = \frac{Q}{N}$, and normal capacity utilization exists when $Q = N$ and $u = 1$. Excess capacity utilization is defined as $X = u\text{-}1 = \frac{(Q - N)}{N}$

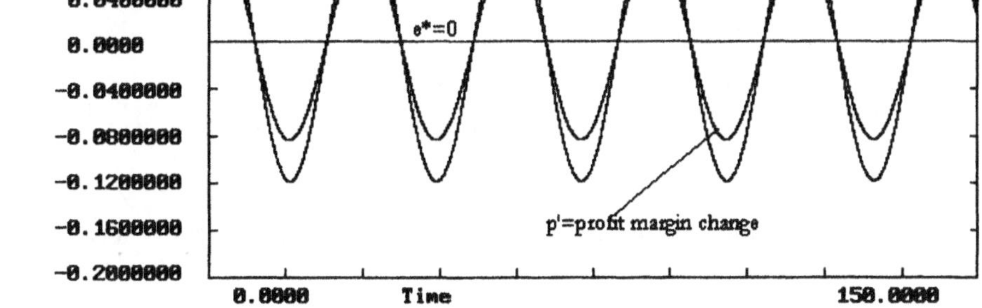


**Figure 10.3 Excess demand/profits and profit margin cycles**

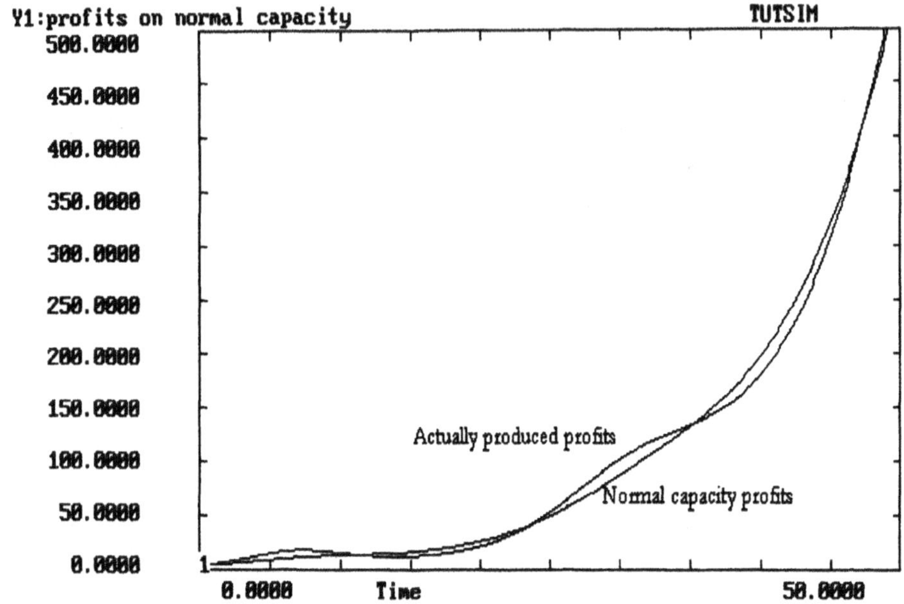


**Figure 10.4 Normal capacity and actual profit cycles: Shaikh's model**

We saw earlier that since the growth rate of produced profits was a function of the rate of accumulation in circulating capital, that is $\frac{\Pi'}{\Pi} = \text{mac}$ and within the fast cycle dynamics, relative excess demand and the excess profit margin, $\mu$, on average approached zero, then $e \approx 0$. Along that critical path the combined rate of accumulation will roughly equal the savings propensity, $a_c(1+v) + a_f \approx s$, and the growth rate of capacity output:

$$\frac{N'}{N} = \left(\frac{q}{N}\right) I_f = \frac{\left(\frac{N}{K_f}\right)}{N} I_f = \frac{1}{K_f} I_f = \left(\frac{I_f}{P}\right)\left(\frac{P}{K}\right) = a_f r = a_f \frac{r}{u} u = a_f r_n u$$

By definition the profit margin on costs, $m = \frac{\Pi}{C}$, and the assumption that m remains constant requires that the profit share, $\frac{\Pi}{Q}$, stays constant. We know that actual output, $Q = C + \Pi$. It follows from these premises that the growth rate of profits will be equal to the growth rate of output, which written in symbols becomes:

$$\frac{\Pi'}{\Pi} = \frac{Q'}{Q} = ma_c \qquad (10.6)$$

As noted in the short-term dynamics, the center of gravity for the cycles of excess demand was defined by $e \approx 0$, a condition requiring the equality between savings and investment. It follows that along this path the savings propensity, $s \approx a_c + a_v + a_f$ . Now since $a_v = va_c$, we can write the savings propensity equation as, $s \approx a_c(1+v) + a_f$ . Then it is evident that given the propensity to save, s and the ratio of inventories to circulating capital, v the accumulation rates in circulating and fixed capital are inversely related.

While the rate of accumulation in fixed capital, $a_f$ is assumed to be constant in the short-term cycle model, it is a state variable in the slower dynamics of capacity adjustments. Shaikh assumes that $a_f' = kX$ and X represents (±) excess capacity utilization, u-1. Therefore its growth rate:

$$a_f' = kX = k(u-1) \qquad (10.7)$$

If capacity utilization is above its normal level, the accumulation rate in fixed capital will rise. A higher accumulation rate in fixed capital, $a_f$ will result in a faster growth of capacity, but at the same time, (given the propensity to save out of profits) will lower the accumulation rate in circulating capital, hence reducing the growth of output. The combined effect, namely a larger capacity and a lower output growth, will cause the rate of capacity utilization to fall back towards its normal level (u=1):

Since $u \equiv \frac{Q}{N}$, and $a_c = \frac{s-a_f}{1+v}$

$$\frac{u'}{u} = \frac{Q'}{Q} - \frac{N'}{N} = \frac{Q'}{Q} - a_f r_n u = \frac{\Pi'}{\Pi} - a_f r_n u = ma_c - a_f r_n u$$

$$\frac{u'}{u} = \frac{X'}{(1+X)} = \frac{(s-a_f)}{(1+v)} - a_f r_n u$$

The change in capacity utilization, u-1 will be:

$$X' = \left[\frac{(s - a_f)}{1 + v}\right](1 + X) - a_f r_n (1 + X)$$

Provided that the pure profit rate (the profit rate minus the interest rate) remains above zero, capacity utilization would converge towards its normal level, but the impact of random shocks will cause it to cycle endlessly around it. Finally Figure 10.5 shows the model simulation for the two cycles, the path of capacity utilization responding to random and exogenous shocks and the path of fixed investment growth cycles. The fixed investment cycle exhibits a slower movement because decisions involving capacity growth require a certain threshold of persistent change in capacity utilization before implementation. Figure 6.8 in Chapter 6 presented the empirical evidence linking the rate of capital accumulation to the degree of capacity utilization in Spanish industry. Regressing the fixed investment/GDP time series on capacity utilization, the correlation is high, the $R^2 = .906$ and the S.E = .0133. It seemed reasonable to assume that changes in fixed capital investment respond to changes in capacity utilization with a discrete time lag.

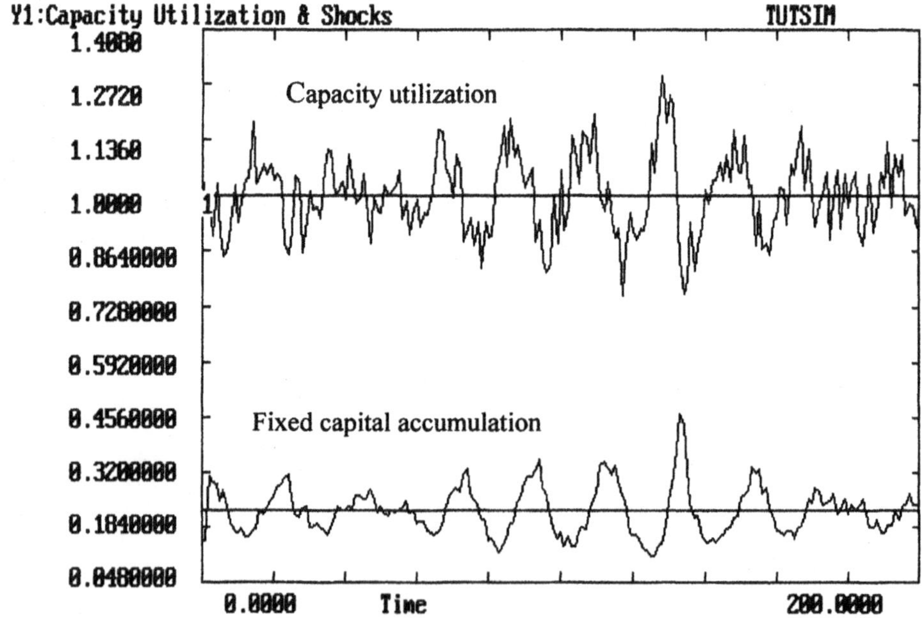


**Figure 10.5** **Capacity utilization and fixed capital cycles: Shaikh's model simulation**

## Excess demand and short-term cycles in Spain

Having presented the guidelines of Shaikh's theoretical structure involving credit, excess demand and debt, my concern now turns to the reconstruction of its empirical underpinnings as applicable to the Spanish economy.

My expressed skepticism regarding the importance of random shocks to explain the medium-term dynamics of growth and income distribution between profits and wages in Spain does not extend to their impact on short-term fluctuations. I find it perfectly acceptable that random shocks having a positive impact on profit expectations would unleash the animal spirits of alert entrepreneurs and trigger increases in investment spending.

To this end, the first step will be to identify the concepts requiring empirical support that are part of the model's structure. A review of the main concepts follows: in Chapter 2, the simplified equation (2.3) for excess demand, $E_t$ contained the following arguments:

$$E_t = Ac_t + If_t + ConR_t - \Pi_t$$

$A_{Ct}$ represents spending on circulating capital; $If_t$ stands for fixed capital investment; $ConR_t$ consumption out of dividends and $\Pi_t$ profits. Dividing the equation through by $\Pi_t$ profits we set the basis for dynamical analysis, since all variables are subject to change, even when the ratios remain constant (equation 2.9 in Chapter 2):

$$\frac{E_t}{\Pi_t} = \frac{Ac_t}{\Pi_t} + \frac{If_t}{\Pi_t} + \frac{ConR_t}{\Pi_t} + \frac{\Pi_t}{\Pi_t} = e_t = a_t + k_t + c_t - 1$$

## Data sources and caveats

There are two important findings derived from the empirical reconstruction of excess demand in Spain. One is that the fluctuations of excess demand derived from the actual data available in Spain coincided with the growth path and fluctuations of the business sector GDP.

The second is that the evolution of total excess demand, calculated according to equation 10.2 fitted the growth and short-term fluctuations of inflation in Spain. I believe that the growth and fluctuations in GDP were caused by the growth and fluctuations in excess demand. As Figure 10.8 reveals, however, the large and positive changes in excess demand, fueled by bank credit granted by banks fearful of their clients' financial distress deepening in the slump, also fanned the flames of inflation in the following years. The large infusion of credit only postponed the structural changes that led to the restoration of profits in the 1980s. Never again, after 1979, did excess demand attained positive values in the Spanish economy.

The problem facing my empirical reconstruction of excess demand in Spain was finding an adequate equivalence between the concepts used in the model and the theoretical assumptions underlying the available data. Thus, I have not found any data related to the levels of desired business inventories, only data pertaining to unintended stock piling. Regarding investment in circulating capital, the available historical series on total annual wages include data from Demo (1954-1988), the Klein Institute (1970-1998) and the OECD Economic Outlook (1960-1998). Shaikh's circulating capital includes spending on materials, which I have interpreted as intermediate goods, and estimated by subtracting from nominal GDP the sum of the Value-added series, as given by Demo (1964-1988) and the data bank *Series* of the Ministry for the Economy (1970-1998). Both Demo and *Series* offered annual data for Value-added covering Agriculture, Industry, Construction and the Service sectors. In the absence of direct data, after aggregation of the sectors I took the difference between the total and the GDP as a proxy for the over-all materials of Shaikh's equation.

What Shaikh calls the rate of accumulation in circulating capital, $a_t$ is the sum of the change in wages and materials from one year to the next, divided by profits. I originally developed my procedure to estimate profit income in my previous investigation (Roman, 1997). Following Shaikh's approach (Shaikh 1989), I calculated aggregate profits using OECD data for the Spanish economy. The OECD publishes yearly figures for the business-sector GDP as well as the relevant deflators, so my estimate of aggregate net profits was $GDP_t$ - (wages + depreciation). The source for the time series on the business-sector GDP as well as the annual depreciation of the capital stock for the period 1960-1998 was the OECD Economic Outlook 66 on diskettes. Taking as reference the inflows of business fixed investment (also available in the OECD Economic Outlook), and the reported stock of fixed capital in the business sector, I solved for the implicit rates of depreciation.

In Shaikh's model the ratio fixed investment/profits, $k_t$, is assumed as constant. Of course, this is not so in the Spanish experience. As far as capitalist consumption $ConR_t$ was concerned, it was necessary to make a number of plausible assumptions, for no direct data are available. I assumed that workers consumption was equal to their wages. Then I subtracted from household consumption data, code CPAA in the OECD Economic Outlook, total wages. Finally I divided the residual over the OECD data on property income, code YOTH. The average for the period 1964-1998 was .53. I calculated capitalist dividends as follows. The Klein Institute's data bank offered a time series for gross business savings, SCP and the BBV bank's annual report reports its own estimates. Dividends paid by firms to capitalist households would be profits net of business taxes minus gross business savings. Dividing household consumption in excess of wages over business profits resulted in an average consumption share of 0.87, higher than the property income share because business profits are smaller than total property income. I settled in favor of 0.85 as an average capitalist propensity to consume out of dividends, ConR.

The model tells us that we should expect actual excess demand to be financed through bank credit. The dynamics of excess demand will then drive the growth and fluctuations of economic activity. Positive excess demand will cause its expansion and negative excess demand will produce declines in the growth path of the GDP. The equation for excess demand can be augmented to include the public deficit relative to profits. Public deficits injected the purchasing power of the borrowed bank credit into the system but carried, as all loans do, the implicit burden of repayment.

While the retirement of the public debt may be prolonged beyond the acceptable limits of the private sector, it is nonetheless a latent commitment. In the absence of direct evidence regarding repayment of business debts, I interpreted the growth of credit as implicitly reflecting the net transactions between borrowers and banks involving the acquisition of new loans after old ones were retired. Once public-deficits were added, the path for excess demand relative to business profits closely matched that of the nominal GDP growth.

There is no reason to suppose that the one-year repayment stipulation of the model should apply in all cases. A flexible repayment schedule could be in place instead depending on the expectations of business firms and banks. What is essential in this regard is that time limits be clearly defined and enforced. There is no doubt that business firms in Spain switched from their deficit spending practice of the 1970s to one of accumulating surplus internal funds, as a result of the discipline of sound finance imposed by the banks. I interpret this transition as one in which firms were forced to reduce their investment spending in order to have the financial wherewithal allowing them the repayment of debt accumulated in previous years.

The rising need for credit finance in the early 1970s was followed by the emergence of surplus funds in the 1980s as investment spending and growth were cut back. Figure 6.7 showed the cyclical growth of profits relative to output and the growth of retained earnings (business savings) relative to profits. It is clear that business savings/investment went up as the growth of credit declined. The evolution of the (±) financial gap-investment ratio justifies the claim advanced regarding a drastic finance switch from deficit spending to the build-up of financial surpluses.

## Empirical findings on excess demand in the Spanish economy

In keeping with the stated caveats, Figure 10.6 shows the empirical estimates for gross excess demand and the growth path of the GDP covering the period 1964-1998. Excess demand here includes the public budget balance. I believe that the data provided by the BBVA annual reports on the credit issued by the banking system to the business sector reflects the requirements of sound finance postulated in Shaikh's model. Of course, absent direct data concerning the actual practices and procedures governing the relationship between banks and business firms, the weight of evidence hinges on plausible inference. I have assumed that a certain discipline prevailed because the results pointed in that direction. All periods of debt build-up were followed with sequential regularity by phases of credit contraction caused by a build-up of internal funds and reductions in investment spending.

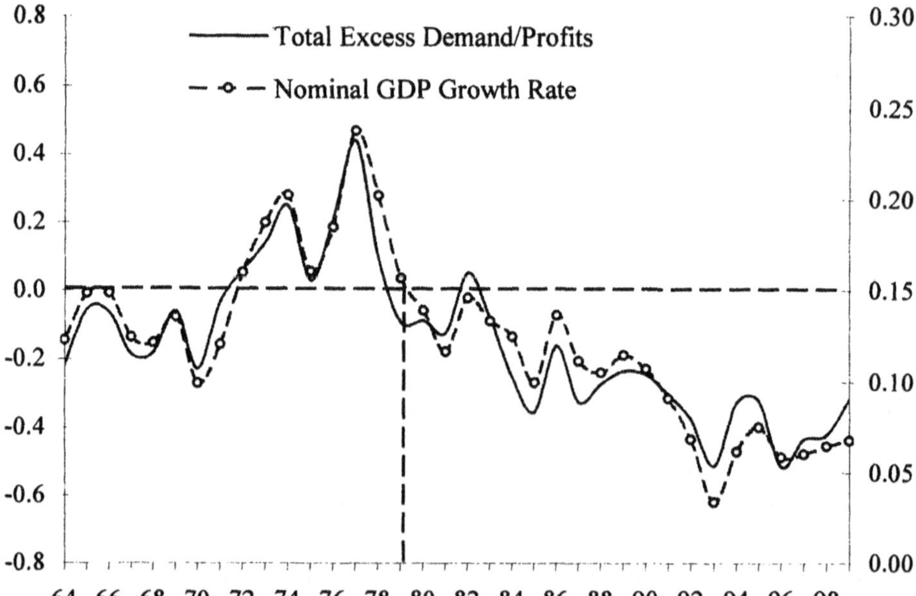


**Figure 10.6 Total excess demand/profits and GDP growth in Spain**

*Sources*: OECD Historical Statistics and Economic Outlook 66.

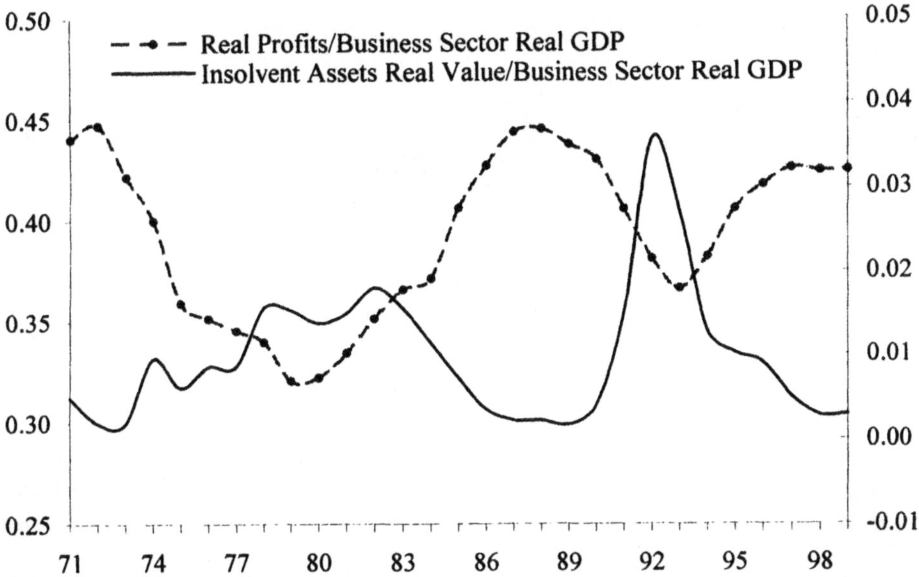


**Figure 10.7 Real profits and insolvent assets/business sector GDP**

*Sources:* Series 254110; OECD Historical Statistics and Economic Outlook 66.

My working hypothesis takes as its point of departure the premise that excess demand was fueled by external credit. The question of how much credit would the banks be willing to extend can be answered in connection with the dynamics of the profit margin. Normally banks would be willing to extend new loans as long as the profit margin was rising relative to its trend. Once this rise was ended, risk-averse banks would reduce their lending and expect firms to build-up their own internal funds in order to preserve their solvency.

It is instructive to observe that, between 1975 and 1978, years in which the collapse of profits started to threaten the survival of many firms excess demand relative to trend reached its highest peak. This was because in those years banks had launched a salvage operation in favor of their best traditional customers. In fact, in the 1980s profit margins recovered while excess demand relative to profits remained negative. As the profit margin net of interest payments continued to decline through the1970s, however, the rescue project was definitely curtailed. The available evidence reveals that rising levels of insolvency accompanied firms' growing exposure to external finance and leverage in the 1970s. This sobering fact would strengthen the resolve of risk-averse banks to enforce measures of sound finance management.

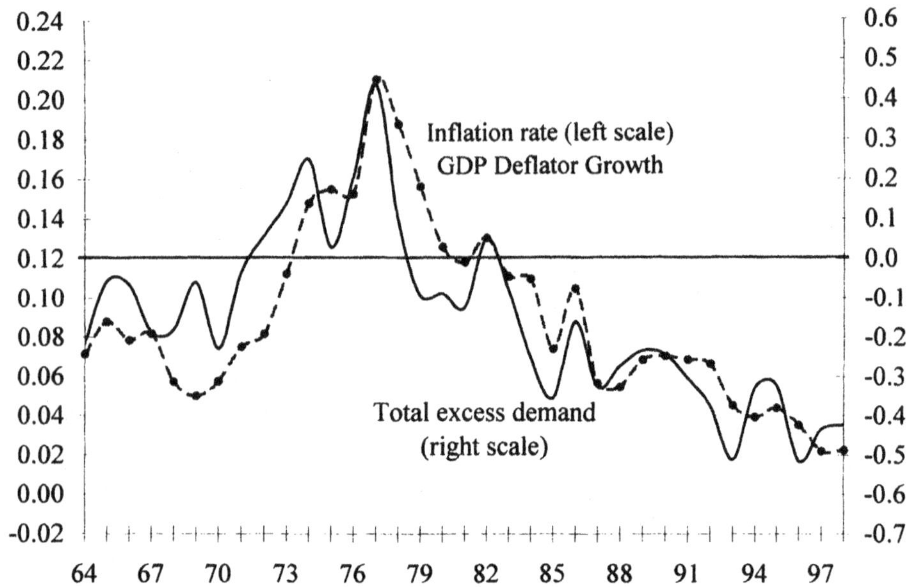


**Figure 10.8 Gross excess demand and the inflation rate**

*Sources:* OECD Historical Statistics and Economic Outlook 66.

## Excess demand and inflation

Figure 10.8 shows the relationship between my estimates for excess demand and the inflation path for the period 1964-1998. My source for the time series in the business sector excess demand calculations, such as GDP, the capital stock, the business sector wages, etc, was the *OECD Historical Statistics and the Economic Outlook* 66 in computer diskettes. I estimated the over-all movement of excess demand according to the specifications developed in Shaikh's model of growth cycles and finance presented in Chapter 2, but added the public sector's budget balance (spending minus taxes). To calculate gross profits I subtracted from the business sector GDP the wages of the labor force employed in the business sector (the difference between total wages and government administration wages) and the annual depreciation estimates of the capital stock. The inflation rate is the yearly percentage change in the GDP deflator, taken also from the *OECD Economic Outlook* 66 database. I think that the empirical link is quite evident. Note that the 1977 peak in inflation indeed coincided with the crest in credit-financed excess demand.

Rising inflation was caused by the fact that the aggregate mass of profits did not grow as fast as total spending, including circulation and fixed capital investment. The onset of the depression phase in the mid 1970s in Spain provided strong empirical support for Shaikh's classical approach to inflation. From the mid-1970s through the early 1980s, the mass of profits in fact declined and the rate of inflation as well as unemployment attained unprecedented growth rates. The massive effort by industry and banks to cushion the collapse in accumulation and assure the survival of their best clients resulted in rising inflation rates but not the recovery of profits. Inflation subsided only when the profits share recovered in the mid-1980s, and excess demand turned negative, that is business spending fell well below the profits mass.

# Bibliography


Akerlof, G. A. and Yellen, J. L. (1985), "A Near-Rational Model of the Business Cycle, with Wage and Price Inertia", *Quarterly Journal of Economics*: 100.

Arestis, P. and Skouras, T. (1985), *Post Keynesian Economic Theory,* Wheatsheaf Books: Sussex.

Arestis, P. (1999), "The Independent European Central Bank", *Working Paper* 274, The Jerome Levy Economic Institute: Annandale-on-Hudson, New York.

Arestis, P. and Sawyer, M. (1999), "The Economic and Monetary Union: Current and Future Prospects", *Working Paper* 282, The Jerome Levy Economic Institute: Annandale-on-Hudson, New York.

Arnon, A. (1991), *Thomas Tooke, Pioneer of Monetary Theory,* The University of Michigan Press: Ann Arbor.

Arrow, K. (1983), *Collected Papers of Kenneth J. Arrow, Volume 2 General Equilibrium*, Harvard University Press: Cambridge, Ma.

Asimakopulos, A. (1991), *Keynes's General Theory and Accumulation,* Cambridge University Press: New York.

Atesoglu, H. S. (2001), "Inflation: Wage-Cost Markup Approach", in *Encyclopedia of Political Economy*, O'Hara, P. A. (ed.), pp. 510-512, Routledge: New York.

Barro, R. J. (1993), *Macroeconomics*, John Wiley: New York.

Bernanke, B. (1981), "Bankruptcy, Liquidity and Recession", *American Economic Review*: 71(2).

Bernanke, B. and Rotemberg, J. (1999), *Macroeconomics Annual 1998*, The MIT Press: Cambridge, Ma.

Bleany, M. (1976), *Underconsumption Theories,* International Publishers: New York.

Caplin, A. and Spulber, D. F. (1987), "Menu Costs and the Neutrality of Money", in *Quarterly Journal of Economics*: 703-725.

Chakravarty, S. (1989) "John von Neumann's Model of an Expanding Economy: an Essay in Interpretation", in Dore, M., H., Chakravarty, S. and Goodwin, R. M. (eds), *John von Neumann and Modern Economics*, Claredon Press: Oxford.

Chick, V. (1983), *Macro Economics After Keynes*, The MIT Press: Cambridge, Ma.

Chick, V. (1985), "Keynesians, Monetarists and Keynes: The End of a Debate—or a Beginning?", in Arestis, P. and Skouras, T. (eds), *Post Keynesian Economic Theory*, Wheatsheaf: Sussex.

Cochrane, J. H. (1999), "A Frictionless View of U.S. Inflation", in Bernanke, B. and Rotemberg, J. (eds), *Macroeconomics Annual 1999,* The MIT Press: Cambridge.

Corrales, A. and Taguas, D. (1989), *Series macroeconomicas para el periodo 1954-1988: un intento de homogeneización*, Instituto de Estudios Fiscales: Madrid.

Council of Economic Advisers (1999), *Economic Report of the President*, U.S. Government Printing Office: Washington.

Davidson, P. (1977), "Post-Keynes Monetary Theory and Inflation", in Weintraub, S. (ed), *Modern Economic Thought,* University of Pennsylvania Press: Pa.

Davidson, P. (1982), *Money and the Real World,* The Macmillan Press: London.

Deleplace, G. and Nell E. J. (1996), *Money in Motion. The Post Keynesian and Circulation Approaches* (eds), St. Martin's Press: New York.

Di Mateo, M. (1984), "Alternative Monetary Policies in a Classical Growth Cycle", in Goodwin, R. M., Kruger, M. and Vercelli, A. (eds), *Nonlinear Models of Fluctuating Growth*, New York: Springer-Verlag.

Dore, M. H. I. (1993), *The Macrodynamics of Business Cycles,* Blackwell: Cambridge, Ma.

Eatwell, J. and Milgate, M. (eds) (1983), *Keynes's Economics and the Theory of Value and Distribution*, Oxford University Press: New York.

Eckstein, O. and Sinai, A. (1986), "The Mechanisms of the Business Cycle in the Postwar Era", in Gordon, R. (ed.), *The American Business Cycle: Continuity and Change*, University of Chicago: Chicago.

Eltis, W. (1984), *The Classical Theory of Economic Growth,* St. Martin's Press: New York.

Fazzari, S. M. (1999), "Minsky and the Mainstream: Has Recent Research Rediscovered Financial Keynesianism?", *Working Paper* 278, The Jerome Levy Economic Institute: Annandale-on-Hudson, New York.

Flores de Frutos, R. and Sebastian, C. (1996), "Un análisis del último ciclo de la Economía Española (1989-1994)", *Documento de Trabajo del ICAE* 9604, Universidad Complutense: Madrid.

Foley, D. (1987a), "Liquidity-Profit Rate Cycles in a Capitalist Economy", *Journal of Economic Behavior and Organization*: North-Holland.

Foley, D. (1987b), "Money in Economic Activity", in *The New Palgrave*, Eatwell, J., Millgate, M. and Newman, P. (eds), The Macmillan Press: London.

Foley, D. (1998), "Hyman Minsky and the Dilemmas of Contemporary Economic Method", Department of Economics, New School University: New York.

Foley, D. and Michl, T. (1999), *Growth and Distribution*, Harvard University Press: Cambridge, Ma.

Fry, M. J. (1995), *Money, Interest and Banking in Economic Development,* The John Hopkins University Press: Baltimore.

Gilchrist, S. and Himmelberg, C. (1999), "Investment: Fundamentals and Finance", in Bernanke, B. and Rotemberg, J. (eds), *Macroeconomics Annual 1998,* The MIT Press: Cambridge, Ma.

Godley, W. (1996), "Money, Finance and National Income Determination: An Integrated Approach", *Working Paper* 167, The Jerome Levy Economics Institute: Annadale-on-Hudson, New York.

Godley, W. and Shaikh, A. (1998a), "An Important Inconsistency at the Heart of the Standard Macroeconomic Model", *Working Paper* 236, The Jerome Levy Economics Institute: Annadale-on-Hudson, New York.

Godley, W. (1998b), "Money and Credit in a Keynesian Model of Income Determination", *Working Paper* 242, The Jerome Levy Economics Institute: Annadale-on-Hudson, New York.

Godley, W. (1999a), "Open Economy Macroeconomics Using Models of Closed Systems", *Working Paper* 281, The Jerome Levy Economics Institute: Annadale-on-Hudson, New York.

Goodhart, C. A. E. (1984), *Monetary Theory and Practice: The UK Experience*, Macmillan: London.

Goodwin, R. M. (1972), "A Growth Cycle", in Hunt, E. K. and Schwartz, J. S. (eds), *A Critique of Economic Theory*, Penguin Books: Baltimore.

Graziani, A. (1996), "Money as Purchasing Power and Money as a Stock of Wealth in Keynesian Economic Thought", in Deleplace, G. and Nell E. J. (eds), *Money in Motion. The Post Keynesian and Circulation Approaches,* St. Martin's Press: New York.

Greenwald, B. and Stiglitz, J. (1993), "New and Old Keynesians", *Journal of Economic Perspectives*: 7.

Gross, D. (1999), "Comment", in Bernanke, B. and Rotemberg, J. (eds), *Macroeconomics Annual 1998*, The MIT Press: Cambridge, Ma.

Hahn, F. H. (1971), "Equilibrium with Transactions Costs", Econometrica: 39.

Hahn, F. H. (1985), *Money and Inflation*, The MIT Press: Cambridge, Ma.

Harris, D. J. (1987), "Classical Growth Models", in Eatwell, J., Millgate, M. and Newman, P. (eds), *The New Palgrave,* The Macmillan Press: London.

Hilferding, R. (1981), *Finance Capital,* Routledge & Kegan Paul: London.

Hinds, M. (1988), "Draft Paper on Financial Crisis in Developing Coutries", World Bank: Washington, D.C.

Hollander, S. (1987), *Classical Economics,* Basil Blackwell: New York.

Jordan, J. L. (1999), "Financial Crisis and Market Regulation", *Economic Commentary*, Federal Reserve Bank of Cleveland: Ohio.

Kaldor, N. (1965), "Capital Accumulation and Economic Growth", in Lutz, F. A. (ed.), *The Theory of Capital*, Macmillan: London.

Kalecki, M. (1971), *Selected Essays on the Dynamics of the Capitalist Economy: 1933-1970*, Cambridge University Press: Cambridge.

Keynes, J. M. (1930), *A Treatise on Money*, Harcourt-Brace: New York.

Keynes, J. M. (1977), *The General Theory of Employment, Interest and Money,* Macmillan: Cambridge.

Keynes, J. M. (1987), *The General Theory and After: Part II*, *The Collected Writings of John Maynard Keynes*, Volume XIV, Moggridge, D. (ed.), Cambridge University Press: Cambridge.

Kiyotaki, N. and West, K. D. (1996), "Business Fixed Investment and the Recent Business Cycle in Japan", in Bernanke, B. and Rotemberg, J. (eds), *Macroeconomics Annual 1996,* The MIT Press: Cambridge, Ma.

Knox, A. D. (1952), "The Acceleration Principle and the Theory of Investment: A Survey", Vol. 19, New Series, *Economica.*

Kopcke, R. W. (1993), "The Determinants of Business Investment: Has Capital Spending Been Surprisingly Low?", *New England Economic Review*, Federal Reserve Bank of Boston: Boston.

Kopcke, R. W. and Howrey M. M. (1994), "A Panel Study of Investment: Sales, Cash Flow, The Cost of Capital, and Leverage", *New England Economic Review*, Federal Reserve Bank of Boston: Boston.

Kregel, J. A. (1971), "J. von Neumann: A model of General Equilibrium", in *Rate of Profit, Distribution and Growth: Two Views*, Aldine: Chicago.

Kregel, J. A. (1996), "The Policy Implications of the Current Bank Crisis", in Deleplace, G. and Nell, E. J. (eds), *Money in Motion. The Post Keynesian and Circulation Approaches,* St. Martin's Press: New York.

Kregel, J. A. (1998), "Yes, "It" Did Happen Again—A Minsky Crisis Happened in Asia", *Working Paper* 234, The Jerome Levy Economics Institute: Annadale-on-Hudson, New York.

Laidler, D. (1981), "Monetarism: an Interpretation and an Assessment", *Economic Journal*: 91.

Laidler, D. (1982), *Monetarist Perspectives*, Harvard University Press: Cambridge, Ma.

Lowe, A. (1954), "The Classical Theory of Economic Growth", Social Research 21, New School for Social Research: New York.

Makarov, V. and Rubinov, A. (1987), "von Neumann Technology", in *The New Palgrave*, Eatwell, J., Millgate, M. and Newman, P. (eds), The Macmillan Press: London.

Marx, K. (1952), *Theories of Surplus Value*, International Publishers: New York.

Marx, K. (1981), *Capital, Volume II*, Vintage Books: New York.

Minsky, H. P. (1984), *Can "It" Happen Again?,* M.E. Sharpe: New York.

Minsky, H. P. (1985), "The Financial Instability Hypothesis: A Restatement", in Arestis, P. and Skouras, T. (eds), *Post Keynesian Economic Theory,* Wheatsheaf Books: Sussex.

Minsky, H. P. (1986), *Stabilizing an Unstable Economy,* Yale University Press: New Haven.

Mirowski, P. (1985), *The Birth of the Business Cycle*, Garland Publishers: New York.

Mitchell, W. (1913), *Business Cycles*, University of California Press: Berkely.

Mitchell, W. (1951), *What Happens During Business Cycles*, National Bureau of Economic Research: New York.

Mitchell, W. (1963), *Business Cycles and their Causes*, University of California Press: Berkely.

Molinas, C. Sebastian, M. and Zabalza, A. (1991), *La Economia Española, una perspectiva macroeconomica*, Antoni Bosch: Madrid.

Moore, B. (1988), *Horizontalists and Verticalists*, Cambridge University Press: Cambridge.

Moore, B. (1996), "The Money Supply Process: A Historical Reinterpretation", in Deleplace, G. and Nell, E. J. (eds), *Money in Motion. The Post Keynesian and Circulation Approaches,* St. Martin's Press: New York.

Moore, G. H. (1978), "Diagnosing the Problem of Inflation and Unemployment in the Western World", in *After the Phillips Curve: Persistence of High Inflation and High Unemployment*, Federal Reserve Bank of Boston: Boston.

Moudud, J. (1998a), "Finance and the Macroeconomic Process in a Classical Growth and Cycles Model", *Working Paper* 253, The Jerome Levy Economics Institute: Annadale-on-Hudson, New York.

Moudud, J. (1998b), "Government Spending and Growth Cycles: Fiscal Policy in a Dynamic Context", *Working Paper* 260, The Jerome Levy Economics Institute: Annadale-on-Hudson, New York.

Moudud, J. (1999a), "Government Spending in a Growing Economy", *Public Policy Brief* No. 52A, The Jerome Levy Economics Institute: Annadale-on-Hudson, New York.

Moudud, J. (1999b), "Finance in a Classical and Harrodian Cyclical Growth Model", *Working Paper* 290, The Jerome Levy Economics Institute: Annadale-on-Hudson, New York.

Moudud, J. and Zacharias, A. (1999c), "The Social Wage, Welfare Policy, and the Phases of Capital Accumulation", *Working Paper* 291, The Jerome Levy Economics Institute: Annadale-on-Hudson, New York.

Mullineux, A. W. (1984), *The Business Cycle after Keynes,* Barnes and Noble Books: New Jersey.

Mullineux, A. W. (1990), *Business Cycles & Financial Crisis,* Harvester Wheatsheaf: London.

Negishi, T. (1989), *History of Economic Theory,* North Holland: Amsterdam.

Novales, A. and Sebastian, C. (1999), *Analisis Macroeconomico II*, Marcial Pons: Madrid.

Papadimitriou, D. B. and Wray, L. R. (1997), "The Economic Contributions of Hyman Minsky: Varieties of Capitalism and Institutional Reform", *Working Paper* 217, The Jerome Levy Economics Institute: Annadale-on-Hudson, New York.

Papadimitriou, D. B. and Wray, L. R. (1999), "Minsky's Analysis of Financial Capitalism", *Working Paper* 275, The Jerome Levy Economics Institute: Annadale-on-Hudson, New York.

Pearce, D. (ed.) (1992), *The MIT Dictionary of Modern Economics*, The MIT Press: Cambridge, Ma.

Peck, J. and Rosengren, E. S. (1995), *Is Bank Lending Important for the Transmission of Monetary Policy?*, Conference Series 39, Federal Reserve Bank of Boston: Boston.

Peck, J. and Rosengren, E. S. (1999), "Japanese Banking Problems", *New England Economic Review*, Jan/Feb: Boston.

Pollin, R. (1986), "Alternative Perspectives on the Rise of Corporate Debt Dependency", *Review of Radical Political Economics*, Vol. 18: URPE.

Pollin, R. (1996), "Marxian and Post Keynesian Developments in the Sphere of Money, Credit and Finance: Building Alternative Perspectives in Monetary Macroeconomics", in Lippit, V. D. (ed.), *Radical Political Economy*. M. E. Sharpe: New York.

Robertson, D. H. (1940), "Effective Demand and the Multiplier", in *Essays in Monetary Theory*, P. S. King: London.

Rogers, C. (1989), *Money, interest and capital,* Cambridge University Press: New York.

Roman, M. (1997), *Growth and Stagnation of the Spanish Economy,* Avebury: Aldershot.

Rousseas, S. (1992), *Post-Keynesian Monetary Economics,* M. E. Sharpe: New York.

Rousseas, S. (1996), "The Spheres of Industrial and Financial Circulation Revisited, and their Implications for Post Keynesian Economic Policy", in Deleplace, G. and Nell, E. J. (eds), *Money in Motion. The Post Keynesian and Circulation Approaches,* St. Martin's Press: New York.

Samuelson, P. A. (1998), "Summing Up on Business Cycles: Opening Address", in Fuhrer, J.C. and Schuh, S. (eds), *Beyond Shocks: What Causes Business Cycles,* Federal Reserve Bank of Boston.

Sawyer, M. (1999), "Minsky's Analysis, the European Single Currency, and the Global Financial System", *Working Paper* 266, The Jerome Levy Economic Institute: Annandale-on-Hudson, New York.

Schiantarelli, F. (1995), "Financial Constraints and Investment: A Critical Review of Methodological Issues and International Evidence", in *Is Bank Lending Important for the Transmission of Monetary Policy?*, Conference Series 39, Federal Reserve Bank of Boston: Boston.

Schumpeter, J. A. (1939), *Business Cycles: A Theoretical, Historical, and Statistical Analysis of the Capitalist Process*, McGraw-Hill: New York.

Sebastian, C. (1997), *Las fluctuaciones de la economia espanola (1971-1996),* Marcial Pons: Madrid.

Seccareccia, M. (1996), "Post Keynesian Fundism and Monetary Circulation", in Deleplace, G. and Nell, E. J. (eds), *Money in Motion. The Post Keynesian and Circulation Approaches,* St. Martin's Press: New York.

Semmler, W. and Sieveking, M. (1988), "Nonlinear Growth-Liquidity Dynamics with Bankruptcy Risk", New School for Social Research: New York.

Semmler, W. (1989), *Financial Dynamics and Business Cycles,* M. E. Sharpe: New York.

Semmler, W. and Sieveking, M. (1993), "Nonlinear Growth-Liquidity Dynamics with Corridor Stability", *Journal of Economic Behavior and Organization*: North-Holland.

Shackle, G. L. S. (1983), *The Years of High Theory,* Cambridge University Press: London.

Shackle, G. L. S. (1988), *Business, Time and Thought*, New York University Press: New York.

Shaikh, A. (1989), "Accumulation, Finance, and Effective Demand in Marx, Keynes, and Kalecki", in Semmler, W. (ed.), *Financial Dynamics and Business Cycles,* M. E. Sharpe: New York.

Shaikh, A. (1990), *Valor, Acumulacion y Crisis*, Tercer Mundo Editores: Bogota.

Shaikh, A. (1992), "A Dynamic Approach to the Theory of Effective Demand", in Papadimitriou, D. B. (ed.), *Profits, Deficits and Instability,* St. Martin's Press: New York.

Shaikh, A. and Tonak, A. (1994), *Measuring the Wealth of Nations,* Cambridge University Press: New York.

Shaikh, A. (1999), "Explaining Inflation and Unemployment: an Alternative to Neoliberal Economic Theory", in *Contemporary Economic Theory*, Vachlou, A. (ed.), Macmillan: London.

Sinai, A. (1977), "Discussion on Papers on the American Economic Environment", in Altman, E. I. and Sametz, A. W. (eds), *Financial Crisis: Institutions and Markets in a Fragile Environment*, John Wiley and Sons: New York.

Solow, R. M. (1996), "Growth Theory", in *A Guide to Modern Economics,* Greenway, D., Bleany, M. and Stewart, I. (eds), Routledge: New York.

Stiglitz, J. E. and Weiss, A. (1981), "Credit Rationing in Markets with Imperfect Competition", *American Economic Review*: 71.

Stiglitz, J. E. (1984), "Price Rigidities and Market Structure", *American Economic Review*: 74.

Stiglitz, J. E. (1988), "Money, Credit, and Business Fluctuations", *Economic Record*: 64.

Strachey, J. (1935), *The Nature of Capitalist Crisis*, Covice-Friede: New York.

Temin, P. (1976), *Did Monetary Forces Cause the Great Depression?*, Norton: New York.

Toporowski, J. (1999), "Monetary Policy in an Era of Capital Market Inflation", *Working Paper* 279, Levy Economics Institute: Annadale-on-Hudson, New York.

Van Duijn, J. J. (1983), *The Long Wave in Economic Life,* George Allen & Unwin: London.

Walsh, C. E. and Wilcox, J. A. (1995), "Bank Credit and Economic Activity", in *Is Bank Lending Important for the Transmission of Monetary Policy?*, Conference Series 39, Federal Reserve Bank of Boston: Boston.

Whalen, C. H. (1999), "Hyman Minsky's Theory of Capitalist Development", *Working Paper* 277, The Jerome Levy Economics Institute: Annadale-on-Hudson, New York.

Wojnilower, A. (1980), "The central Role of Credit Crunches in Recent Financial History, *Brookings Papers on Economic Activity*, 2, Brookings: Washington.

Wojnilower, A. (1985), "Private Credit Demand, Supply and Crunches: How Different Are the 1980s?", *American Economic Review*: 75.

Wolfson, M. H. (1994), *Financial Crisis,* M. E. Sharpe: New York.

Wray, R. L. (1990), *Money and Credit in Capitalist Economies,* Edward Elgar: Vermont.

Wray, R. L. (1998b), *Understanding Modern Money: The Key to Full Employment and Price Stability*, Edward Elgar: Aldershot.

Wray, R. L. (1999a), "Theories of Value and the Monetary Theory of Production", *Working Paper* 261, The Jerome Levy Economic Institute: Annandale-on-Hudson, New York.

Zarnowitz, V. (1996), *Business Cycles, Theory, History, Indicators and Forecasting,* The University of Chicago Press: Chicago.

# Index

For Product Safety Concerns and Information please contact our EU representative GPSR@taylorandfrancis.com Taylor & Francis Verlag GmbH, Kaufingerstraße 24, 80331 München, Germany

**Batch number: 10726009**

Printed by Printforce, the Netherlands